Usable Pasts

Historical Materialism Book Series

The Historical Materialism Book Series is a major publishing initiative of the radical left. The capitalist crisis of the twenty-first century has been met by a resurgence of interest in critical Marxist theory. At the same time, the publishing institutions committed to Marxism have contracted markedly since the high point of the 1970s. The Historical Materialism Book Series is dedicated to addressing this situation by making available important works of Marxist theory. The aim of the series is to publish important theoretical contributions as the basis for vigorous intellectual debate and exchange on the left.

The peer-reviewed series publishes original monographs, translated texts, and reprints of classics across the bounds of academic disciplinary agendas and across the divisions of the left. The series is particularly concerned to encourage the internationalization of Marxist debate and aims to translate significant studies from beyond the English-speaking world.

For a full list of titles in the Historical Materialism Book Series available in paperback from Haymarket Books, visit: www.haymarketbooks.org/series_collections/1-historical-materialism.

Usable Pasts

Social Practice and State Formation in American Art

Larne Abse Gogarty

Haymarket Books
Chicago, IL

First published in 2022 by Brill Academic Publishers, The Netherlands
© 2022 Koninklijke Brill NV, Leiden, The Netherlands

Published in paperback in 2023 by
Haymarket Books
P.O. Box 180165
Chicago, IL 60618
773-583-7884
www.haymarketbooks.org

ISBN: 978-1-64259-900-8

Distributed to the trade in the US through Consortium Book Sales and Distribution (www.cbsd.com) and internationally through Ingram Publisher Services International (www.ingramcontent.com).

This book was published with the generous support of Lannan Foundation and Wallace Action Fund.

Special discounts are available for bulk purchases by organizations and institutions. Please call 773-583-7884 or email info@haymarketbooks.org for more information.

Cover design by David Mabb. Cover art is a detail from a photograph of the International Ladies Garment Workers Union dance group at Unity House in 1924, from the Edith Segal papers, Jerome Robbins Dance Division, the New York Public Library.

Printed in the United States.

10 9 8 7 6 5 4 3 2 1

Library of Congress Cataloging-in-Publication data is available.

Contents

Acknowledgements   VII
List of Illustrations   IX

Introduction: Historicising Social Practice   1
   1   The New Deal Imaginary   2
   2   The Stakes of Social Practice   8
   3   Prevented Futures and Usable Pasts   16

1 Rehearsals for Real Life   25
   1   Performance and Critical Realism   25
   2   *The Roof Is on Fire*   32
   3   *Code 33*   40
   4   *Injunction Granted*   48
   5   Conclusion: Legislation and Rehearsals   66

2 Social Practice / Social Reproduction   73
   1   Introduction   73
   2   Cells in Organisms/Cogs in Machines   74
   3   *Black and White* at the Rockland Palace: The Body against the Belt   85
   4   Dance and Domestic Labour   91
   5   Expectations and Welfare Reform   101
   6   'Each Week We started with the Body'   106
   7   *Expectations* at Capp Street Gallery   114
   8   Conclusion: Reproducing Culture, Reproducing Life   119

3 Housing, Homelessness and Documentary   122
   1   *If You Lived Here …*   125
   2   *One-Third of a Nation*   144

4 Race, Nation and Usable Pasts   159
   1   Documentary and Nationalism   160
   2   Blackness and the Limits of a Usable Past   169
   3   Project Row Houses   183

Coda: Utility and Social Practice   197

Bibliography   209
Index   226

Acknowledgements

The development of this book was initially shaped by two experiences. In 2008, I started working with Rachel Anderson in the Interaction department at the art organisation Artangel. At the time, Rachel was producing ambitious, participatory projects that introduced me to the world of social practice in a way that was explicitly politicised, especially with the first project I worked on: Noor Afshan Mirza and Brad Butler's *The Museum of Non Participation*, a project which ran over an eighteen month period, and shuttled between London and Karachi, collaborating with street vendors, Urdu translators, architects, housing activists, lawyers, hairdressers, filmmakers, wedding photographers, newspaper printers, artists and writers. I am grateful to Rachel, Noor and Brad for introducing me to questions which are at the heart of this book concerning the difficulties and possibilities involved in trying to situate art as a conduit for social change and cooperation. Concurrent to working on *The Museum of Non Participation*, I began an MA in the History of Art department at UCL and was taught by Professor Andrew Hemingway on a course called *Class Formation in American Art: From the New Deal to the Eisenhower Period*. In studying the New Deal art programmes with Andrew, I was struck by the shared concerns of artists, administrators and participants that mark that history, with the work I was doing alongside Rachel, Noor and Brad. Despite the very different socio-political context of 1930s America, and London, or indeed Karachi, in 2008, it was clear to me that there were shared problems around the instrumentalisation of art, institutional limits, and the idea of aesthetic experience as intimately connected with pedagogy and politics, leading me to write the comparative history contained here. Andrew went on to supervise my PhD which forms the basis of this book, and I am immensely grateful for his support, and all I have learned from him.

A doctoral award from the Arts and Humanities Research Council made my PhD research in the History of Art Department at UCL possible, and the department was a stimulating and supportive home during the course of my graduate studies. I am particularly grateful to Stephanie Schwartz for her precise and thoughtful co-supervision of my PhD alongside Andrew, and all her invaluable support since. Comments from Gail Day and Michael Hatt assisted in reshaping this manuscript for publication and gave me the confidence to develop this book. I would also like to thank Angela Miller for her helpful feedback on an earlier draft. A postdoctoral fellowship from the Terra Foundation for American Art, based at the Institut für Kunst- und Bildgeschichte at the Humboldt University, Berlin from 2016–2018 provided invaluable support while writing this book, as did support in 2012 from the Terra Foundation to conduct research in the US. Since 2018, I have been lucky enough to work at the Slade School of Fine Art and would like to thank my colleagues and students for engaging me in new ways of thinking about the questions explored in this book.

I want to thank the following archives and art institutions for making their materials available: The Tamiment Library, The Theatre Division and Jerome Robbins Dance Division at New York Public Library, The Special Collection and Archives at George Mason University, The Schomburg Center for Research in Black Culture and the Capp Street Project Gallery Archives at CCA, Oakland. Warmest thanks to Suzanne Lacy for her generosity with her time, apartment, image and video resources. Unique Holland, Chris Johnson, Rick Lowe and Martha Rosler generously gave time for me to interview them. Many thanks to Martha, Suzanne and to Project Row Houses for also supplying images for use in this book. I would also like to thank Arcilla Stahl at the South Side Community Art Centre in Chicago for her generosity in assisting my research there, and Skyla Hearn for her help in accessing related collections at the Vivian G. Harsh Research Center.

While doing my MA, my thinking was transformed by studying alongside Sonel Breslev, Danielle Monks, Jenny Nachtigall, Giulia Smith, Andrew Witt, who remain some of my closest friends and have all been important during the development of this book, from hosting me on research trips, to being excellent holiday companions, to all reading, listening to and engaging with what I have written at various points. The Marxist Feminist reading group I was part of was an invaluable space, and I still think of it as the collective intellectual project I have learned the most from. Thanks especially to Hannah Black, Christina Chalmers, E.C. Feiss, Rose-Anne Gush, Dimitra Kotouza, Hannah Proctor, Zoe Sutherland, Marina Vishmidt and Josefine Wikström, who were all either part of that reading group, or have been similarly important as friends and interlocutors. Thanks to Hannah Lustig and Emile Kelly, for their friendship and for listening to me talk about this project over the years. I would also like to thank Danny Hayward for his careful editing of this manuscript.

Thanks to my parents Susanna Abse and Paul Gogarty, and my brother Max for their constant support, as well as to my aunt, Keren Abse for always being engaged and encouraging. This book is dedicated to the memory of my grandmother, Joan Abse, whose relationship to art and politics provided a formative role in my life. I only wish I could have discussed everything here with her. Most of all, with love, thanks to Adam Lane for his intellectual engagement, love and kindness, and for being interested in what I have been working on the whole way through.

Illustrations

1 Suzanne Lacy, Annice Jacoby, and Chris Johnson, *The Roof is on Fire*, 1993–94, from The Oakland Projects, 1991–2001. Oakland, California. Photo by Gary Nakamoto. Courtesy of Suzanne Lacy   33
2 Suzanne Lacy, Annice Jacoby, and Chris Johnson, *The Roof is on Fire*, 1993–94, from The Oakland Projects, 1991–2001. Oakland, California. Photo by Nathan Bennett. Courtesy of Suzanne Lacy   33
3 Suzanne Lacy, Annice Jacoby, and Chris Johnson, *The Roof is on Fire*, 1993–94, from The Oakland Projects, 1991–2001. Oakland, California. Photo by Nathan Bennett. Courtesy of Suzanne Lacy   34
4 Suzanne Lacy, Julio César Morales, and Unique Holland, *Code 33: Emergency, Clear the Air!*, 1997–99, from The Oakland Projects, 1991–2001. Oakland, California. Photo by Kelli Yon. Courtesy of Suzanne Lacy   43
5 Suzanne Lacy, Julio César Morales, and Unique Holland, *Code 33: Emergency, Clear the Air!*, 1997–99, from The Oakland Projects, 1991–2001. Oakland, California. Photo by Lily Rodríguez. Courtesy of Suzanne Lacy   44
6 Final scene, *Injunction Granted*, Biltmore Theatre, New York City, 1936. Photographer unknown. Courtesy of the Arnold Goldman Living Newspaper Collection, Special Collections and Archives, George Mason University   49
7 Clown with cigar, *Injunction Granted*, 1936. Photographer unknown. Courtesy of the Arnold Goldman Living Newspaper Collection, Special Collections and Archives, George Mason University   50
8 Demagogue scene. *Injunction Granted*, 1936. Photographer unknown. Courtesy of the Arnold Goldman Living Newspaper Collection, Special Collections and Archives, George Mason University   56
9 Clown giving gherkin to Heinz, *Injunction Granted*, 1936. Photographer unknown. Courtesy of the Arnold Goldman Living Newspaper Collection, Special Collections and Archives, George Mason University   58
10 Hearst vs. Jennings, *Injunction Granted*, 1936. Photographer unknown. Courtesy of the Arnold Goldman Living Newspaper Collection, Special Collections and Archives, George Mason University   61
11 Edith Segal and ILGWU members at Unity House, 1924. Photographer unknown. Courtesy of the Jerome Robbins Dance Division, New York Library for the Performing Arts   76
12 Dance Group of the Needle Trades Workers' Industrial Union, page from the Workers Dance League Spartakiade program, Sunday June 4th 1933. Photographer unknown. Courtesy of the Jerome Robbins Dance Division, New York Library for the Performing Arts   78
13 Trui H. Uruma, Edith Segal, and Allison Burrough's in rehearsal for *Black &*

White, 1928. Courtesy of the Jerome Robbins Dance Division, New York Library for the Performing Arts   86
14   Programme for the Second Annual Interracial Dance at the Rockland Palace, 1930. Courtesy of the Jerome Robbins Dance Division, New York Library for the Performing Arts   88
15   Photo of the New Duncan Dancers performing Kinder Küche Kirche, printed in the *New Dance League Bulletin*, summer issue, 1936. Courtesy of the Jerome Robbins Dance Division, New York Library for the Performing Arts   92
16   Red Dancers, *Dance of the Washerwomen*, 1935. Photographer unknown. Courtesy of the Jerome Robbins Dance Division, New York Library for the Performing Arts   93
17   Suzanne Lacy with Leslie Becker, Lisa Findley, Amana Harris, Leuckessia Hirsh, Unique Holland, Annice Jacoby, Sheila Jordan, and Maxine Wyman, photo of summer school workshop within the *Expectations* project, 1996–97. Photo by Suzanne Lacy. Courtesy of Suzanne Lacy   108
18   Suzanne Lacy with Leslie Becker, Lisa Findley, Amana Harris, Leuckessia Hirsh, Unique Holland, Annice Jacoby, Sheila Jordan, and Maxine Wyman, image of drawing made by summer school programme participant within the *Expectations* project, 1996–97. Photo by Jeff McLane. Courtesy of Suzanne Lacy   114
19   Suzanne Lacy with Leslie Becker, Lisa Findley, Amana Harris, Leuckessia Hirsh, Unique Holland, Annice Jacoby, Sheila Jordan, and Maxine Wyman, *Expectations*, 1996–97, installation at Capp Street Gallery, San Francisco, California. Photo by Suzanne Lacy   115
20   Martha Rosler, Installation view of "Home Front" in Martha Rosler, *If You Lived Here ...*, Dia Art Foundation, New York 1989 (photograph © Martha Rosler, provided by the artist)   130
21   Martha Rosler, Installation view of "Homeless: The Street and Other Venues" in Martha Rosler, *If You Lived Here ...* Dia Art Foundation, New York 1989 (photograph © Martha Rosler, provided by the artist)   131
22   Martha Rosler, Installation view of "City: Visions and Revisions" in Martha Rosler, *If You Lived Here ...* Dia Art Foundation, New York 1989 (photograph © Martha Rosler, provided by the artist)   131
23   Martha Rosler, Installation view of "Home Front" in Martha Rosler, *If You Lived Here ...*, Dia Art Foundation, New York 1989 (photograph © Martha Rosler, provided by the artist)   134
24   Installation by the The Urban Centre for Photography, *Demolished by Neglect*, on display in Martha Rosler, *If You Lived Here ...* Dia Art Foundation, New York 1989 (photograph © Martha Rosler, provided by the artist)   137
25   The Mad Housers erecting shelter in Brooklyn (photograph © Martha Rosler, provided by the artist)   139

ILLUSTRATIONS　　　　　　　　　　　　　　　　　　　　　　　　　　　　　　　　XI

26　The Mad Housers shelter installation at "Homeless: The Street and Other Venues" in Martha Rosler, *If You Lived Here ...* Dia Art Foundation, New York 1989 (photograph © Martha Rosler, provided by the artist)　140
27　Staging *One-Third of a Nation*, Seattle, 1938. Courtesy of the Federal Theater Project Photograph Collection, University of Washington Special Collection　148
28　'The city grows', in *One-Third of a Nation*, New York City, 1938. Courtesy of the Federal Theatre Project Collection, Special Collections and Archives, George Mason University Libraries　150
29　Irish family scene, in *One-Third of a Nation*, Detroit production 1938. Courtesy of the Jerome Robbins Dance Division, New York Library for the Performing Arts　153
30　Dance of the Washerwomen, choreography by Edith Segal, in *One-Third of a Nation*, Detroit production, 1938. Courtesy of the Jerome Robbins Dance Division, New York Library for the Performing Arts　154
31　*One-Third of a Nation*, Philadelphia, Pennsylvania, 1938. Courtesy of the Federal Theatre Project Collection, Special Collections and Archives, George Mason University Libraries　156
32　Berenice Abbot, *Huts and Unemployed*, from the series *Changing New York*, (Federal Art Project) 1935. Courtesy of the New York Public Library　165
33　Berenice Abbot, *Shelter on the Water Front, Coenties Slip, Pier 5, East River, Manhattan*, from the series *Changing New York*, (Federal Art Project) 1938. Courtesy of the New York Public Library　166
34　Aaron Siskind, 'Brotherhood of the Sleeping Car Porters', from *Harlem Document*, gelatin silver print, ca. 1935, George Eastman Museum, gift of Aaron Siskind. © Virginia Museum of Fine Art　177
35　Aaron Siskind, 'Church Interior', 1938, from *Harlem Document*, gelatin silver print, printed 1980 by Michaela Allan Murphy under the supervision of Aaron Siskind. George Eastman Museum, Gift of LIGHT Gallery. © Virginia Museum of Fine Art　178
36　Russell Lee, *Bedroom*, Chicago, FSA, from Richard Wright and Edwin Rosskam, *12 Million Black Voices: A Folk History of the Negro in the United States*, New York: Viking Press, 1941. Photo: Emile Ebrahim Kelly　181
37　Aerial view of Project Row Houses in 2015. Photograph by Peter Molick courtesy of Project Row Houses　184
38　Row houses before renovations. Photograph by Sheryl Tucker Vasquez courtesy of Project Row Houses　185
39　Drive by Exhibit at Project Row Houses – Installation of work by Israel McCloud 1993 courtesy of Project Row Houses　188
40　Young Mothers Residence at Project Row Houses. Photo by Peter Molick. Courtesy of Project Row Houses　190

Introduction: Historicising Social Practice

It is 1938 in New York City, and a group of government-employed actors, directors, writers and researchers produce a play named *One Third of a Nation*. Titled after President Franklin Delano Roosevelt's second inaugural speech in January 1937, the play responds to calls for an extension of the New Deal on the grounds that Roosevelt still saw 'one-third of a nation ill-housed, ill-clad, ill-nourished'. The play uses cinema projection, modern dance, vaudeville and elaborate sets, in order to both satirise and applaud the Wagner-Steagall Housing Act, which extended public funding for housing, and was signed into law on 1 September 1937 as a partial answer to the problems laid out in Roosevelt's speech. Within the play, a 'Little Man' character carries the audience through an episodic, expanded documentary that seeks to discover the cause of the housing crisis in order to propose solutions. Early on, the Little Man time-travels back to the 1800s in order to witness the parcelling out of New York City to wealthy landowners, with this forming an origin point for *One Third of a Nation*'s account of contemporary dispossession. The play goes on to explore the capacities of state welfare as a solution to the housing crisis. For those on stage as well as in the audience, the stakes of this narrative not only pertained to the uses of public funds for housing, but also to the use and meaning of government sponsored art and culture.

Some 55 years later, organised by the artist Rick Lowe and working under the title of *Project Row Houses*, a group gets together in the Third Ward of Houston, Texas to begin a project rebuilding dilapidated shotgun shacks. Firstly, the shacks are commandeered for artists' studios, and later, young mothers with limited housing options are invited to move in with their families. From its inception in 1993 to the present, *Project Row Houses* remains a powerful force in the Third Ward, reshaping the relationship between art and life. Both *One Third of a Nation* and *Project Row Houses* received support from the United States government, the first through the Works Progress Administration Federal Theatre Project, and the second through the National Endowment for the Arts. However, in the first instance, that funding and the work it supported came under such a degree of public and legal scrutiny that the Federal Theatre Project was closed in 1939. In contrast, the support *Project Row Houses* gained from the National Endowment for the Arts emerged at a historical moment where socially engaged art projects were perceived as a salve to the controversies of the culture wars, which had raged over the morals of publicly funded culture from the end of the 1980s. Since 1993, *Project Row Houses* has become an exemplary artwork within the field that has come to be known as social practice, meaning artworks that take social interaction as their material.

Both *One Third of a Nation* and *Project Row Houses* sought to address a crisis in housing and living conditions; both projects were organised by large, collaborative groups; both projects positioned art and cultural work as capable of contributing solutions to social issues; and both projects were supported through government funds. In examining the disparate yet connected artistic and social possibilities of such initiatives, this book offers a new perspective on the relationship between art and state formation in the United States. By examining the growth of socially engaged art and culture in both the 1930s and 1990s, we can gain a more complex view of the surge in art, criticism, and curating that takes social relations as its material since the 1990s in the United States. Written as a comparative history, I analyse artworks by Suzanne Lacy, Rick Lowe and Martha Rosler in relation to performance, experimental theatre, modern dance, and photography produced within the leftist Cultural Front of the New Deal era. During both periods, there was increased financial support from the state for community-based art, as well as a proliferation of grassroots and self-organised projects.

1 The New Deal Imaginary

The continued relevance of the political situation during the 1930s has become particularly evident following the crash and economic crisis that began in 2007, in ways that also enables a reappraisal of the immediately preceding administrations of President George W. Bush and President Bill Clinton. For example, the significance of President Clinton's 1999 repeal of the 1933 Glass-Steagall Act has been a central motif within analysis of the post-millennial crisis. Brought into law to ensure separation between commercial and investment banks, the Act was introduced during the first New Deal to safeguard deposits in commercial banks and prevent speculation. As Robert Pollin explains, the effective removal of Glass-Steagall in 1999 by President Clinton helped fuel rampant speculation and contributed to the 'precarious financial pyramid' that crashed spectacularly in 2007–8.[1] Since then, the rise and fall of Glass-Steagall has come to symbolise de-regulation and the decline of a post-war economic order in the US, with the result that the re-introduction of regulatory measures by President Barack Obama in 2010 was heralded by many liberals as a new 'Glass-Steagall'

---

1   Pollin 2000, pp. 27–8. Most notoriously, the removal of Glass-Steagall enabled deregulation of the financial sector, allowing banks to take on debt and lend money kept in commercial banks against unreliable collateral. See also Blackburn 2008, p. 64.

and a triumphant return to New Deal era politics.² Equally, right-wingers and free marketeers decried Obama's reforms as a sign of encroaching state controls and sought to downplay the role of deregulation in precipitating the crisis.³ Beyond the Glass-Steagall Act, the 1990s saw the final dismantling of the New Deal welfare state, as Aid to Families with Dependent Children, the last vestige of the Social Security Act, was eliminated.⁴ Since the 2007 crash, then, the Depression and the New Deal have both frequently been invoked as a warning about the ravages of economic decline, and as an argument against neoliberalism in favour of an expanded state.

Rather than the social realist painting that many view as the sum total of art in the US during the New Deal era, this book addresses dance, performance, photography and innovative exhibitions which frequently interacted with radical politics and community organising during the period. By considering such activity in relation to the flowering, and subsequent institutionalisation of, social practice in the 1990s – the decade that saw the final dismantling of the New Deal order – this book examines the antinomies of the 1930s as a terrain of struggle within the cultural imaginary of art and politics in the US. The New Deal took shape through a series of government programmes, legislative acts, financial reforms and public works which sought to alleviate the crisis of the Depression. The first New Deal, enacted in 1933 after President Roosevelt's election, focused on financial reforms, addressing the unemployment crisis through the Public Works Administration (PWA) and reforming agricultural production. The projects dating to the 1930s addressed in this book, however, were mostly produced through the Works Progress Administration, which was enacted during the Second New Deal, beginning in 1935 within the context of what Michael Denning describes as the Cultural Front.⁵ With this phrase, Denning describes a social formation composed of plebeian artists and intellectuals, usually the second generation of a second wave of immigrants to the US, as well as African Americans, who formed an allegiance with an older generation of American modernists within the context of the Popular Front. While the phrase Popular Front designates a particular period within international Communist history, that is, a set of policies and approaches primarily marked by a coalitional drive uniting the centre and far left as a response to the growth of fascism, it also refers to a social movement. In the US, this social movement encompassed activity such as Communists working within the cultural pro-

---

2   Treanor 2010.
3   Pearlstein 2012.
4   Pateman 2005.
5   Denning 1998.

grammes of the New Deal; marches through Harlem in opposition to the Italian invasion of Ethiopia; a flowering of experimental 'little magazines'; summer camps where children learned dances designed to raise class consciousness; labour struggles presented on the silver screen; and interracial balls in Harlem, sound-tracked by Duke Ellington and his orchestra.

Within this book, the Living Newspaper unit of the Works Progress Administration Federal Theatre Project WPA-FTP (1936–9) stands as a central case study within the Cultural Front and exemplifies the syncretic nature of that formation. At its origins, the Living Newspaper was a theatrical form developed in the Soviet Union in response to the March 1919 decree of the Central Committee of the Communist Party that established a far-reaching apparatus for the distribution of news, information and revolutionary propaganda during the civil war.[6] Between 1923 and 1928, the Living Newspaper was the most popular form within amateur proletarian theatres, and by 1927 over seven thousand amateur groups had sprung up through Soviet Russia.[7] The formation of the Blue Blouse Living Newspaper troupe by the Moscow School of Journalism was partly responsible for the rapidity of this growth. Blue Blouse performances began with a parade of 'headlines' that were followed by eight to fifteen short episodes that interrogated, satirised and explained those stories presented in the media. Through their episodic structure, these performances recreated the format of a newspaper and the Blue Blouses incorporated satirical songs, dance, pantomime and pageantry, aspects that were tied together by the narrativising 'Voice of the Living Newspaper'. Such characteristics were constant through the Americanisation of the Living Newspaper, as was the use of exaggerated props to codify the social types under examination: a top hat represented a capitalist, whilst an absurdly oversized red pen stood for a bureaucrat.[8] At the end of sketches, spectators were asked to give their thoughts and determine the ending. Actors were also planted in the audience to either disrupt the drama or act as a kind of community leader – tropes common with the drive towards participation in many of the social practice works from the 1990s discussed in this book, as well as the case studies drawn from the Cultural Front.[9]

After a tour through Germany in 1927, the Blue Blouses returned to the Soviet Union to find their productions had fallen into disfavour, as the aesthetic

---

6 Cosgrove 1982, pp. 5–6.
7 Cosgrove, 1982, p. 9.
8 Mally, 2008, p. 5.
9 Cosgrove, 1982, p. 14.

policies of the Comintern moved towards Socialist Realism.[10] The Living Newspaper subsequently declined in the Soviet Union, with official support withdrawn in 1932 and the Moscow Blue Blouse troupe shut down in 1933. Charges centred on complaints that the use of types – rather than rounded characters – made the Blue Blouse Living Newspaper too humorous, frivolous and satirical of the revolution. However, as the Living Newspaper began to decline in the Soviet Union, its reputation increased in the US, both within the proletarian theatre movement and, from 1935 onwards, in the Living Newspaper Unit of the WPA-FTP. It is not clear when or by whom the Living Newspaper was first performed in the US, but there was a lively proletarian theatre movement from the 1920s onwards, formed mostly by communities of immigrants. In addition, Hallie Flanagan, director of the WPA-FTP, saw several Blue Blouse presentations whilst visiting Russia on a Guggenheim Fellowship in 1926, affirming that those performances had 'the precision of machines and the zeal of those who spread the faith'.[11]

As Stuart Cosgrove explains, almost everybody who worked on the early formation of the WPA-FTP claimed the Living Newspaper unit as their idea.[12] Flanagan's appointment of Elmer Rice as director of the New York Federal Theatre Project unit was surely central to its creation. Rice had made a significant contribution to expressionist theatre in the US with his play *The Adding Machine* of 1923, which told the story of an accountant replaced by a machine, and also *Street Scene* of 1929, which concerned the lives and relationships in a working-class community in New York. In Flanagan's account, she proposed the Living Newspaper unit as a solution to Rice's concerns that the WPA-FTP would discriminate over hiring actors and only require a limited number of workers.[13] Because the Living Newspaper required large numbers of workers with different skills in film, music, acting, staging, writing and research, this solved Rice's qualms about taking on the role of Director, and fully cohered with the role of the WPA-FTP as a relief programme for theatre workers.

Emulating the partnership of the Soviet Living Newspaper with the Moscow School of Journalism, Rice invited Morris Watson, the leftist national vice president of the American Newspaper Guild, a union for journalists and newspaper workers, to head the Living Newspaper Unit. Flanagan later stated that Watson knew very little about theatre, but his appointment by Rice meant the Unit

10   Ibid.
11   Cosgrove 1982, p. 18.
12   Cosgrove 1982, p. 46.
13   Flanagan 1973, p. vii.

gained sponsorship from the Newspaper Guild, which pleased her.[14] Staffing of the unit was set up like a 'large city daily'; there was an editor-in-chief, managing editor, city editor, reporters and copy readers and as a collective unit they began 'to shake the living daylights out of a thousand books, reports, newspaper and magazine articles' in their approach to mass media.[15] The issues presented were often closely tied to Depression-era, Popular Front causes such as housing, unemployment, labour, international struggles and lynching, with the latter two concerns never making it to the stage due to censorship.

Flanagan emphasised that from the outset the Living Newspaper 'was concerned not with surface news, scandal, human interest stories, but rather with the conditions back of conditions'.[16] *Ethiopia*, the first production by the Living Newspaper Unit, was directed by Rice and written by Arthur Arent, and scheduled to open in January 1936. However, the play did not make it past the final dress rehearsal due to its portrayal of Benito Mussolini and Haile Selassie, with this representation of foreign government leaders drawing the attention of Flanagan's superior Jacob Baker, who was the assistant to Harry Hopkins, director of the WPA. Baker flagged his concerns with the State Department because he was worried that the play might inflame diplomatic relations, and *Ethiopia* was swiftly scrapped. Subsequently, the WPA issued a decree stating that no dramatic representation could be made on the Federal Theatre stage of a sitting foreign minister or cabinet politician. Alongside *Ethiopia*, Rice was also in the stages of planning a Living Newspaper called *The South* about lynching and sharecropping with Joseph Losey.[17] Recognising that this would be even more inflammatory than *Ethiopia*, Rice resigned from the Unit, stating he would not comply with censorship.[18]

Following the false start of *Ethiopia*, the Living Newspaper Unit embarked on an intense period of work in order to prepare an amenable first production, and to avoid coming under further scrutiny from the Federal Emergency Relief Administration (FERA) for inactivity.[19] On 14 March 1936 *Triple-A Plowed Under* opened, drawing its title and subject matter from the controversies around the Agricultural Adjustment Act (AAA). Brought into legislation in 1933, the AAA raised crop prices by reducing production. Farmers were paid subsidies to leave some of their land unplanted, and farm animals were slaughtered.

---

14   Ibid. and Bentley 1988, p. 211.
15   Flanagan 1973, p. vii.
16   Ibid.
17   For details of other Living Newspapers not produced, see Nadler, 1995, pp. 615–22.
18   Flanagan 1973, pp. vii–viii.
19   Cosgrove 1982, p. 57.

INTRODUCTION: HISTORICISING SOCIAL PRACTICE 7

These policies left sharecroppers disadvantaged and provoked public outcry towards the cutting of production whilst many went hungry. The Supreme Court declared the AAA unconstitutional in January 1936, an event played out in *Triple-A Plowed Under*. Agrarian poverty was presented in *Triple-A* not as a 'natural' disaster, but instead as something engineered by traders in the wheat pit of Chicago, who oppressed both farmers and the proletarian industrial workers for whom bread prices rose. The play presented a story of solidarity between farmers and the unemployed and remained open for 85 performances over nearly two months at the Biltmore Theatre in New York City. The performance ends with a dialogue between a chorus of the unemployed and a chorus of farmers, each affirming 'we need you' to one another, repeating this statement of projected unity until it culminates in the formation of a Farmer-Labor party before the curtain goes down.[20]

The formation of a Farmer-Labor Party was Communist Party USA (CPUSA) policy during the start of the Popular Front in 1935–6, and it was this final scene of unity, amongst others, that led *Triple-A Plowed Under* to be denounced as 'the most outrageous misuse of taxpayers money that the Roosevelt Administration has yet been guilty of' by the William Randolph Hearst-owned *New York Evening Journal*.[21] The representation of figures such as Earl Browder, General Secretary of the CPUSA, also made *Triple-A Plowed Under* vulnerable to charges of un-Americanism. In one performance, a member of the Veterans Association arose at Browder's appearance on stage and began singing the 'Star Spangled Banner' in protest.[22] As the director, Losey was singled out for criticism, with his participation in CPUSA-associated theatre groups making him particularly vulnerable. Prior to his work with the WPA-FTP, Losey had been immersed in the proletarian avant-garde performance scene in New York, was friends with Bertolt Brecht, and also knew Erwin Piscator.[23] The controversies around the Living Newspaper unit and wider WPA-FTP eventually led to Flanagan being called to testify in front of the House Un-American Activities Committee, popularly known as the Dies committee, in December 1938. In the Dies committee hearing, Flanagan was quizzed about her visits to the Soviet Union and the communist leanings of WPA-FTP productions, and following budget cuts

---

20   Editorial Staff of the Living Newspaper Federal Theatre Project for New York City, script for *Triple-A Plowed Under*, 1936.
21   Cosgrove 1985, p. 248.
22   Flanagan 1973, p. x.
23   Cosgrove 1985, p. 57. Also see Lyon, 1983 for details of Losey and Brecht's 1947 collaboration during the first US theatre production of *Galileo*. Later on, Losey became a well-known film director in the UK after being blacklisted from the US during the McCarthy period.

and further scrutiny, the WPA-FTP closed in 1939.[24] The Living Newspaper Unit attracted particular suspicion due to its Soviet origins. However, all performances produced within the Unit intertwined characteristics from the American performance avant-garde, as well as popular forms of entertainment such as vaudeville and slapstick. To a greater or lesser extent, all the Living Newspapers staged by the WPA-FTP can be viewed as exemplary of the syncretism Denning identifies as foundational to the Cultural Front and its status as an avant-garde formation of primary importance.[25] Its rise and decline also speaks to the political stakes of culture during the New Deal era, and the means by which this period can be viewed as a resource for thinking through the growth of social practice in the US during the 1990s. By focusing on how the Left – particularly the CPUSA – responded culturally to the Depression and the New Deal, this book explores the interaction between the state, radicalism and artistic production. This assists in analysing the composition of the participants in the works I discuss, and establishes a problematic concerning the relationship between race and class formation. From the outset, it must be said that the orientation of radical politics towards an industrial working class in the 1930s and the presence of an active Communist Party and lively culture of the left differs significantly from the subjects, practices and forms of organisation that comprise the artistic activity I discuss dating from the 1990s. However, as will become clear, despite the decline of an organised left, this book does not favour projects dating to the 1930s, nor does it seek to add to the reformist admiration of the New Deal as a political order.

2   The Stakes of Social Practice

Since the early 1990s, there has been a significant growth of artists working with social relations as their material and an equivalent expansion in art historical and critical discourse that attempts to theorise, historicise and evaluate such practices. As writers, curators and artists have positioned themselves as identifying and defining a new 'movement', a range of terminology has proliferated. In no particular order, some of the labels devised for this work include participatory art, collaborative art, socially engaged art, dialogical art, new genre public art, relational aesthetics, littoral art, collective artistic praxis and social practice. There are differences between these terms, but overwhelmingly the

---

24   Browder p. 154.
25   Denning 1997, p. 65.

practices to which they refer are collaborative, ephemeral and usually involve an encounter between artists, and a group of non-artists that may be identified with a particular social group. The work is process-based and durational, usually coming in the form of a project that analyses issues binding the group together, or alternatively will act as a touchstone for collaboration between previously unfamiliar individuals. In light of such consistent formal conventions, it is tempting to read the persistent re-naming of such practices as either a case of historical amnesia or simply a quest for scholarly novelty. In this book I use the term 'social practice', as it is currently the least attached to a particular scholar, artist or curator, as well as being the term that enjoys widest currency in the US.

The French curator Nicolas Bourriaud presented one of the first theorisations of this tendency in his book *Relational Aesthetics* (English publication: 1998). For Bourriaud, relational aesthetics describes artworks that take social relations as their material and transfer some power to spectators and audiences, with these practices helping us learn 'how to inhabit the world in a better way'.[26] Drawing on Karl Marx's analysis of trading communities not fully subsumed within capitalism, Bourriaud describes relational art as a 'social interstice' marked by connections and meetings, conviviality and encounters, with the aesthetic posed as a form of emancipatory play that draws on, but somehow exceeds everyday interactions.[27] Bourriaud views this 'relational aesthetic' as evading commodification through its dematerialised and ephemeral form, suggesting that such art can counter reification, commodification and alienation by replacing objects with subjects and affirming social relations that appear to step outside the logic of capital. Bourriaud's *Relational Aesthetics* has been widely criticised, most persuasively by Stewart Martin.[28] As Martin explains, Bourriaud's affirmation of non-object oriented art as less subject to the laws of value misses the point that value is produced through social relations. Following Karl Marx, Martin stresses the dialectic between subject and object in order to emphasise that commodification is a process where social relations become reified, and objects fetishised, meaning that artistic appeals to dematerialisation as an ethical gesture capable of swerving capital are more complex than Bourriaud suggests.

It was precisely this yoking of aesthetics to ethics and politics that led Claire Bishop to author her attack on Bourriaud's *Relational Aesthetics*. This was followed by her article 'The Social Turn: Collaboration and its Discontents' which

---

26   Bourriaud 1998, p. 13.
27   Bourriaud 1998, p. 16.
28   Martin 2007, pp. 369–86.

appeared in *Artforum* in early 2006, and then the development of these arguments in *Artificial Hells* in 2012.[29] As one of the most prominent writers on socially engaged and collaborative practice, Bishop believes this art 'forms what avant-garde we have today', yet remains wary of how 'There can be no failed, unsuccessful, unresolved or boring works of collaborative art because all are equally essential to the task of strengthening the social bond'.[30] Across her writing on the subject, Bishop's primary concern is to contest the way in which aesthetic criteria have supposedly been supplanted by ethical judgments and sociological analysis.[31]

Bishop's position was clarified through her debate with Grant Kester in *Artforum* in 2006. Another significant voice within the field, Kester coined the term 'dialogical aesthetics' in his 2004 book *Conversation Pieces: Community and Communication in Modern Art*, in which he draws upon the terminology of Brazilian educator and activist Paulo Freire to express the pedagogical element within the practices he affirms.[32] Freire's *Pedagogy of the Oppressed* (1970) remains a seminal text for education activists and has been taken up widely within community-based and pedagogical art practices. For Freire, the basic principle of dialogical education rests on a belief that 'banking' education – in which the teacher stores 'deposits' of knowledge in the student – must be abolished in order to make way for 'problem-posing' or dialogical education, which promotes 'acts of cognition' rather than transfers of information. In problem-posing education, reality can be viewed dialectically and therefore appears capable of transformation.[33] Accordingly, Kester suggests dialogical artworks cannot be judged through 'pleasure-based' art historical methodologies that emphasise the visual, and should instead be evaluated through criteria that redefine aesthetic experience as durational.[34] He also supports the introduction of an ethical evaluative frame that stresses the difference between practices espousing a paternalistic model of social reform, and truly dialogical works which establish an equitable exchange between artist and community.[35]

As demonstrated by his elevation of the dialogical over the paternalistic, Kester is attached to ethical criteria for artworks insofar as these emphasise the cultivation of non-hierarchical relations. In contrast, Bishop views ethics

---

29 Bishop 2004, Bishop 2006 and Bishop 2012.
30 Bishop 2012, p. 13.
31 Bishop 2012, p. 17.
32 Kester 2004, p. 10.
33 Freire, 1970.
34 Kester, 2004, p. 12.
35 Kester, 2004, pp. 131–40.

INTRODUCTION: HISTORICISING SOCIAL PRACTICE   11

as the dominant and therefore normative register through which this work is assessed and seeks to re-introduce aesthetic judgment. Significantly, she views the attachment to ethics within the evaluation of social practice as inextricable from the instrumentalisation of art by the state, and makes particular reference to New Labour cultural policy in the UK.[36] In opposition to this bureaucratisation of art's ameliorative capacities and the liberal promotion of 'inclusion', Bishop valorises work that pursues an aesthetic centred on antagonism, indeterminacy and the limits of political discourse. Consequently, Kester argues that there can be no legitimate engagement between artists and political struggles for Bishop, lest they become 'doomed to represent in the most naïve and facile manner possible, a given political issue or constituent'.[37]

Bishop's aversion to art produced or circulated in affinity with political struggles is related to how she historicises the social turn in art and aesthetics. She links the rise of social practice in the early 1990s to the fall of Communism, which 'deprived the Left of the last vestiges of the revolution that had once linked political and aesthetic radicalism'.[38] This confirms her aversion to revolutionary politics, allowing Kester to characterise her position as 'typical of post cold-war intellectuals embarrassed by work that evokes leftist ideals'.[39] In *Artificial Hells* Bishop triangulates her association of the rise of social practice with the fall of Communism alongside two artistic precedents. The historical avant-garde following the Russian Revolution of 1917 forms the first reference point, the second being the neo avant-garde that developed in relation to the upheavals of 1968. For Bishop, these dates – 1917, 1968 and 1989 – are a continuum marking the rise and eventual 'collapse of a collectivist vision of society'.[40] After this so-called collapse, Bishop argues that social practice can only become the true inheritor of the avant-garde and neo-avant-garde by pursuing shock, absurdity and rupture rather than amelioration (which would fall under the paternalistic, as defined by Kester) or social transformation (which would fall under Kester's ambitions for the dialogical.) As will become clear, my account diverges from Bishop's due to the way her argument mobilises the aesthetic as a generalised and abstract category that can be applied to evaluate artworks in a uniform and ahistorical manner. Politically, I refuse her belief that because the forms of ideology binding state to citizen are totally encompassing, resistance can now only be located in micro-gestures.

---

36 Bishop, 2012, pp. 14–15.
37 Kester 2006, p. 22.
38 Bishop 2006, p. 179.
39 Kester 2006, p. 22.
40 Bishop 2012, p. 3.

Despite Kester's and Bishop's differences, both writers present a similar genealogy of social practice that incorporates the European, inter-war avant-gardes and then 1960s conceptualism as key precedents. Whilst Bishop is more attached to an avant-gardist model that emphasises aesthetic and political rupture, Kester emphasises continuity by situating dialogical art at the end of a timeline that begins with the concept of minimalist theatricality proposed in Michael Fried's *Art and Objecthood*.[41] Famously, Fried argued that the scale and materiality of sculptures by Tony Smith, Donald Judd and Robert Morris produced an anthropomorphic effect, functioning as 'surrogate persons' through their hollowness, size and responsiveness to their physical environment in terms of light, space and scale.[42] Fried's disapproving claim that minimalist sculpture produced a 'new genre of theater' was centred on his observation that visuality was withdrawn and accompanied by an aesthetic shift towards the 'literal' or everyday.[43] For his purposes, Kester *affirms* Minimalism's theatricality as the beginning of an 'increased emphasis on art as a process of collaborative interaction' which reprises the tenets of the avant-garde in a more exploratory, less antagonistic mode.[44] Tracing the consequences of this, Kester describes how conceptual artists such as Hans Haacke and Adrian Piper politicised the minimalist inquiry into the cognitive effects of space and scale in the 1970s, also citing the video and performance work of artists including Vito Acconci and Dan Graham as precedents to dialogical art through their emphasis on duration.[45]

Following this formative debate, Shannon Jackson has more recently argued that understanding social practice as a revision of sculpture, theatre or dance produces a range of different meanings.[46] In contrast to Bishop and Kester, Jackson writes from the perspective of performance and theatre studies, and highlights a continued aversion towards theatre within the art world, a position inherited not only from Fried's seminal *Art and Objecthood* essay (1967), but also a much longer intellectual history.[47] In her view, the assumptions made within the visual arts rarely take stock of either the historical or current com-

---

41   Kester 2004, p. 153.
42   Fried 1998, p. 153.
43   Fried 1998, p. 136.
44   Kester 2004, p. 53.
45   Ibid.
46   Jackson 2011, p. 18.
47   Jackson identifies a 'prejudice' against theatricality in Western intellectual history from Plato through Rousseau to J.L. Austin and Theodor Adorno. Her argument does not seek to affirm theatre over the visual arts, but rather to insert theatre and performance history more fully into the development of social practice. Jackson 2011, p. 20.

plexity of theatre; in response Jackson suggests we need to bring different genealogies into 'high relief'.[48] In addressing works that have been situated as art, theatre, photography and dance alongside one another, this book takes up Jackson's challenge. Unlike other art historical accounts that analyse the growth of social practice as a global phenomenon that obediently succeeds the inter-war avant-gardes, minimalism, conceptualism and video, this book centres on one nation, providing a concrete response to the crucial issues Bishop raises around instrumentalisation by focusing on the rapid growth in socially engaged cultural activity during two divergent state formations.[49] Because social practice art has been so bound up with issues of state formation, in particular around labour, race and welfare, my contention is that we can deepen our history of the field by drawing case studies from one nation state.

If artistic responses to the Depression, the influence of a European avant-garde and the establishment of the WPA cultural programmes supported the flourishing of socially engaged cultural practice in the 1930s, the political coordinates around the growth and codification of social practice in the US during the 1990s are markedly different. While the projects I address by Lacy, Lowe and Rosler in this book unarguably have an art historical and aesthetic relationship to the histories of minimalism, conceptualism and performance as laid out by Bishop and Kester, they also find their formation through the political and social context of the culture wars of the late 1980s and the restructuring of the National Endowment for the Arts (NEA) in the years following. Established in 1965 as part of President Lyndon Johnson's Great Society, the NEA formed part of a mid-1960s re-imagining of New Deal welfare programmes. The creation of the NEA and the National Endowment for the Humanities fell within this vision, but were also, from the outset, implicated within a Cold War culture that situated artistic and cultural freedom in the US against the strictures of cultural production in the Soviet Union. By 1989, however, the necessity of promoting America's cultural freedom in contrast to the repressiveness of their rival hegemon was coming to an end, and in its place, the NEA spent much of the 1990s shifting towards the prioritisation of utilitarian values and social impact in response to domestic, conservative attacks on the funding of culture.[50]

The conservative attacks on the NEA began in 1989, following the controversy over Robert Mapplethorpe's exhibition *The Perfect Moment* at the Corcoran

---

48 Jackson 2011, p. 17.
49 Other significant publications within this discourse include Lacy (ed.) 1995; Kwon 2002; Stimson and Gregory Sholette (eds.) 2007; Sholette 2011; Kester 2011 and more recently, La Berge 2019.
50 Yúdice 1999.

Gallery of Art in Washington DC, and the exhibition of Andres Serrano's *Piss Christ* (1987) the same year. Mapplethorpe's exhibition had received NEA funding, and included photographs of interracial intimacy, gay sex, and S&M practices, while Serrano had indirectly received NEA funds via the Southeastern Centre for Contemporary Art.[51] Senators Jesse Helms and Alfonse D'Amato led those attacks, and also targeted Marlon Riggs' film *Tongues Untied* (1989), which explored Black gay life and had received $5,000 from the NEA. By 1990, projects by the so-called 'NEA Four' – Karen Finlay, Holly Hughes, John Fleck and Tim Miller – were all pre-emptively vetoed for funding by John Frohnmayer, the head of the NEA. What overwhelmingly links these artists' work is their focus on sexuality and LGBT+ experience during the growing AIDS crisis. The attacks on NEA funding forms part of the increase in power the religious right enjoyed during the period, and by 1996, with a Republican dominated congress, the NEA suffered forty percent cuts and the elimination of almost all individual artist grants.[52]

The homophobic, sexist and racist agendas driving these attacks on NEA funding should also be viewed in relation to the broader undermining of state spending, which had begun in the late 1970s, shortly after President Johnson's Great Society reforms. As Lewis Hyde explains, the de-funding of the NEA can be linked with the tax revolt that began in California in 1978 through the passage of Proposition 13, which radically decreased property taxes, and limited future increases.[53] By cutting taxes, less money was available to support education, parks, libraries and social security, meaning city councils had to decide what services would continue to be funded, and what would be cut, decisions that would be driven by increasing scarcity. Therefore, while the growth in power of the religious right may have ideologically legitimised forty percent budget cuts to the NEA in 1996, this not only took place after what George Yúdice describes as a crisis in the meaning of state sponsorship for the arts at the close of the Cold War, but also during a period where the logic of scarcity imposed by Proposition 13 had provided a model of defunding.[54]

---

51   Hartman, 2015, pp. 191–7.
52   National Endowment for the Arts 1996 Annual Report, p. 4.
53   Hyde 1999, p. 265.
54   Yúdice, 1999, p. 20. Allan Sekula makes a compelling case for the relationship between the homophobia involved in the attacks on the NEA, and distaste towards public funding as non-productive, noting that the NEA was attacked for its 'profligacy', falling in line with the conservative intellectual Gertrude Himmelfarb's suggestion of a 'connection between the (supposed) spendthrift shortsightedness of Keynesian economics and John Maynard Keynes' personal life as a homosexual'. See Sekula 1989.

Such forces underpinned the ideological redefinition of the NEA's remit, most clearly captured in the 1997 *American Canvas* report, authored by Gary Larson. *American Canvas* responded to the right-wing assault on arts and culture by arguing that if public funds were to survive, art and culture must be translatable into 'civic, social and educational' terms.[55] Responding to the growth in socially engaged art since the beginning of the 1990s as well as the crisis over what public funding for culture meant, Larson advocated that artists should continue to penetrate the 'civic structure ... far afield from the traditional aesthetic functions of the arts'.[56] Describing an 'extended role for culture' where art organisations could partner with civic, charitable and state bodies, Larson affirmed the aims of the report as follows:

> No longer restricted solely to the sanctioned arenas of culture, the arts would be literally suffused throughout the civic structure, finding a home in a variety of community service and economic development activities – from youth programs and crime prevention to job training and race relations – far afield from the traditional aesthetic functions of the arts. This extended role for culture can also be seen in the many new partners that arts organizations have taken on in recent years, with school districts, parks and recreation departments, convention and visitor bureaus, chambers of commerce, and a host of social welfare agencies all serving to highlight the utilitarian aspects of the arts in contemporary society.[57]

Through this rhetoric, *American Canvas* shifted blame for the culture wars away from the outrage of religious right, and onto the institutions of the art world and art education, which it repeatedly painted as elitist and out of touch with communities. Two communities clearly emerge in the report: the art community, and then all other communities, amorphously defined. The report is primarily concerned with how a chasm seems to have emerged between these blocs, and how to close this gap. Its solution is posed in the form of partnerships that could work towards, as Yúdice writes, a situation where the arts and culture sector attempts to solve America's problems, to 'enhance education, salve racial strife, help reverse urban blight through cultural tourism, create jobs, reduce crime, and perhaps even make a profit' in order to legitimise its funding and presence.[58]

---

55 Gary Larson, *American Canvas*, National Endowment for the Arts, 1997.
56 Larson 1997, p. 127.
57 Larson 1997 pp. 127–8.
58 Yúdice 1999, p. 26.

In the same way that the WPA arts projects formed a central organising structure in the 1930s that fed off and into a broader range of activities, the shifts in NEA ideology in the 1990s also affected how non-governmental and private funding for the arts would be allocated. This dynamic is important to bear in mind, as the projects discussed in the following pages were not all funded through the WPA, or the NEA, and yet nonetheless remain part of the same climate where funding priorities are synchronised through decisions made by the state. As Robert Hughes noted in 1995, just prior to the 1996 NEA budget cuts, private philanthropy would largely follow suit with NEA policy, a trend exemplified by the newsletter *Corporate Philanthropy*'s declaration that 'We no longer "support" the arts. We use the arts in innovative ways to support the social causes chosen by our companies'.[59]

3 Prevented Futures and Usable Pasts

At this point, some of the differences as well as similarities between the interaction of cultural and civic issues within the context of the Cultural Front, and the climate of the post-culture wars 1990s, should be coming into focus. By presenting a comparative analysis of both periods, this book allows us to test assumptions about the relationship between the production of artworks and broader social concerns in each period. As Rick Halpern and Jonathan Morris write, comparative analysis necessitates focusing on a constellation of factors, rather than privileging a single variable as capable of providing a totalising explanatory power.[60] Instead of presenting a historical model that rests upon either rupture or continuity – models that have tended to dominate our primary accounts of social practice – this book stresses a historical materialist method of comparative analysis, which emphasises the persistent blind spots in how both eras have been historicised and understood to bear upon the current conjuncture. By examining works from the boom and codification of social practice during the 1990s in relation to those drawn from the 1930s, we gain a clearer view of the possibilities and limits of these responses to frequently comparable social crisis under two distinct state formations, as well as the divergent subjects and communities they seek to engage. This approach also enables us to consider how earlier works continue to deliver meaning in the present, an undertaking which responds to Lucy Lippard's description of cultural amne-

---

59   Hughes 1995.
60   Halpern and Morris 1997, pp. 4–5.

sia as a form of censorship. Describing the discovery of *Art Front* – a magazine published by the Artists Union, which was formed by those employed by the WPA Federal Art Project (WPA-FAP) – by the Art Workers Coalition in the 1960s, Lippard writes:

> We would have been a lot further along in our own ideological debates and strategic aesthetics had we known which of their actions worked and which didn't, despite the obvious differences between the historical moments. But, as is often the case, lessons weren't learned and the same mistakes continue to be made over and over again.[61]

In this book, I attempt to work against such cultural amnesia by drawing on Ernst Bloch's concept of *Ungleichzeitigkeit* – translated as non-simultaneity or non-contemporaneity – which tries to grasp the social character of capitalist development and its relation to history as multi-temporal rather than teleological, or structural. On the one hand, Bloch describes how non-simultaneous contradictions can subjectively manifest themselves in accumulated rage, conjuring up earlier social and economic formations as harmonising solutions.[62] Bloch views these non-simultaneous contradictions as unthreatening to capital because they draw on declining social remnants whose greatness is long gone, and he associates this tendency with attempts by the bourgeoisie to revoke the excesses of capitalism or subordinate it to their needs, with German fascism forming his primary example.[63] On the other hand, Bloch describes how revolutionary non-simultaneous contradictions are manifested in the notion of prevented futures, and the potential liberation of these from the past.[64] By prevented futures, Bloch means nothing less than the very 'existence of the proletariat itself, the discrepancy between the forces of production unleashed by capitalism and the capitalist circumstances of production'.[65] This contradiction reveals itself when the worker recognises herself as a commodity, and thus at the same time uncovers the commodity character of capitalist society and the potential for self-abolition. Although Bloch argues that this recognition can arise from the same experience that provokes the anachronistic, reactionary drive of non-simultaneity, he stresses that revolutionary non-simultaneity rests upon a relational understanding of prior forms of community. The past

---

61 Lippard 1999, p. 41.
62 Bloch 1991, p. 109.
63 Ibid.
64 Bloch 1991, p. 110.
65 Bloch 1991, pp. 110–11.

becomes 'part of the matter which seeks a life undestroyed by capital', a utopian element which has not as yet found fulfilment at any time – indeed, a prevented future rather than a nostalgic longing for the past.[66]

History for Bloch is evidently open and dynamic, and this assists with analysing the projects discussed here in relation to class formation in the United States. Women, people of colour and the dispossessed all form 'subject-participants' in the works I discuss across both periods and all are variously positioned as non-simultaneous to the dominant time of capital. This dominant time is synchronised by the state, and as David Harvey describes, the production of a 'structured coherence' through various social infrastructures that support the reproduction and circulation of capital.[67] In the projects discussed here, this exclusion from the 'structured coherence' of capital is always encountered first as oppression, and then as a means to develop a shared consciousness. As will become clear, this does not always unleash the kinds of antagonisms promised in Bloch's description of the worker's self-recognition through the experience of non-simultaneous contradictions. Instead, because of the historical circumstances under which these projects were produced – circumstances in which the state actively embraced the 'usefulness' of culture as a social and pedagogical force – this process of developing something like a shared consciousness often leads to more reformist propositions, that is, calls for recognition and inclusion within the structured coherence of the state. My argument is that during the 1930s, this reformist response was strongly tied to the specifically American, nationalistic conjuring of the past in order to provide a structured coherence, whereas the projects produced during the 1990s that I treat most critically are those which naturalise the indivisibility of state and capital under neoliberalism as this is experienced by individuals and communities.

While the conditions of the latter process of state formation should be familiar to most readers, it is crucial to register that the construction of community through the state during the Depression years was largely articulated through appeals to a 'usable past'. This was supported at a national level through the Works Progress Administration, and as already indicated, this book engages with aspects of the Federal Art Project (WPA-FAP) and Federal Theatre Project (WPA-FTP). Other branches of the WPA-FAP such as the Index of American Design sought to create an atlas of folk cultures across the nation, and the Community Art Centers (CACs) were established with the aim of celebrating localism whilst creating a structured coherence. Jonathan Harris's account of the

---

66 Ibid.
67 Harvey 1989, p. 145.

construction of community through the WPA-FAP situates this as a Machiavellian project to extend the tentacles of the state into every community across the US. As Harris writes, 'Art activity in a CAC was intended both to embody and to prefigure a state of participatory democracy. Within such a society, order would be based on the elimination of antagonisms between cultures, on a plurality of different but equivalent social positions and subjectivities'.[68] As identified by Alfred Howarth Jones, this notion of 'different but equal' was present in the idea of a usable past within New Deal ideology, and expressed through a belief that the levelling effects of the Depression permitted an affirmation of national, over ever-fragmenting class, ethnic, religious or racialised experience.[69] This idea of a national 'levelling' allows Harris to claim that the CACs transformed art and the social relations involved in its production 'from objects of conflict and antagonism in industrial-capitalist society into objects of reconciliation, bringing order, reason and collective will'.[70] In this light, Harris' reading is strikingly similar to Bishop's criticisms of social practice as uniformly instrumentalised, in her depiction of participants and artists as docile and pliant subjects, ideologically manipulated by a monolithic state.[71]

The problem of endowing the state with this power is neatly captured by Raymond Williams, who stresses that if ideology were 'only the isolable meanings and practices of the ruling class ... occupying merely the top of our minds, it would be – and one would be glad – a very much easier thing to over-throw'.[72] Because Harris and Bishop both lack a materialist account of domination and exploitation, their view of the state is inadequate to analysing any *particular* relationship between state and capitalism, let alone the means by which individuals and groups might begin to subvert or challenge such arrangements. The aim here is not to elevate the 1930s as a better time for socially engaged culture, and the 1990s as a hopeless decline towards neoliberal impoverishment and cultural recuperation, but rather to think through – to paraphrase Bloch – the most promising of these projects as prevented futures. As Fred Moten writes, 'There are all kinds of little holes and tunnels and ditches and highways and byways *through the state* that are being produced and maintained constantly by the people who are also at the same time doing this labor that ends in the production *of the state*'.[73] The themes which structure my chapters seek to excavate

---

68   Harris 1995, p. 61.
69   Haworth Jones 1971, p. 718.
70   Harris 1991, p. 257.
71   Harris 1995, p. 20.
72   Williams 1973, p. 9.
73   Harney and Moten 2013, p. 145.

this relationship between the *through* and the *of* by addressing projects that engage social and political struggles which extend across both periods. Through examining these points of commonality and disjuncture, my contention is that we will have a better history of social practice in the US and a new model of how to address contemporary art practice that seeks to work 'socially', particularly in relation to the state. *Usable Pasts* is divided into four chapters that take law, gendered social reproduction, housing and race as their focus. Each chapter addresses projects engaging with these issues dating to the 1930s and the 1990s. The social issues into which the work under discussion has sought to intervene guide these themes, and as I have begun to explain here, also form key battlegrounds within the rise and fall of the New Deal order.

Law is the theme for Chapter One, which discusses two projects that sought to rehearse the transformation of repressive legislation and policing. The chapter begins with Lacy's *The Oakland Projects* (1991–2001) which has become a paradigmatic work within histories of recent social practice, and one I discuss across two chapters. This ten-year long project involved collaborating with primarily African American and Latinx teenagers to address issues of police violence, race, gender and the demonisation of youth by popular media. In Chapter One, I focus on two large-scale public performances from *The Oakland Projects*: *The Roof is on Fire* (1994) and *Code 33* (1999), both of which engaged with police violence. I address the formal qualities of these performances, focusing on their episodic structure, quilt-like staging, and their use of the automobile as a performance space. The second half of the chapter turns to *Injunction Granted* (1936), a performance detailing the history of labour struggles in the US that was produced by the Living Newspaper unit of the WPA-FTP. Through its episodic structure, *Injunction Granted* presented a teleological narrative of labour struggles in the United States, from slavery to the contemporaneous formation of the AFL-CIO labour union, which merged a craft union with an industrial union. I analyse how *Injunction Granted* integrated film projection, innovative stage design and techniques drawn from Bertolt Brecht and the Russian avant-garde, mixing those aspects with the vaudeville tropes of North American performance. The chapter continues by stressing how in both *The Oakland Projects* and *Injunction Granted*, the performers were implicated in the drama. In *The Roof is on Fire* and *Code 33*, policemen and youth played themselves. Similarly, in *Injunction Granted*, the performers – as organised labour allied with the Workers' Alliance union and employed by the WPA-FTP – were directly implicated in the labour struggles presented on stage. In order to theorise the shared status of these performances as rehearsals for real life, Chapter One engages with Bertolt Brecht's and Georg Lukács's 1930s debates on realism. The chapter concludes by addressing historical, political and aesthetic differences, asking who forms the viable subject-participant for politicised performance practices in the 1930s and 1990s. In contrast with the figure of the primarily white, male industrial worker who struggles against the law in *Injunction Granted*, African American and Latinx youth take centre stage in *The Roof is on Fire* and *Code 33*.

Chapter Two takes the concept of social reproduction as its rubric, expanding this Marxist-feminist concept to discuss not only the reproduction of life and capital, but also the reproduction of counter-hegemonic cultures. We begin with the proletarian, female-dominated amateur dance groups organised by Edith Segal during the 1930s. Within these groups, which had close links to the Communist Party USA (CPUSA) and labour unions, Segal and her fellow dancers conceived of dance as an activity that could assist in transforming the political consciousness of both participants and audiences. Following on from the questions of temporality I began to outline here in the introduction, I analyse Segal's performance of *Black and White* at the 1930 Harlem Interracial Ball in relation to Bloch's concept of non-simultaneity, and the historical formation of race and gender in the United States. The chapter continues with a discussion of domestic labour through Segal's dances *Kinder, Küche, Kirche* (1935) and *Dance of the Washerwomen* (1935). I situate these in relation to struggles over social reproduction from that period, as well as writing by Mary Inman, an author who addressed women's oppression within, and in conflict with the CPUSA during the 1930s and early 1940s. The chapter then turns to Lacy's *Expectations* (1997), a part of *The Oakland Projects* that involved collaboration with teenage mothers, and which began a year after the passage of the Personal Responsibility and Work Opportunity Reconciliation Act, a piece of welfare legislation that eliminated the Aid to Families with Dependent Children Program, a form of federal assistance established in 1935 via the Social Security Act. Concurrent to the passage of this legislation, teenage mothers – particularly Black and Latinx teenage mothers – were routinely scapegoated in the mass media as embodying the breakdown of a Fordist, nuclear family. I examine what it meant for Lacy and her collaborators to produce an exhibition and project that directly responded to this, and how the artistic labour of *Expectations* was proximate to the very forms of gendered labour that state-provided welfare had supported since the New Deal. The chapter concludes by arguing that the codification of social practice as a medium in the 1990s must be understood alongside the concurrent encouragement of arts organisations and artists to produce socially engaged projects during a period where the state-led support of social reproduction via welfare provision was in retrenchment.

Housing, homelessness and the aesthetics of social documentary form the theme for Chapter Three. The chapter begins with a discussion of Martha

Rosler's *If You Lived Here* (1989–90), which dealt with homelessness and gentrification in the form of a year-long project involving residents, housing activists and artists at the brink of the culture wars. By approaching the project in relation to Rosler's engagement with depression-era documentary photography, I emphasise how social practice in the 1990s frequently attempted to sidestep the burden of representation, whilst addressing issues similar to those that concerned the documentarians of the 1930s. The chapter proceeds with an analysis of *If You Lived Here* ... through Fredric Jameson's concept of the cognitive map, stressing how both Rosler's and Jameson's work relies on aesthetic and theoretical models dating to the 1930s, newly revived for the neoliberal era. The second case study here is *One-Third of a Nation* (1938), which I mentioned above. Similar to *If You Lived Here*, *One-Third of a Nation* was concerned with the role of financial speculation in the housing crisis of the Depression and relied on documentary tropes as its mode of critique. In examining *If You Lived Here* ... and *One-Third of a Nation* together, we can recognise that land value and finance capital – despite its 'fictitious' status – always involves a claim on future labour through the form of rent or a mortgage. Through this, the chapter criticises the persistent idea that labour in the west under neoliberal governance is entirely immaterial, and that social practice simply reflects de-industrialisation and finance capital.[74] I nuance both the negative articulation of this position as well as the belief that social practice can offer a salve to current labour conditions. The chapter concludes by addressing how documentary mobilises a particular model of history in both *If You Lived Here* ... and *One-Third of a Nation*. This model is that of a usable past, a concept, as already described, that gained strength during the Depression. Through this, I stress how the recourse to a usable past within social documentary of the 1930s provided a seedbed for some founding tenets within social practice during the 1990s.

Chapter Four follows on from Chapter Three in its focus on housing and urban space, but does so here in order to tackle questions of race, labour, community and nation, taking up Ira Katznelson's suggestion that there is frequently a 'radical separation in people's consciousness, speech, and activity of the politics of work from the politics of community'.[75] This chapter engages with projects that disrupt the national-populist dimensions within mobilisa-

---

[74] For examples of this argument, see Bishop 2012, pp. 216 and 231; and Fraser 1997, pp. 111–16. Along similar, but more Marxist lines, Leigh Claire La Berge provides an account of social practice as intrinsically linked to what she calls 'decommodified labor', a term used to describe the diminishing of the wage alongside the increase in demands of work. See La Berge 2019.

[75] Katznelson 1981, p. 6.

tions of a usable past, as well as the claim to objectivity and political legibility that frequently underpin both social documentary and social practice. The chapter begins with a discussion of works by Berenice Abbot and the Photo League Feature Group that were displayed in the exhibition *Roofs for 40 Million* (1938). By addressing the reception of that exhibition, I demonstrate the nationalist dimensions within the quest to produce a usable past. The chapter then turns to the Photo League Feature Group's *Harlem Document* (1938–9) and Richard Wright's *12 Million Black Voices* (1941) as works that have a more complex relationship to the pursuit of an idealised teleology and nationalist rhetoric within the latter period of the Cultural Front. Although both *Harlem Document* and *12 Million Black Voices* fall within the bounds of a documentary practice, their tone and method are markedly different in that both works put the subjectivity of their makers into the picture, eschewing the quest for objectivity in favour of directly confronting the viewer. The second half of the chapter addresses Rick Lowe's *Project Row Houses* (begun 1993). *Project Row Houses* has significantly altered the fabric of the Third Ward in Houston and exists as a tentative contradiction to the world that surrounds it. *Project Row Houses* has wavered between the utilitarian and the utopian during its lifespan, and I close the chapter by examining the utilitarian logic of social practice in relation to the demand for art to act as a weapon within the Cultural Front.

Usable Pasts closes with a coda that addresses the contemporary stakes of social practice in the US, focusing on artists including Tania Bruguera and Theaster Gates. In particular, I address the emphasis on 'usefulness' in social practice as it has become increasingly institutionalised within American art from the late 1990s onwards. The conclusion also examines what it means to address two periods together, and calls for this method of analysis to become a broader art historical project in order to rethink issues of periodisation, temporality, nostalgia and nationhood.

My motivation for writing this book came from dissatisfaction with recent art historical and theoretical accounts of social practice, as outlined above. Initially, this was underpinned by the notion that more complex histories could be uncovered, which would allow for a closer reading of particular artworks and also form a retort to the cultural amnesia Lippard describes. Addressing two periods together therefore became a means to supplement the histories we have received, but in the process of writing, my approach to history and questions of temporality shifted. In analysing projects that work with subaltern subjects, I found that the rhetorics around art and community from both reactionary and mainstream left-liberal perspectives often display surprising affinities that rely on nostalgia as well as a developmental logic that views progress as inherent to the dynamic of capital. I have found such teleological thinking hard to maintain when considering cultural work produced by, and addressing subjects, who are continuously positioned outside the dominant logic of capital and the state. During both periods I discuss, these remain women, people of colour and the dispossessed, yet the way that artists who work socially have engaged these groups differs. This is partially due to the changing character of state formations in the US, as well as transformations in artistic production. In what follows, I analyse such patterns, in order to provide a ground for understanding how social practice interacts with aesthetics, politics and state formation in the US.

CHAPTER 1

Rehearsals for Real Life

> Perhaps the theatre is not revolutionary in itself, but it is surely a rehearsal for the revolution.
> AUGUSTO BOAL, *Theatre of the Oppressed*, 1974[1]

∵

1   Performance and Critical Realism

As the quotation above suggests, I am mobilising the concept of rehearsal in this chapter to discuss performances that were situated as preparation for real-life struggles over the law as a repressive apparatus. I begin with *The Roof is on Fire* (1994) and *Code 33* (1999), two performances drawn from Suzanne Lacy's *The Oakland Projects* (1991–2001), a decade long artwork organised by the artist that addressed race, policing, education, welfare, parenting and violence with young people in Oakland, California. The second half of the chapter turns to *Injunction Granted* (1936), a Living Newspaper examining the history of labour relations in the US produced by the WPA-FTP. Like the Federal Art, Music and Writers projects, the WPA-FTP was initiated in 1935 under the umbrella of the Works Progress Administration, existing both as a relief programme for unemployed actors and theatre workers, as well as a means to create theatre that was egalitarian, accessible and responsive to contemporary issues. As described in the introduction, the Living Newspaper unit was the most radical branch of the WPA-FTP and its productions were marked by the use of film, documentary, mass performance, collective script writing and experimental staging and music.

This chapter analyses the episodic form and multiple stage-settings in *The Roof is on Fire*, *Code 33* and *Injunction Granted* as shared formal characteristics, along with the way the performers in these works all had a real-life investment in their drama. Through emphasising these similarities, we expand our understanding of American performance history. Early North American takes

---

1   Boal, p. 97.

on the aesthetic forms and debates associated with the pre-war and inter-war European avant-gardes were unique. Cities such as New York developed a lively culture of performance in the 1920s and 1930s, partly due to the presence of exiled and immigrant Germans, Russians and Eastern Europeans. Within these communities, European avant-garde performance was inevitably syncretised into new forms appropriate to the social, political and economic culture of the US. This is not just an invocation of the tired cliché of the American 'melting pot'. Rather, American performance of the 1930s such as *Injunction Granted* grew out of the internationalism of the left, and the radical performance scene of the 1930s that I discuss in this chapter and the following had strong ties to the CPUSA, and was often supported by the WPA-FTP after 1935. Crossovers were frequent between dance, theatre, agit-prop, vaudeville and amateur performance, and this activity formed part of the Popular Front cultural movement. Notably, performance was figured as a proletarian activity, and incorporated into everyday life far more than traditional theatre or the visual arts, as evidenced within advertisements in the CPUSA associated *New Masses* for events such as the 'New Theatre Anti-Fascist Dance' and the Workers' Laboratory Theatre 'Theatre of Action' Ball. In the latter, 'shock troupe shows', music and 'mass games' are promised to the punter, blending popular dancing and participatory performance.

Alongside these social occasions, reviews and features in the communist-affiliated press such as *New Masses* make clear the centrality of performance to the Popular Front through the regularity of their appearance. This writing helped sustain a debate about the aesthetic and political meaning of performance, with critics such as Stanley Burnshaw and Edna Ocko often highlighting the cross-pollination between revolutionary groups such as the New Dance Group and the Red Dancers, and the modernist dance of Martha Graham and those associated with the bourgeois DelSarte School. Such critics oscillated between praising the political commitment of leftist performers, and berating them for not reaching the technical heights of Graham and her peers.[2] The challenge to make theatre and dance accessible, open to amateurs and related to working-class struggle whilst retaining a level of aesthetic integrity corresponds strongly with the debates shaping the reception of social practice in the 1990s discussed in the introduction.

Yet, this early history of US performance remains overwhelmingly absent from noteworthy primers of the medium such as Roselee Goldberg's *Perform-*

---

2 See for example Burnshaw 1935, p. 27 and Ocko, 5 March 1935, p. 26.

ance: 1909 to the Present.³ Goldberg's account typically begins with the European avant-gardes of the early twentieth century in order to situate performance, modern dance and experimental theatre as closely interwoven, exemplified by her description of Alfred Jarry's *Ubu Roi* as a nineteenth-century predecessor. The origin of performance art is further attributed to the Futurists in Italy and Russia; Constructivist theatre and dance in the Soviet Union including the Blue Blouse troupes and the re-enactment of the *Storming of the Winter Palace*; Dada's Cabaret Voltaire; Surrealism; and Oskar Schlemmer's work within the Bauhaus. Though these European, politicised avant-gardes are positioned as foundational, the American story outlined briefly above is markedly absent. Instead, Goldberg's account only incorporates and then swiftly becomes dominated by North American artists after 1945, following the typical trajectory of twentieth-century Western art history. The presence of Bauhaus exiles such as Josef Albers at Black Mountain College is held to be overwhelmingly responsible for the birth of performance in the US, embodied in the work of figures such as John Cage, Merce Cunningham, Allan Kaprow, Jim Dine, Claes Oldenburg and Robert Rauschenberg. Goldberg's history proceeds by detailing the codification of performance as a 'movement' within the visual arts from the 1960s onwards through Robert Morris, Yvonne Rainer, Trisha Brown, Vito Acconci, Dan Graham, Hannah Wilke, Laurie Anderson, Adrian Piper, Paul McCarthy and Matthew Barney.⁴ Within this narrative, American performance art is inextricably tied to body art and frequently focused on the staging of individual, rather than collective experience. This narrative is not only inhospitable to the development of collective performance by artists such as Lacy in the 1990s, but also overlooks the vitality and legacy of American performance during the 1920s and 1930s.

This chapter therefore presents an intervention into the historiography of American performance art. I suggest that the absence of scholarly attention towards an internationalist and largely leftist American performance culture of the 1930s remains a crucial blind spot within our capacity to theorise the growth of social practice in relation to performance history. By paying attention to the transmission of European avant-garde forms and debates into the US via this cosmopolitan, radical culture we can expand the scope of performance history from below, going beyond the more familiar story of how European exiles reshaped American culture in the interwar years, such as in the narrative of Albers at Black Mountain. The emphasis on the left adds a different dimen-

---

3   Goldberg 2001.
4   Ibid.

sion because the debates around political impact, the popular, and aesthetic form which coursed through that milieu, help us to understand the interpenetration of avant-garde devices with American entertainment such as vaudeville, slapstick and jazz. This mix was crucial to how the left sought to produce a working-class culture that was as experimental as it was popular, and bears strongly on the mobilisation of popular culture within social practice, as we shall see with the references to rap music, television and car culture in Lacy's *The Roof is on Fire* and *Code 33*.

In order to address how *The Roof is on Fire*, *Code 33* and *Injunction Granted* criticised and denaturalised the workings of the law for performers and audiences, I draw on Bertolt Brecht, and particularly the Brechtian emphasis on interruption, which underpins how I view the performances discussed in this chapter as rehearsals. As Robert Baker-White has noted, the open activity of the rehearsal is 'inherently interruptible' and marked by the possibility of participants repeatedly rethinking their roles in relation to one another.[5] More recently, Sabeth Buchmann and Constanze Ruhm have addressed how the rehearsal has become a trope in contemporary art, often forming the means for artists to collaborate with social groups beyond the 'classical exhibition visitor'.[6] In their account, this stems from the rehearsal as a theatrical space that offers the potential for breaking down divisions of labour between technicians, director, actors and so on. Their proposals are strikingly close to Brazilian dramatist Augusto Boal's claim in the epigraph at the beginning of this chapter that the techniques he founded with Theatre of the Oppressed operated as rehearsals for revolution.[7] In particular, Buchmann and Ruhm's statement that the rehearsal 'enables one to overcome idle habits, routines, and role relationships by visibly acting them out and revising them' echoes Boal's emphasis that revolutionary theatre should involve participants changing the drama, trying out solutions and ultimately training for 'real action' through acting out what that might look like.[8] In my view, this aesthetic investment in the rehearsal within contemporary art must be understood as a corollary of the growth in social practice over the last two decades, and also helps to illuminate the privileged relationship of that genre to performance history.

In addition to Brecht, Georg Lukács's writing helps us explore how the use of 'types' in *The Roof is on Fire*, *Code 33* and *Injunction Granted* function as a form of ideology critique. In May 1936, the 'types' of the WPA-FTP Living News-

---

5 Baker-White 1999, p. 49.
6 Buchmann and Ruhm 2013.
7 Boal 2009, p. 97.
8 Buchmann and Ruhm, and Boal, p. 97.

paper were described by the critic John Mullen in *New Theatre*: 'each character is an individual with problems and needs, representing not only himself but a large group of people'.[9] This bears comparison to Lacy's comment that the process of performing in *The Oakland Projects* was to 'step into the role of yourself not only as an individual but as a member of a particular group'.[10] Since their well-known disagreement over the aesthetic form realism should take, the characterisation of the Brecht-Lukács debate as marked by bitter antagonism has been frequently challenged. As Lukács himself acknowledged in 1968, their positions grew closer through their ongoing dialogue up until Brecht's death.[11] Given that their disagreement has often been interpreted as a difference over style, Brecht's belief that realism is 'wide and political, sovereign over all conventions' should be kept in mind.[12]

In terms of their dispute over what form realism should take, Lukács viewed avant-garde techniques such as montage and fragmentation as failing to go beyond merely reflecting 'the immediate experience of chaos, dehumanisation and alienation in advanced capitalist society'.[13] Lukács particularly opposed Brecht's *Lehrstücke* (learning plays) for presenting characters seemingly devoid of subjectivity.[14] Instead, Lukács called for realism to create – as in the novels of Honoré Balzac, Miguel de Cervantes and Ivan Goncharov – 'types' that stand for a social group larger and more meaningful than themselves, but which nevertheless retain the qualities of plausible, rounded individuals, thus showing the potential for humans to be fully rounded subjects in a post-capitalist society.[15]

Fredric Jameson progressed the Brecht-Lukács debate by suggesting that Lukács's 'realism' is closely connected to his earlier text, 'Reification and the Consciousness of the Proletariat' (1920). As Jameson explains, realism 'is the bearer of the force of de-reification, which suggests that our stereotypical idea of Lukácsean realism as a 'form' in its own right, and a constraining and anti-

---

9   Mullen 1936, p. 25. In 1935, the Workers' Theatre League and *Workers' Theatre* journal were renamed in accordance with the policies and strategy of the Popular Front, as had been adopted by the CPUSA who supported the League and journal. Renamed *New Theatre*, the journal continued to provide a platform for discussion of proletarian theatre, dance, film and photography and also, from the inception of the WPA-FTP, began to cover a range of those productions.
10   Lacy, personal interview, 27 April 2012.
11   Lukács 2011, p. 9.
12   Brecht 1977, p. 82.
13   Lunn 1982, p. 83.
14   Lunn 1982, p. 85.
15   Lukács 1977, p. 56. Also see pp. 49–50 of this essay for an account of how Lukács understood his position on realism to have transformed from his early 'idealist' phase, as displayed in Lukács 1994.

quated one at that, may not be altogether accurate'.[16] Jameson's observations seem particularly pertinent when considering passages from the 'Reification' essay where Lukács argues that class-consciousness consists of the 'appropriate and rational reactions 'imputed' (*zugerechnet*) to a particular typical position in the process of production'.[17] Despite Lukács's own, later disavowal of his 'Reification' essay, Jameson argues that the conception of consciousness articulated therein remains present in Lukács's later writings on realism, allowing for a connection with Brecht's claim that realism needs to be free from aesthetic restrictions. Indeed, as with Lukács's belief in realism as a force of de-reification, Brecht emphasised that realism should expose 'society's causal network'.[18]

The notion of catharsis in the work of both Brecht and Lukács seemingly provides another point of disagreement. For Lukács, communists ought to be invested in the idea of catharsis from an ethical and aesthetic viewpoint; indeed in his belief, cathartic activity produces a 'moral crisis' in the aesthetic receiver, which leads to a transformation.[19] Peter Thomas asserts that Lukács's emphasis on catharsis is founded on a belief that it can provoke a 'shaking of subjectivity' that breaks up 'the previously fetishising contemplation of the world', a perspective closely linked to the 'Reification' essay.[20] In contrast, Brecht viewed catharsis as a mystical, individualising process that could not achieve the dialectic of distance and empathy his theatre sought to construct. Nevertheless, we can again observe a conceptual parity between Lukács's commitment to a 'shaking of subjectivity' as essential to de-reification and Brecht's *Verfremdungseffekt*: the alienation, or distancing effect. Beyond Lukács and Brecht's shared belief in realism as a cognitive experience rather than a fixed style, it is important to reserve a point of difference. Lukács's humanism is met with an incipient anti-humanism in Brecht. For as much as Lukács believed realism needed to present the possibility of wholeness, Brecht's theatre contains a dual attack on bourgeois and socialist humanism.[21] Yet, rather than mapping their political and philosophical difference onto the formal techniques and styles they affirm, my intention is to work from their points of commonality, primarily located in the *experiences* they want works of realism to engender, and the fundamental connection this has to consciousness.

---

16   Jameson 2009, p. 204.
17   Lukács 1971, p. 51.
18   Brecht 1977, p. 82.
19   Mittenzwei 1973, p. 219.
20   Thomas 2009, p. 262.
21   Zhang and Jameson 1998, pp. 353–83.

This chapter seeks to analyse what form of realism is present in *The Roof is on Fire*, *Code 33* and *Injunction Granted*, and how these performances were all situated as rehearsals for the transformation of reality. Their realism and status as rehearsals is significantly complicated by the fact that the performers involved were all actually implicated in the drama presented on stage. In *The Roof is on Fire* and *Code 33*, policemen and youth played themselves. Similarly, in *Injunction Granted*, the performers – as organised labour allied with the Workers Alliance of America and employed by the WPA-FTP – were directly implicated in the labour struggles presented on stage. This quality links to the craze for civic pageantry in the early twentieth century in the US, when that form was mobilised to establish common ground between individuals of diverse backgrounds as a means to engender American citizenship. Many towns used pageantry to act out episodes from their history and to try and create a sense of how the community related to the state; individuals would play themselves in order to underscore their role within a particular social formation.

The *Paterson Strike Pageant*, which took place on 7 June 1913 in Madison Square Gardens, provides a contrast to the dominant history of civic pageantry as a means to form bonds between the state and citizen. As Martin Green has stated, the strikers 'had taken over, for one night, one of the palaces of the ruling class'.[22] Conceived by journalist John Reed and organised by the Industrial Workers of the World (IWW), the pageant involved more than 1,000 striking workers from silk factories in Paterson, New Jersey performing the story of the strike in front of over 15,000 spectators. The pageant both raised funds for the strike relief by charging the public to witness the spectacle, and also attempted to bridge the gap between New York's bohemian, radical intellectuals and the working-class rank and file IWW members.[23] The pageant had six 'episodes', each addressing an aspect of the strike's history; from scenes of mass meetings to May Day protests and fights between police and strikers. The sixth episode, titled 'Strike Meeting in Turn Hall', showed the strikers legislating for themselves and passing a law that guaranteed an eight-hour day that no court could declare unconstitutional. Several of the real strike leaders, including prominent IWW members Elizabeth Gurley Flynn and Carlo Tresca, performed 'typical strike speeches' after acting out this legislation.[24] This diverged from the dominant use of the pageant as a frequently exclusionary and conservative invocation of a usable past, which depended on nationalist sentiment in order to promote assimilation. Like the *Paterson Strike Pageant*, the pageantry of *The*

---

22   Green 1988, pp. 199–200.
23   McNamara et. al. 1971, p. 60.
24   Ibid.

Roof is on Fire, *Code 33* and *Injunction Granted* also created oppositional communities by criticising prevailing conditions, and each similarly collided with broader social struggles against the law.[25] In *The Roof is on Fire* and *Code 33* the unwavering figure of the policeman dominates, and the prison cell hovers as a constant threat. Legal and illegal struggles for workers' rights form the backbone of *Injunction Granted*, and scenes within courtrooms frequently punctuate the performance. In all three, law is presented as a fetish and as the supposedly civilised veneer for violent coercion. In the following, I analyse how raced and classed subjects experience these systems of exploitation and domination, and how these works use performance as a means to rehearse the transformation of such conflicts.

2 The Roof is on Fire

On the evening of 9 June 1994, 220 teenagers ascended to a rooftop garage in downtown Oakland, and took their positions in 100 cars that formed a succession of small, semi-accessible stages. (Fig. 1) Arranged in a haphazard fashion, the cars pointed towards one another and lacked uniformity. Jeeps, convertibles, saloons and estate cars were populated with groups of between two and five youths, mixed in gender, race and age, although most performers were between 15 and 17 years old. Beginning at 7 p.m., the initial sections of the performance were lit by evening sunlight, progressing through twilight, and by the end the roof was in darkness, aside from overhead lighting. (Fig. 2) An audience composed primarily by adults roamed between the cars and listened to rehearsed conversations on topics including sex, violence, the police, their neighbourhoods, families and futures. Within the cars, the young people performed a heightened dialogue that self-consciously verbalised their daily reality and experience. Video documentation shows adults awkwardly leaning into partially closed windows to listen, and the spectators were largely free to wander in and out, to talk to one another, and to move around the cars at their own pace.[26] (Fig. 3)

---

25 This emphasis on the pageant within the proletarian avant-garde in the US was part of a broad project to concretise the existence and meaning of a working-class revolutionary community. As Ellen Graff notes in her study of proletarian dance in 1930s New York, 'The pageant was trumpeted as a model of proletarian theatre, its effectiveness deriving from the twin techniques of mass participation and audience identification' (Graff 1997, p. 27).

26 The documentary video of the performance can be accessed on Lacy's Vimeo site https://vimeo.com/39865636 (Accessed 14/03/2015).

FIGURE 1   Suzanne Lacy, Annice Jacoby and Chris Johnson, *The Roof is on Fire*, 1993–94, from The Oakland Projects, 1991–2001. Oakland, California
PHOTO BY GARY NAKAMOTO. COURTESY OF SUZANNE LACY

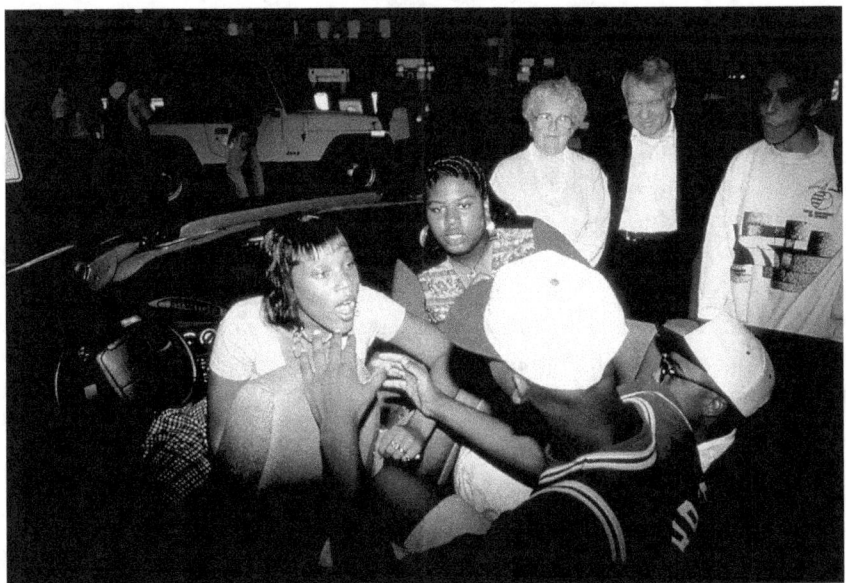

FIGURE 2   Suzanne Lacy, Annice Jacoby and Chris Johnson, *The Roof is on Fire*, 1993–94, from The Oakland Projects, 1991–2001. Oakland, California
PHOTO BY NATHAN BENNETT. COURTESY OF SUZANNE LACY

FIGURE 3   Suzanne Lacy, Annice Jacoby and Chris Johnson, *The Roof is on Fire*, 1993–94, from
The Oakland Projects, 1991–2001. Oakland, California
PHOTO BY NATHAN BENNETT. COURTESY OF SUZANNE LACY

The Roof is on Fire was the second public performance within *The Oakland Projects* after *Teenage Living Room* (1992), which had also sought to make visible otherwise private conversations between teenagers. Each phase of *The Oakland Projects* involved long periods of research and workshops prior to a public performance, and both the more rudimentary *Teenage Living Room* and the larger scale *The Roof is on Fire* gestated out of media literacy workshops Lacy coordinated in 1991–2 with the photographer Chris Johnson at Oakland Technical High School. These workshops aimed to develop methods for teenagers to analyse and criticise negative stereotypes of youth in the mass media, a project that emerged in response to extreme levels of over-reporting on youth crime: in 1990–8 in California, 68 percent of stories about violent crime in the mainstream media focused on youth gangs, while only 14 percent of arrests for violent crime actually involved young people.[27] Gang violence of course carries heavily racialised overtones, and this media spectacle formed part of the overall criminalisation and mass incarceration of Black people that accelerated in the US after the 1970s. As Löic Wacquant writes, media representations of crim-

27   Espiritu 2005, p. 194.

inal activity in the 1990s were marked by sensational 'Lombroso-style mythologies ... and the wide diffusion of bestial metaphors', in reports peppered with buzzwords including 'superpredators', 'wolfpacks' and the generic description of criminals as 'animals'.[28] In the workshops convened by Lacy and Johnson, young people listed common notions of youth and their activities – 'drug dealers', 'violent', 'sex-crazed maniacs', 'babies having babies' – on cut-out figures, accumulating to form a series of stereotypes. As we shall see, the progression of *The Oakland Projects* was marked by a sharpening of the political limitations of a moralising critique of media stereotypes that fails to address their function in a broader material reality. Though the initial activity around *The Roof is on Fire* took aim at the media, the subsequent phases of the project addressed policing and family life, meaning that the project as a whole has to be taken as attempt to analyse how media representation of Black and Latinx youth as criminals in the US is integral in preparing those subjects for the reality of their existence within a nation dominated by the racist prison-industrial complex. As Wacquant wrote in 2002 about the period in which *The Oakland Projects* took place, the lifelong 'cumulative probability of "doing time" in a state or federal penitentiary based on imprisonment rates from the early 90s is 4% for whites, 16% for Latinxs and a staggering 29% for Black Americans'.[29]

While the media literacy workshops were private, *The Roof is on Fire*, organised by a committee of teenagers, working with Lacy, Johnson and Annice Jacoby under the label of TEAM (Teens, Educators, Artists, Media Makers) made that process public. Though *The Roof is on Fire* was collectively developed, Lacy alone directed the staging on the night of the performance. A week before the performance, Oakland saw a large-scale riot erupt after a summer festival. Despite later investigations revealing that the police's behaviour had escalated a minor fistfight between youths, the enduring media representation of the riot was a news clip of a young man putting his foot through a glass window.[30] As a result, the performance of *The Roof is on Fire* coincided with this event, becoming both a general critique of media stereotypes and scapegoating and a particular response to that incident which inevitably shaped local audience perception and responses.

The movement of the audience at the performance was tightly controlled. Spectators were not allowed to intervene or stick their heads into the cars and if

---

28   Wacquant 2002, p. 56.
29   When class is considered, Wacquant also stresses that a majority of African American (sub-)proletarian males will face a prison term at some point in their life. Wacquant, p. 45.
30   Suzanne Lacy's *The Roof is on Fire* text is available at http://theoaklandprojects.wordpress.com/the-roof-is-on-fire-1993-94/.

they did, a member of TEAM would explain that they were there to give space to the young people. This decision gestured toward the uneven relation between performers and spectators in this work, and stood as an exploration of the differential attainment of privacy through class, race and property ownership.[31] As Lacy has expressed, this prohibition on aspects of spectators' participation was a theatrical decision that kept them within their prescribed role in the performance.[32] As they moved from car to car, spectators experienced *The Roof is on Fire* as a series of episodes and a distancing effect was achieved by making them aware of their implication in the performance. This episodic structure can be related to Brechtian theatrical devices. In *The Messingkauf Dialogues* (1939–42), Brecht explained that he cut his plays into 'a series of little independent playlets', often announced by theme.[33] In addition to the audience's experience of these conversations, the participants listened to each other, with this rehearsal and recounting of reality on behalf of the performers as much part of the work as the flickering view given to the spectator. The braggadocio of some of the young people's performance acknowledged and exaggerated those stereotypes inscribed on the cut-out figures and presented in the media. Equally, others justified or contradicted them. Yet the point is not that *The Roof is on Fire* provided a corrective to the mainstream marginalisation of mostly Black teenagers for the audience.[34] Rather, the significance of *The Roof is on Fire* lies in constructing a space for performers to analyse how their individual realities related to those of a whole social group. As a performance rather than a taught lesson, workshop or meeting, *The Roof is on Fire* presented a heightened environment where the young people participating could examine how their social group was constructed, and the meaning of why they were set up as types by the mass media and law enforcement.

---

31 We might compare this with Martha Rosler's 1980 video *Secrets from the Street: No Disclosure*, shot in a gentrifying San Francisco. As Rosler's narrative to the video states, 'There's a culture in the streets and a culture behind closed doors. It's a privilege to close doors'. The video of *Secrets from the Street: No Disclosure* (1980) is available online at: http://artfem.tv/id;14/action;showpage/page_type;video/page_id;secrets_from_the_street_no_disclosure_by_martha_rosler_flv/ (Accessed 06/03/2015).
32 Suzanne Lacy, personal interview, 27 March 2012.
33 Brecht 1977, p. 74.
34 Alongside the live performance, *The Roof is on Fire* was later aired as a one-hour documentary by Oakland's local NBC-affiliated TV station. This sought to directly engage the stereotyped media representation of youth. I do not discuss the documentary as in comparison to the performance I believe it can be viewed more straightforwardly as a simple corrective measure, produced in line with a liberal politics of representation. I do however draw on the documentary as source material for describing the appearance of the performance, and for the dialogue it captures between performers.

One parallel that might be drawn to the use of cars as a private stage within a public arena in *The Roof is on Fire* is the spectacle of the drive-in movie, a format that remained popular in California long after its steady decline from the 1950s onwards elsewhere in the US.[35] Owners of drive-ins frequently solicited spectators who were ignored by mainstream movie theatres including children, housewives, disabled people, African Americans, and most notoriously, teenagers.[36] The mode of spectatorship in watching a film at a drive-in has been linked to the variety programming of early cinema, episodic in its nature through the extra-cinematic distraction of on-site entertainment like pony rides, a dance floor, baby parades, dare-devil car rides, circus attractions and fireworks.[37] The effect of engaging in these extra-cinematic attractions, alongside the permission to smoke, fool around, talk and eat, produced a discontinuous, and distanced mode of reception, similar to the effect of moving from car to car as a spectator in *The Roof is on Fire*.

The car is also politically significant as a staging device, particularly with regards to the intersection of race, law and the mass media in the US. Cars can lend a public visibility that begets the very police harassment addressed in the later performance of *Code 33*, as well as having a central place within African American popular culture. As Paul Gilroy argues, the centrality of cars as objects of conspicuous consumption within hip-hop videos, for example, can be analysed in relation to 'the distinctive history of propertylessness and material deprivation' within those communities that 'has inclined them towards a disproportionate investment in particular forms of property that are publicly visible and the status that corresponds to them'.[38] Within *The Roof is on Fire*, the appearance of the car chimes with this racialised, proletarian popular culture outlined by Gilroy. Yet in *Code 33*, the car as staging device was further awash with meaning because the performers were not only youth, but also police officers, therefore bringing the question of police harassment when 'driving while Black' to the fore.[39]

Code 33 ran from 1998 to 2000 and my focus here is specifically on the performance that staged a dialogue between youth and police on 7 October 1999. This was the culmination of two years of police-youth workshops, a youth art and leadership programme and the creation of a training video for police made by young people. Like *The Oakland Projects* as a whole, these activities slid into

---

35   Giles 1983, p. 68.
36   Morley Cohen 1994, p. 479.
37   Morley Cohen 1994, p. 472.
38   Gilroy 2001, p. 84.
39   David A. Harris.

one another and were propelled by Lacy and a core group of participants, with the performances acting as flashpoints that made the process, or rehearsal, public. As Lacy explained, *Code 33*'s focus on police-youth relations was guided by how within *The Roof is on Fire*, African American teenagers repeatedly stressed difficulties in their relationship with the police.[40] To understand properly the conflict between young people and police as it is addressed in *Code 33*, it is necessary to review the history of resistance to police violence in Oakland alongside further details of the socio-economic backdrop to the project.

In late 1966, Huey P. Newton and Bobby Seale founded the Black Panther Party for Self-Defense in Oakland, a revolutionary group committed to organising and emancipating Black communities. Their initial actions involved conducting armed surveillance patrols against the Oakland police force, and they also ran numerous community initiatives including free breakfasts for children, free dental care as well as their own schools.[41] Arguably, no organised, street-level resistance to racist policing of equal significance has emerged since the disintegration of the Black Panthers due to the combined pressure of internal schisms and the effects of the Counter Intelligence Program (COINTELPRO), a covert and often illegal project conducted by the FBI that involved the surveillance, infiltration and disruption of domestic political organisations. To the present, the Oakland Police Department remains notorious for corruption, brutality and misconduct, as illustrated by the homicide of the unarmed Oscar Grant in 2009, which provoked riots in the city. In 2011, the Occupy Oakland movement was also met with excessive force by the police and since then, regular 'Fuck the Police' marches have continued to take place.[42]

Ghettoisation and a crack epidemic ravaged Oakland from the late 1980s and as Chris Rhomberg explains, this has partially obfuscated the legacy of the emancipatory politics of the 1960s, a contrast perhaps most starkly rendered in the 1989 death of Black Panther founder Huey Newton at the hands of a petty drug dealer on the streets of West Oakland.[43] During the 1990s there was a continued suburbanisation of the city, and extensive job losses as the Federal Government closed the majority of the military bases in the Bay Area, leading to 12,000 military and 6,000 civilian job losses.[44] Despite this, a wave of

---

40   Suzanne Lacy, personal interview, 27 March 2012.
41   Rhomberg, p. 154.
42   Harris 2011. Since the August 2014 killing of unarmed teenager Michael Brown by Officer Darren Wilson in Ferguson, Missouri and the subsequent Grand Jury trial where Wilson was not charged, there have also been regular solidarity demonstrations in Oakland, associated with the Black Lives Matter movement. See Ticker and Ho et. al. 2014.
43   Rhomberg 2004, p. 187.
44   Ibid.

gentrification began to take hold and by the end of *The Oakland Projects*, *Forbes* magazine ranked Oakland the tenth best place to do business in the US due to low costs.⁴⁵ For the first time in fifty years, the 2000 census showed an increase in the city's white population and average apartment rents increased by 65 percent from 1995 to 2000, a drastic turnaround from the post-war 'white flight' that continued up until the 1970s.⁴⁶ These changes were partly engineered by Mayor Edmund Jerry Brown's '10K' programme, which boosted development in order to attract ten thousand new residents through the building of 6,600 new housing units within four years. By the late 1990s, Oakland was being aggressively re-branded as a viable alternative to San Francisco for private developers. Brown, long thought of as a solid centre-left politician, disappointed many who had voted for him and excused his neo-liberal push for developer-led gentrification by explaining that 'In capitalism, capital counts, and as Mayor I can't repeal that law'.⁴⁷

These neo-liberal economic policies failed in every aspect to create a trickle-down effect amongst the largely Black and Latinx youth with whom Lacy was working. Instead, many of them suffered not only from growing up in communities beset by drug-related crime, violence and disinvestment, but also a damaged education system still reeling from the effects of Proposition 13. Passed in 1978, Proposition 13 lowered property taxes in California and limited increases, thus radically reducing public revenue and causing California's public schools to fall dramatically in per-pupil spending, from fifth in the country during the 1960s to 45th by the 1990s.⁴⁸ As already discussed in the introduction, Proposition 13 provided a model for defunding, which assisted in legitimising welfare reform as well as cuts to the NEA. As one young man describes in the video documenting the workshops leading up to *Code 33*, welfare had been 'chopped off' – a reference to the 1996 Personal Responsibility and Work Opportunity Reconciliation Act, which removed all Federal Aid to the Families with Dependent Children programme, popularly identified with the Black poor. Such restructuring was part of the economic re-alignments that took place under the Clinton administration, securing a neoliberal consensus dressed up as a 'third way', which in effect meant a further shrinking of the state and a promotion of the third sector, said to be capable of compensating for diminished welfare spending.⁴⁹

---

45   Rhomberg 2004, pp. 189–90.
46   Rhomberg 2004, p. 153.
47   Ibid.
48   Meyerson and McLaughlin et. al. 2009, pp. 42–3.
49   As Pollin states, the number of people receiving food stamps declined from 1995–7, yet this

Beyond these transformations in state spending and welfare, the criminalisation of teenagers in the US had a particular impact in California following Proposition 21 (2001), an act legislating that one could commit a crime simply by associating with others who belonged to what the police labelled a 'criminal street gang'.[50] As Steve Martinot writes, clothing, gestures and certain colours were listed as 'signifying gang status' within this law, meaning 'it is not what a person does, nor even who they are, but who or what they are associated with by others (the police) that comes under judicial control'.[51] Though Proposition 21 was legislated at the very end of *The Oakland Projects*, the principles at play were already widely accepted within California law enforcement and formed the thematic drive of *Code 33*. The imbrication of aggressive policing with damaged education and welfare systems in the 1990s is illustrative of Henry Giroux's argument that neoliberal economic policy has stripped the role of the state primarily down to a surveillance function, a shift which coincided with the further marketisation of prisons during this period: by 2000 over a hundred cells were being built every day, and much of the work was outsourced to private providers such as the Corrections Corporation of America.[52] These developments had a serious bearing upon the young people participating in *The Oakland Projects*, particularly young Black men. As private investment in prisons continued apace, public resources for education and welfare dwindled, having a direct effect on the kind of institutions young people interacted with. By 1993, 708,000 young Californians were attending college whilst 930,000 were held on felonies in prison, on probation, or parole.[53] Within *Code 33*, youth explored their own criminalisation through both rehearsed and unrehearsed interactions with the police performing in the event.

3 *Code 33*

Code 33 was a far larger production than *The Roof is on Fire* in terms of its length, multi-level staging, and the number of participants and spectators. The stakes

---

number was five times greater than the drop in the number of people living in poverty. The truth of such anomalous statistics can be found in the dramatic increase in the pressure on private soup kitchens and food pantries during the period, demonstrative of the way recourse to the 'third sector' often masks the social impact of economic crisis within state-produced statistics. Pollin 2000, p. 26.

50 Martinot 2003, p. 210.
51 Ibid.
52 Giroux 2001, p. 80.
53 Lacy and Wettrich 2010, p. 223. See also Males 1996.

of *Code 33* and the atmosphere within the performance was drastically affected by the last-minute cancellation of a parade of low-rider cars initially planned as a first act.[54] Low-riders invited from a local car club were going to drive around the perimeter of the garage in opposite direction to circling police cars as the spectators and performers entered the site. Each car's sound system was to blast out a soundtrack designed by artist David Goldberg, composed of found sound, pre-recorded music and conversations between police and youth from the workshops.[55] However, the parade was cancelled following police anxieties about a demonstration that had gathered below the garage. The protest was demanding justice for Mumia Abu-Jamal, a former Black Panther and journalist who had been on death row since 1981 for supposedly shooting a police officer, following a trial that many deemed controversial.[56]

The protesters were of course responding to *Code 33*'s focus on policing, and as recalled by Moira Roth, art historian and participant, it was initially unclear what was happening. A passer-by asked her 'What's going on? A protest?' and Roth responded 'No, no. It's a community performance', only becoming aware of the demonstrators as their chanting of 'Justice for Mumia' became more audible.[57] As Roth explained, suddenly there were 'two events in the street between the Federal Building and the City Centre West Garage. Both events [were] about police, prisons, youth, and race'.[58] Like the riot that exploded in Oakland a week before *The Roof is on Fire* and which made the performance part of a constellation of events within the city, the October 4th Supreme Court denial of Abu-Jamal's appeal had come just three days prior to the performance, prompting the assembly outside *Code 33*.

As Lacy explains, between the demonstration and the planned low rider procession, the police got nervous, partly because many of them already felt disgruntled about being made to 'participate in this bizarre performance' by the Chief of Police, keen to improve the image of the police among Oak-

---

54   Low-riders are classic cars with their hydraulic suspension modified so that the height can alter, and the car can bounce. In the 1990s, Oakland became known for its 'sideshows': informal and illegal demonstrations of automobile stunts, usually using low-rider cars. This subculture is closely linked with the Bay Area genre of 'hyphy' rap music which rose to prominence in the 1990s; the rapper Keek da Sneak is credited with coining this term in 1994. For an analysis of hyphy, poetics and police violence see Bernes, Clover and Spahr 2014.
55   Roth 2001, p. 50.
56   After a sustained campaign, Abu-Jamal was taken off death row in December 2011.
57   Roth 2001, p. 56.
58   Ibid.

land's youth.[59] After receiving strong advice from the Chief, who was nervous a protestor might 'scratch' one of the low-rider cars and prompt a 'riot', Lacy cancelled the procession.[60] However, the cancellation of this first act did not provide a kind of hermetic seal between art and life, or protest and performance, as the police prevented anybody wearing a 'Free Mumia' sticker from entering the garage. According to Grant Kester, who attended the performance, the majority of officers absconded from their roles as 'performers' in order to carry out their usual functions in public order situations. Scores of would-be spectators and participants were turned away from the performance as the police 'aggressively secured and cordoned off the space around the garage, and packed off handcuffed protestors in a police van'.[61]

Lacy was less surprised than Roth by the 'interruption' of the Free Mumia protest as many members of TEAM, herself included, belonged to the same kinds of circles as the organisers of the demonstration. According to Lacy, many of the Free Mumia protestors 'were not even to the left of most of our politics' and prior to the start of the performance, when the demonstration first assembled, Lacy and members of TEAM suggested 'creating platforms within the performance for them to express their voices'.[62] Yet, Lacy readily admits that the Free Mumia demonstrators were at least partially staging the protest outside *Code 33* in response to what they surely viewed as the liberal, reformist collaboration TEAM had undertaken with the Oakland Police Department.[63] As Lacy acknowledges, she had worked long enough in Oakland to know that 'working with the city or the police was highly questionable in some quarters'.[64]

As with *The Roof is on Fire*, the vehicles which formed part of the staging of *Code 33* were assembled and arranged in blocks of colour on the roof of a garage in downtown Oakland, with their headlights lighting the performance as darkness fell. The central act of the performance presented partially rehearsed, partially improvised conversations between youth and police, sited

---

59   Suzanne Lacy, personal interview, 27 March 2012.
60   Ibid.
61   Kester 2004, p. 185.
62   Suzanne Lacy, personal interview, 27 March 2012.
63   Although portions of the demonstration were perhaps close to Lacy's position, it was organised primarily by the Critical Resistance prison abolition movement, students from UC Santa Cruz and community leaders such as Van Jones, a founder of Bay Area Police Watch, all of whom at that time primarily viewed collaboration with the police and city council as unthinkable.
64   Suzanne Lacy, personal interview, 27 March 2012.

FIGURE 4   Suzanne Lacy, Julio César Morales and Unique Holland, *Code 33: Emergency, Clear the Air!*, 1997–99, from The Oakland Projects, 1991–2001. Oakland, California
PHOTO BY KELLI YON. COURTESY OF SUZANNE LACY

around the cars in small circles. Woven in between the cars were 100 police officers and 150 young people discussing questions of crime, retribution, policing and authority. Unlike *The Roof is on Fire*, the dialogues were not enclosed within the vehicles, but staged in a more accessible, less private manner for the 1000 spectators who attended, and were also implicated as performers by the final act. (Fig. 4) Once the performance began, conversations about police brutality against the protestors coalesced to form an entirely unrehearsed counter-narrative. As Roth described, 'three determined Mumia protesters gained entry and travelled from group to group trying to interrupt the conversations … Many rumours fly around; for instance, of three arrests on the 7th floor of the garage'.[65] The protest as 'interruption' thus destabilised the collaboration that had been established with the police by shifting the terrain of the performance beyond its pre-established boundaries, and, unsurprisingly, the dialogues following that interruption were far more heated than those within the self-contained workshops. (Fig. 5) As a young woman performer explained, the trust established between youth and police in the workshops broke down, partly due to the performance involving a larger group of officers who made clear they did not want to be part of the performance, but had been instructed by their

---

65   Roth 2001, p. 58.

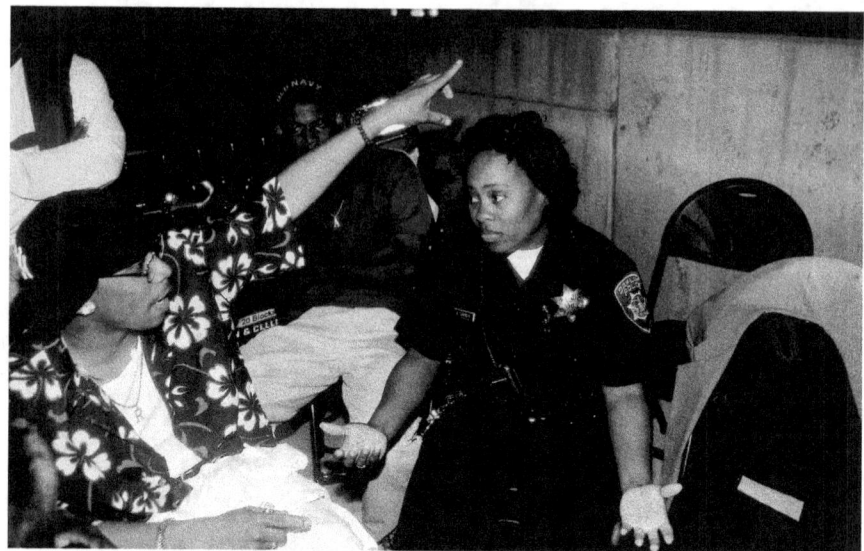

FIGURE 5 Suzanne Lacy, Julio César Morales and Unique Holland, *Code 33: Emergency, Clear the Air!*, 1997–99, from The Oakland Projects, 1991–2001. Oakland, California
PHOTO BY LILY RODRÍGUEZ. COURTESY OF SUZANNE LACY

superiors to participate.[66] Similarly, not all the young people performing had attended the workshop, and in many cases brought suspicion, fear and anger at the police with them, unmediated by the ameliorating effects the workshops had for some of the young participants' relationship with the police.

To give an example of the dialogue in *Code 33*, one young man described how he saw a policeman repeatedly punch a handcuffed person and asked how it was possible for the police to get away with this violence. When a police officer responded by saying that he had never seen such behaviour in ten years of being in the force and claimed officers were always penalised for brutalising the public, another young man interjected, stating that 'It happened in Riverside to a young girl, what are you talking about that never happens?'[67] This referred presumably to the shooting of 19-year-old African American woman Tyshia Miller by four white police officers in December 1998.[68] As Lacy explains, the primary risk during *Code 33* was 'that the police might freeze up' follow-

---

66 From video documentation of *Code 33*, available online at Lacy's vimeo site: http://vimeo.com/4041923.
67 Ibid.
68 The police killed Tyshia Miller in December 1998 in Riverside, California. The four policemen involved in the murder were cleared of charges in May 1999.

ing such tense exchanges.⁶⁹ This 'freeze-up' was expressed in how the police handled the Free Mumia protestors. The 'cops got vigorous not letting people in' and abdicated their role in the performance whilst those remaining found the conflict seeped into the staged conversations.⁷⁰ This clarifies that participation by the majority of the police was directed from above by their Chief as a public relations stunt, and as unrehearsed performers they swiftly assumed their structural role in the wake of the Free Mumia interruption.

The end of this central episode was signalled by loud rap music, following which the spectators descended three stories down to another parking lot. During this interval, youth participants staged a mass dance that was spot-lit by police helicopters circling overhead. The final segment of the performance invited audience members to respond to the first act in rehearsed 'neighbourhood conversations'. This involved a different kind of staging, as performers took their positions on grass-covered platforms surrounded by picket fences. These platforms were laid out in a quilt-like arrangement, akin to the staging of the cars in *Code 33* and *The Roof is on Fire*, as well as earlier performances by Lacy such as *The Crystal Quilt* (1987). Within this much more suburban setting, pre-selected groups from eight Oakland neighbourhoods discussed the conversations they had overheard between youth and police.

Like *The Roof is on Fire*, the overall staging and organisation of *Code 33* was episodic, a quality which means the work implicitly absorbed the interruption by the Free Mumia protest into its structure, supporting my analysis of this performance as a rehearsal. In Brecht's account, the rehearsal is marked by the relative independence of distinct theatrical elements (performers, text, staging) with their mutual alienation enabling the process of development and learning.⁷¹ This was exemplified in the disjuncture between workshop and performance in *Code 33*. The Brechtian qualities can also be seen in the dual role of the police participants as police on duty, and police as performers, the teenagers' performance of themselves, and the implication of the audience into the drama. For Brecht, actors were not waiters who serve up their parts as 'meat', but rather, their 'job as political human beings was to use art or anything else to further their social cause'.⁷² Brecht was intent on actors bringing their own life and concerns into the work to further enable a critique of social conditions. Of course, Brecht's actors were professionals, distinguishing them from the performers in *The Roof is on Fire* and *Code 33*. However, the status of youth and

---

69 Suzanne Lacy, personal interview, 27 March 2012.
70 Ibid.
71 Baker-White 1999, p. 51.
72 Brecht 1977, p. 71.

police as performing themselves complicates Brecht's command, since despite being non-professionals these performers were potentially better able than an actor to portray their roles. *The Roof is on Fire* and *Code 33* integrate, and then eclipse, the Brechtian call for actors to inflect a character with personal experience.

More so than *The Roof is on Fire*, *Code 33* made extensive use of tropes and media drawn from popular culture. Along with the music marking the breaks between episodes, one of the posters promoting *Code 33* had the tagline 'Yo! This ain't no MTV rap', referring to the show 'Yo! MTV raps!' which played a significant role in the global popularisation of rap music. Structurally however, the performance recalls a different show airing on MTV during the 1990s: *The Real World*, which ran from 1992 and stands as one of the first successful reality TV shows. In working with performers who played themselves, the process of performing reality in *The Oakland Projects* demonstrated that teenagers could assume many roles. Conversely, the breaking down of police stereotypes proved close to impossible, as the final performance of *Code 33* adequately demonstrates. Here, types materialise through defining themselves against one another, forming realistic characters by their ability to, in Jameson's account

> [S]tand ... for something larger and more meaningful than themselves, than their own isolated individual destinies. They are both concrete individualities, and yet at the same time maintain a relationship with some more general or collective human substance.[73]

Such strategies of typification are present in *The Roof is on Fire* and *Code 33*. However, the events surrounding the latter exemplify some of the inherent problems in Lacy and TEAM's ambitions of working with the police as an ameliorative measure. The initial cooperation did not result in a less abrasive relationship. Instead, the police demonstrated their inability to move beyond their coercive duties. Moving from stage to stage, they continually expressed themselves as a flattened or shallow type, boiled down to representatives of a force more meaningful than themselves as individual officers. In Lukácsean terms, the police participants fully enacted the role 'imputed' to them within the reproduction of capital – that of property protection – holding the web of domination in the 'hollow of their hands'.[74] The experience of this within the space of the performance concretised the broader social reality of the police

---

73 Jameson 1970, p. 25.
74 This metaphor is drawn from Lukács's description of the characters of Gaubertin and Rigou, the capitalist usurers in Balzac's *The Peasants*. See Lukács 1972, pp. 28–9.

for the teenage participants, as well as the meaning of the type that had been assigned to them as youth – particularly Black and Latinx youth – by the law and media. While the process leading up to the performance had perhaps temporarily shifted relations into a more dialogical encounter, the performance of *Code 33* failed to present or temporarily enact an idealised, projected or parallel reality, despite its status as an artwork. Instead, the media stereotype of young people that spurred on *The Oakland Projects* was revealed as a component of a broader social process, rather than as ideological epiphenomena simply capable of being deconstructed through reframing the dominant media narrative about teenagers. As the already-known truth of the police's role in Oakland appeared with renewed and clarified force in *Code 33*, the legislative and carceral system propelling those stereotypes bubbled to the surface.

The unmovable reality of the police's role in the United States cannot be disconnected from their existence as a racialising force. As Martinot and Jared Sexton write, racialisation is a system of meanings assigned to the body, and 'police spectacle' – by which they mean brutality and harassment – is a 'banal', everyday form of this violence. Legal impunity means that the actions of individual police officers within a broader force serves to codify and constitute the 'distinction between those whose human being is put permanently in question and those for whom it goes without saying'.[75] *Code 33* demonstrates that because the police exist to maintain and reproduce racial and class subjugation, they cannot be reformed within the reality that has assigned that role to them. As Martinot and Sexton explain, 'The truth is that the truth is on the surface, flat and repetitive, just as the law is made by the uniform'.[76] The investigation of the police as types concretised this truth through the episodic, rehearsal-like function of the performances, with both *Code 33* and *The Roof is on Fire* being mutable and responsive to the political dramas of the city. Though I have described the formal characteristics of these performances as inheriting Brechtian techniques of interruption, montage and estrangement, my suggestion is that their realism can also be conceived along Lukácsean lines. Describing Balzac's *Comédie Humaine*, Lukács wrote that although the cycle was composed by a succession of singular parts, the whole is constantly present in each novel, therefore producing a web of 'immensely complex motivations, interrelations and combinations' within the world Balzac portrays.[77] This is how I want to conceive of the performance discussed from *The Oakland Pro-*

---

75 Martinot and Sexton particularly stress the impact of 'probable cause' statutes in enabling police impunity. Martinot and Sexton 2003, p. 174.
76 Martinot and Sexton 2003, p. 178.
77 Lukács 1962, p. 99.

jects in this chapter, in order to carry forth this relation between the overall cycle and their individual meaning when I turn to another segment of that work, *Expectations*, in Chapter Two. By shifting focus now to the Living Newspaper, I explore the historical continuities and transformations in such an approach to making realist, collective performance works. The attempt here is to illuminate points of connection, enabling a more open reading of how performance has been mobilised as a rehearsal for a broader social critique, and an examination of continuities and gaps in these works' engagement with law.

4 *Injunction Granted*

Injunction Granted was the second Living Newspaper directed by Joseph Losey and the third production by the Living Newspaper Unit, following *Triple-A Plowed Under* and *1935*.[78] The script was collectively written by the Living Newspaper Unit, supervised by Arthur Arent and produced by Morris Watson. *Injunction Granted* opened on 24 July 1936 at the Biltmore Theatre in New York City, and played to full houses for three months.[79] A chronicle of labour struggles in the US, it ended on a polemical note by arguing that all workers should unite behind the newly formed Congress of Industrial Organizations (CIO). In the final scene, over one hundred performers playing steel workers, female garment workers and coal miners along with other groups of workers took the stage. Symbolising the formation of the CIO as an umbrella organisation for industrial unions, this theatrical formation of mass unity across trades was reminiscent of a picket line or rally, suggesting that struggle produced unity across social groups, a quality shared with the oppositional pageantry of the Paterson Strike Pageant. (Fig. 6)

Like *Code 33* and *The Roof is on Fire*, the structure of *Injunction Granted* was episodic. If the spectators in Lacy's work had to move from car to car, *Injunc-*

---

78 For a brief discussion of *Triple-A Plowed Under* see the introduction to this book. *1935* was a minor production that ran for only 34 performances, and the least successful of the Living Newspapers. Losey and other Living Newspaper staff distanced themselves from *1935* as it patronised the audience, assuming their interest in tabloid subjects of crime, society weddings and dangerous voyages. As Cosgrove explains, poor audience attendance also suggests that Depression-era theatregoers were 'not simply on the lookout for escapism but had a developed interest in culture that generated pleasure through knowledge. The tabloid Living Newspaper was an abject failure; it was never tried again, and the Unit returned once more to political theatre'. See Cosgrove 1982, p. 61.

79 Brown and O'Connor 1980, p. 77.

FIGURE 6   Final scene, *Injunction Granted*, Biltmore Theatre, New York City, 1936
PHOTOGRAPHER UNKNOWN. COURTESY OF THE ARNOLD GOLDMAN LIVING
NEWSPAPER COLLECTION, SPECIAL COLLECTIONS AND ARCHIVES, GEORGE
MASON UNIVERSITY

tion Granted generated a similar effect through revue-like skits and pageantry. Many scenes began with a tableau vivant that would then be activated by the disembodied 'Voice of the Living Newspaper' explaining the action, providing contrary details or a pre-history. The Voice of the Living Newspaper also played a practical function, as the speed of the performance necessitated some form of narration. Anticipating the use of captions in Brecht plays such as *Mother Courage* (1939), the shifts between episodes in *Injunction Granted* were announced by the booming Voice of the Living Newspaper, grounding each section historically. Throughout *Injunction Granted* the actor Norman Lloyd assumed the role of a mute clown, who supplemented the Voice through frequently satirical visual commentary. Inspired by Harpo Marx and the Barnum and Bailey circus, Lloyd suggested to Losey that a clown would liven up *Injunction Granted*, counselling that the history of labour in the courts was 'hardly something to bring an audience in'.[80] Losey agreed, and built Lloyd a trapdoor on set from which the Clown popped out at key moments, wielding props that typified the other char-

---

80   Lloyd 2003, p. 29.

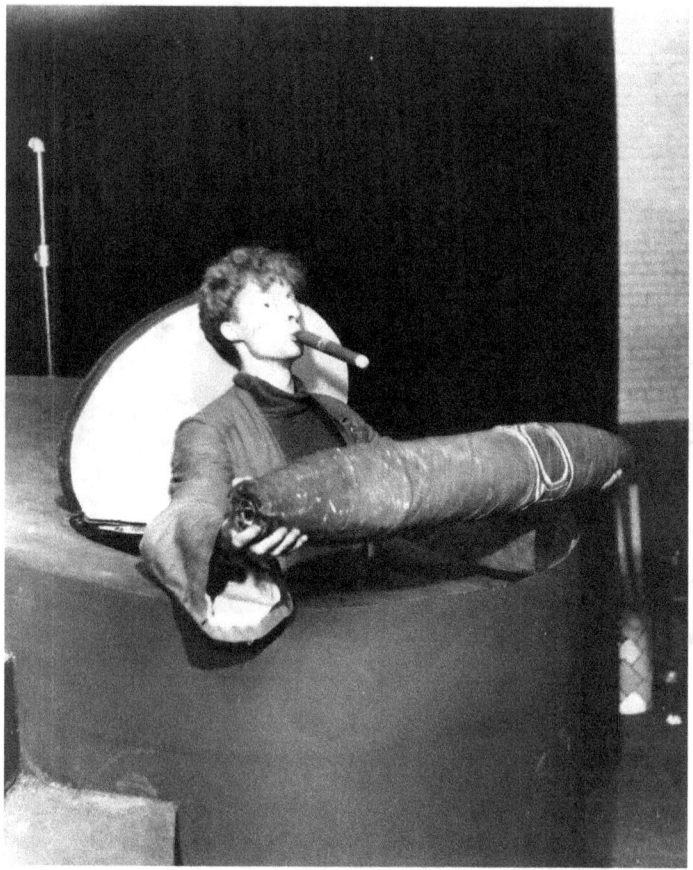

FIGURE 7   Clown with cigar, *Injunction Granted*, 1936
PHOTOGRAPHER UNKNOWN. COURTESY OF THE ARNOLD GOLDMAN LIVING NEWSPAPER COLLECTION, SPECIAL COLLECTIONS AND ARCHIVES, GEORGE MASON UNIVERSITY

acters on stage, such as a giant cigar during an interaction with stockbrokers. (Fig. 7) Unlike the Voice of the Living Newspaper, which remained neutral for much of *Injunction Granted*, merely relaying facts and dates, the Clown's commentary mocked, lampooned and rubbed up against the action on stage. The Clown stood firmly on the side of labour, thus acting as a conduit between the Living Newspaper theatre workers and their proletarian audience, of whom many came through block bookings organised by unions.[81] The clown's

---

81   Cosgrove 1985, p. 249.

role was to assist in the formation of a bloc by repeatedly breaking the fourth wall and encourage a discussion about social conditions within the audience. Along Brechtian lines, *Injunction Granted* asked the audience to 'justify or abolish' the conditions they saw on stage.[82]

The inclusion of magic tricks, film projection and a cacophonous array of sound effects prompted the CPUSA associated cultural journal *New Masses* to describe *Injunction Granted* as carrying 'suggestions of the Greek chorus, burlesque, the *March of Time*, Symbolism, the miracle plays, and Charlie Chaplin'.[83] This eclectic range of references indicates how *Injunction Granted* cohered with the stylistic hallmarks of the proletarian avant-garde described by Denning, mixing popular American forms with the European avant-gardes. The staging consisted of platforms, runways and steps that composed ten separate acting areas. These areas could be individually lit, which was particularly conducive to the rapidity of scene changes and the episodic nature of the performance, as well as in accommodating the large cast of 125 performers.[84] Losey described the staging as inspired by the Russian theatre director Vsevolod Meyerhold, and the 'totally flexible and plastic' design he had seen in Russia at a production directed by Nikolay Okhlopkov.[85]

The score for *Injunction Granted* was by Virgil Thomson, a leftist composer who had studied with Erik Satie, spent time among the Parisian avant-garde of the 1920s and also composed the soundtrack for Pare Lorentz's Resettlement Administration film, *The Plow that Broke the Plains* (1936). Thomson's percussive score formed a necessary punctuation within *Injunction Granted*. As he described:

> What you wanted to do was use industrial sounds. Also with a script that jumps about in tiny little pieces it is valuable to punctuate everything, so I used those percussion instruments to separate one thing from another, or to hit something on the nose, or to salt the whole thing up. I think there was something like 496 music cues.[86]

As Lloyd recalled, the score was composed of 'ratchets, sirens, drums, ship's bells, trombones and trumpets', and when the sound 'all went off at one time the first night' complaints from the neighbours caused the police to storm the

---

82   Brecht 1964, p. 139.
83   Taylor 1936, p. 29.
84   Brown and O'Connor 1980, p. 82.
85   Joseph Losey interview with Arnold Goldman, 1972.
86   Virgil Thomson, quoted in Brown and O'Connor 1980, p. 80.

theatre in alarm, guns drawn.[87] Thomson's score mimicked the industrial landscape of much of *Injunction Granted* and contributed to the episodic nature of the performance, playing a similar function to the music that signalled the end of the first act in *Code 33*. Through the episodic nature, pantomimic acting style, use of props, fast-paced action alongside captions, projection and the Voice of the Living Newspaper, *Injunction Granted* produced multiple effects intended to constantly jolt the audience, rather than offering harmonious accompaniment.

Injunction Granted begins in seventeenth-century England and shows workers being encouraged by 'officials' to emigrate to the US. The New World is described as an 'earthly paradise', with this phrase repeated mechanically in response to workers' questions about the passage to America.[88] As the performance shifts to the US in scene two, multiple figures take the stage, playing bidders in a slave auction. Here, a slave owner refers to a document and asks the Captain why the nineteen children – described as 'twelve years of age and older' – are listed for sale but not present. The captain of the ship explains they all died in passage, to which the owner replies by instructing the Captain that he will need 'another hundred', and to ensure they are over fourteen as 'they'll be able to stand it better'.[89] Rear projection lends a cinematic atmosphere as a group of 'indentured servants' are illuminated against a screen; this is captured for five counts before a blackout and the boom of the Living Newspaper announces 'More ships, more men, women and children. So begins the slave labour ... black and white ... on which the agriculture of the colonies is based ... These laborers, employed by the great landowners, have no vote in their government because they own no property, and they work from SUNRISE to SUNSET'.[90] Emphasis is added to the final phrase through the lowering of a banner onto the stage, emblazoned with the caption 'SUNRISE to SUNSET'. As David Roediger explains, in the mid-eighteenth century, the degrees of unfreedom among whites in the US included indentured servitude, apprenticeship, convict labour, farm tenancy as well as emergent combinations of wage labour with the aforementioned conditions. Despite this continuum of oppressions experienced by poor whites, the horrors of chattel slavery ensured an ontological distinction from the oppression of Black people.[91] This difference is barely parsed in *Injunction Granted*, and the play also declines to register the begin-

---

87 Lloyd 2003, p. 29 and also Brown and O'Connor 1980, p. 78.
88 Editorial Staff of the Living Newspaper, script of *Injunction Granted*, 1936. Scene 1.
89 Editorial Staff of the Living Newspaper, script of *Injunction Granted*, 1936, Scene 2, p. 3.
90 Editorial Staff of the Living Newspaper, script of *Injunction Granted*, 1936, Scene 2, p. 3.
91 Roediger, p. 25.

nings of settler colonialism in the US as one involving the dispossession and murder of a native population. Instead, the teleology of the drama papers over such distinctions in order to emphasise unity among proletarians.

By opening with this scene, the writers introduced an origin point against which the gradual and continuous improvement of 'free' working conditions through the emergence and stabilisation of wage labour could be set. Within this history and the emergence of organised labour in the US, the idea of slavery became crucial to how white workers expressed their oppression. As long as slavery existed in the US, attempts to criticise the emergence of wage labour lapsed into both inflated metaphors comparing it to slavery, and on the other hand, emphatic denial of such comparisons. As Roediger notes, the oppression of white workers was primarily articulated as 'white slavery', followed by the terms 'slavery of wages' with the more recognisable 'wage slavery' least present in the Democratic press of the 1840s.[92] After emancipation, a more thoroughgoing critique of wage labour in its specificity could emerge, as well as a struggle over the meaning of free labour.[93] However, by that time, the conceptualisation of what free labour entailed was frequently bound up with whiteness. Furthermore, terms like 'white slavery' were rarely used in an act of solidarity with Black people, but were more often deployed as a call to arms to end the 'inappropriate oppression of whites'.[94] The historical progression of *Injunction Granted* corresponds to the historical development of these terms, and the necessity of Black slavery to conceptualising wage labour as both free, and white. As discussed further in Chapter Two, the development of wage labour in the US was a critical element in maintaining a distinct, 'primitive' existence for people of colour as well as women, with Black women experiencing this most forcefully in their working conditions as well as cultural representation. By stressing the relation between these terms and material histories of how class formation interacted with race in the 1930s, my intention is to present a more complex view of the transformations we also witness across those categories of race, class and gender in the 1990s.

The first scene of *Injunction Granted* thus establishes an extreme against which subsequent modes of exploitation could be measured, but also stands as the moment of 'primitive accumulation' from which the history on stage emerges. Thereafter attention quickly shifts to the passage of the first American labour law in Massachusetts in 1630, and *Injunction Granted* proceeds

---

92   Roediger 1999, p. 72.
93   Roediger 1999, p. 87.
94   Roediger 1999, p. 68.

through a whistle-stop tour of early American legislation pertaining to workers' struggles. This is portrayed by a wide range of historical actors and through a series of landmark cases; Nathan Bacon, King Charles II and John Adams appear on stage, and the first five scenes move from the Philadelphia Shoemakers strike and subsequent trial of 1806 to the Haymarket Massacre of 1886.[95] Also included before the intermission are scenes detailing the trumped-up trial of the Molly Maguires in 1875, and the emergence of anti-labour spies and the Pinkerton Detective Agency. The boom of the Living Newspaper summarises these events: 'The first labor spy in history. The ten Molly Maguires were hanged. The wheels of industry turn again. The Knights of Labor become the largest union of workers in the country'.[96] Accompanying the Voice was a stereopticon projection – similar to a magic lantern – which stressed certain phrases within the narration, flashing up 'wheels of industry' and then 'Knights of Labor'. The Voice then announces 'The federated Trades Union of America springs up. Its leader is a cigar maker named Samuel Gompers'. An actor playing Gompers walks onstage as does a worker, and the light arcs to illuminate them meeting centre stage and shaking hands. The caption 'one united union' is projected as the Voice announces 'This union is to be called ... The American Federation of Labor', and a final projection of the seal of the AFL appears before the close of the scene with a blackout.[97] The next scene showed the organisation of the American Railway Union and the Pullman strike of 1894, led by Eugene Debs, followed by a scene played between two workers where one explained to the other what an 'injunction' from a judge meant; the capacity to break a strike by gaining a court order declaring it illegal, meaning any picketing or striking can result in an immediate jail sentence, without trial by a jury.

The following scenes play out this drama in the courts, before culminating in the repressions outlined in scene seventeen, set in 1925. Entitled 'Labor counts up', here a 'Second Loudspeaker' joins the Voice of the Living Newspaper, providing an additional voice that announces the massacre of striking coal miners and their families in Ludlow, Colorado in 1914, the life imprisonment of labour organiser Tom Mooney in 1916, and then the death sentences given to Nicolo Sacco and Bartolomeo Vanzetti in 1921. The scene ends with the following speech from Vanzetti:

---

95   Editorial Staff of the Living Newspaper, script of *Injunction Granted*, 1936, scenes 1–5.
96   Editorial Staff of the Living Newspaper, script of *Injunction Granted*, 1936, scenes 6 and 8.
97   Editorial Staff of the Living Newspaper, script of *Injunction Granted*, 1936, Scene 8, p. 29.

If it had not been for this case, I might have lived out my life talking at street corners to scorning men. I might have died, unmarked, unknown, a failure. Now we are not a failure. This is our career and our triumph. Never in our full life could we hope to do such work for tolerance, for justice, for man's understanding of man as now we do by an accident. Our words – our lives – our pains – nothing! The taking of our lives – lives of a good shoemaker and a poor fish-peddler – all! That last moment belongs to us – that agony is our triumph.[98]

The martyrdom of Sacco and Vanzetti closes this scene and is followed by a blackout, closing the first half of the play. Up to the half-way point, the audience had watched the progression of various modes of oppression, exploitation and resistance from the beginnings of settler colonialism in the US to almost the present-day. As they bustled out for the intermission, what kind of relation did the audience feel to this history? Or even, what kind of debt did they feel they owed to those workers' struggles which came before them? And how would their implications for the present carry through to the second half of the play?

After the interval, *Injunction Granted* firmly moves into the contemporary conjuncture and adopts a more satirical and acerbic tone, shedding the solemn historicism of the first half. Scene eighteen, dated 1929, is entitled 'Partnership', and satirises the overly cosy relationship between craft unions such as the AFL and capitalist firms. It opens with a 'demagogue' standing on a platform dressed in an outfit split down the middle. This is intended to reflect his listeners, who on the right represent capital, and on the left a group of workers. The side facing capital wears a pinstriped trouser, jacket, slicked-back hair and half a moustache whilst the side facing labour dons an overall leg, half a blue shirt, tousled hair and one horn-rimmed glass. The demagogue personifies the types of 'worker' and 'capitalist', thereby functioning as a schizophrenic embodiment of class conflict. (Fig. 8) He gives a speech to the capitalists and workers with each side's applause 'deafening, in unison, automatic', as conducted by the Clown. The demagogue's saccharine dialogue affirms that

> Capital is wonderful – and Labor is wonderful too! We cannot do without Labor, and we cannot do without Capital! They are both wonderful! Nine-tenths of the difficulties between Labor and Capital spring from the lustful loins of

---

98 Editorial Staff of the Living Newspaper, script of *Injunction Granted*, 1936, Scene 17, p. 61.

FIGURE 8 Demagogue scene. *Injunction Granted*, 1936
PHOTOGRAPHER UNKNOWN. COURTESY OF THE ARNOLD GOLDMAN LIVING NEWSPAPER COLLECTION, SPECIAL COLLECTIONS AND ARCHIVES, GEORGE MASON UNIVERSITY

>   – Bolshevism –
>   (Capital applauds)
>   – Fascism –
>   (Labor applauds)
>   – Socialism –
>   (Capital applauds)
>   – and un-Americanism! –
>   (Both applaud, extra loud)[99]

This scene is punctured by the Clown blowing a horn, causing the demagogue to raise his voice, before closing with the Clown inflating a balloon to bursting point. As it pops, he brandishes a bouquet towards the demagogue, perforating the sentimental nationalism of his hot air speech.

---

99 Editorial Staff of the Living Newspaper, script of *Injunction Granted*, 1936, p. 63.

Following a blackout, the lights come up as John D. Rockefeller appears on stage. Rockefeller proceeds to echo the demagogue's sentiments that Labour and Capital should put their petty gripes behind them, a statement met with the Clown solemnly handing a giant dime to Rockefeller, satirising the multiple images which circulated of him handing out dimes to children and the poor. Next, Mr Howard Heinz of the H.J. Heinz Company – an archetype of capitalist paternalism – enters the stage, announced by the Voice of the Living Newspaper, and declares that capital and labour are 'co-partners'. The Clown meets Heinz's pronouncement by handing him a giant gherkin. (Fig. 9) Brandishing their humiliating booby-prizes, Heinz and Rockefeller bow to one another before a blackout. As the lights come up on the third episode within this scene, a 'President of the University' is announced by the Voice, who strolls onstage in mortar board and gown to make a speech which consists of statements proclaiming that 'in the year of 1929 there are no limits' to achieving success for young people, in a nation that is now 'experiencing an era of expansion and prosperity that will endure until the end of time'.[100] The Clown too wears a mortarboard in this episode and impersonates a 'naïve college student, farcically overjoyed at the President's statement'.[101] However, at the President's announcement that prosperity will endure, the Clown/college student, dumbfounded, strikes himself over the head with his diploma and lies flat out on the ramp stage.

Throughout this scene, '1929' – marking the beginning of the Great Depression – is projected in large letters on the scrim. The Clown's ridiculing of the demagogue, Heinz, Rockefeller and the University President provide humour and incite antagonism towards bourgeois notions of expertise, success and reform, pulling the audience into alliance with the workers onstage, while, on the other hand, cementing the protagonists of these scenes into a hegemonic social group composed of types which represent the interests of capital. Through the demagogue in particular, scene eighteen mobilises the appearance of the 'type' as a form of self-education for the performers and audience, with an uncompromising attitude towards the notion of corporatist partnerships between capital and labour.

---

100 Editorial Staff of the Living Newspaper, script of *Injunction Granted*, 1936, Scene 18, p. 65. The University Professor was likely intended to mock Nicolas Murray Butler, the President of Columbia. Butler was a staunch Republican who sought the presidential nomination on a number of occasions. He was also an anti-Semite and admirer of Mussolini, inviting the Nazi ambassador on campus in 1933 and enforcing a strict Jewish quota among the faculty. See Mallon 2006.

101 Editorial Staff of the Living Newspaper, script of *Injunction Granted*, 1936.

FIGURE 9   Clown giving gherkin to Heinz, *Injunction Granted*, 1936
PHOTOGRAPHER UNKNOWN. COURTESY OF THE ARNOLD
GOLDMAN LIVING NEWSPAPER COLLECTION, SPECIAL
COLLECTIONS AND ARCHIVES, GEORGE MASON UNI-
VERSITY

Scene twenty-four of *Injunction Granted* focuses on the 1934 General Strike in San Francisco and further illustrates the developing ties between the state, legislature, and capital in repressing workers' struggles. Here, National Guardsmen attack striking dock workers who are blocking access to ships when strike breakers turn up to unload cargo, and this sparks a general strike as announced by the Voice of the Living Newspaper. General Hugh Johnson, the right-wing head of the National Recovery Administration (NRA) appears on stage and, as he begins to speak, becomes aware of the fact he is standing in a red light; he 'indignantly' jumps down stage into a green light. Johnson was the head of the NRA from 1933–5 and along with his Deputy Donald Richberg, who later took over as head, was renowned for his pro-capital handling of disputes between trade unionists and their employers. Richberg began as a supporter of trade unions but moved to the right, issuing several anti-labour edicts during his time in office.[102]

In Johnson's first scene he pontificates that the general strike is a 'threat to community ... menace to government ... it is a civil war!'[103] The scene progresses with industrialists discussing how to break the strike, interrupted by four newsboys tearing across the stage yelling 'Extra! Revolution! Revolution!' Two men buy newspapers and read aloud the coverage about 'foreign agitators' and conclude that this 'unlawful rebellion' must be put down by them as American citizens.[104] This ominous announcement is followed by a blackout as the action moves quickly to depict a group of policemen arresting a man at his typewriter. One policeman whispers 'You're sure he's a Red?' and another responds 'I tell you, he writes all night!' lampooning the anti-intellectualism of anti-communism.[105] Another blackout follows before the third episode within this scene, opening on a woman describing to her professor husband that she has just seen the militia fire on a group of strikers. The professor, distracted, announces 'I have to read up on this new theory of Douglas on social credit. One of my students asked about it ...' He is interrupted by a crash of glass and a brick coming through the window, attached to which is a note signed by the 'Citizens Vigilante Committee' that reads 'Leave this community immediately or drastic action will be taken. All undesirables such as Communists, Bolsheviks, radicals, agitators and other anti-government groups will be abolished at once'. The wife chastises the husband: 'I *told* you not to have that Russian doctor here to dinner last week!'[106]

The lights are cut again before coming up on Johnson, who waves his arms, declaring 'this is a bloody insurrection' by 'one half of one percent of our population', causing a worker to laughingly declare that Johnson's mathematics are 'perfect'. The worker explains that an insurrection is indeed being carried out by the 'one half of one percent', arguing that those who are blocking the action by 'sixty million people who work for a livin'' and want to get paid for the work' are really responsible for the disturbance. Mocking Johnson further, the President of the University of California, aided by the clown wielding a giant Phi

---

102 Dubofsky 1994, p. 112.
103 Editorial Staff of the Living Newspaper, script of *Injunction Granted*, 1936, scene 24, p. 83.
104 Editorial Staff of the Living Newspaper, script of *Injunction Granted*, 1936, scene 24, p. 84.
105 Editorial Staff of the Living Newspaper, script of *Injunction Granted*, 1936, scene 24, p. 85.
106 Editorial Staff of the Living Newspaper, script of *Injunction Granted*, 1936, scene 24, pp. 85–6.

Beta Kappa key, presents Johnson with the honour of joining the fraternity for, as the worker interjects, his 'proficiency in mathematics!' As the Voice of the Living Newspaper declares General Johnson's resignation from the National Relief Administration, the Clown strikes Johnson over the head with the key, who stumbles, murmurs 'crack down' and rolls down the ramp.[107]

As with the appearance of the University Professor in the demagogue scene, the appearance here of the Professor positions the academy as disconnected from a social reality that becomes viscerally present in the form of a brick and a smashed window. The Professor only gains awareness when the 'Community Vigilante Committee' indicts him as a possible 'Red'. The episode stresses the pitfalls of careerist individualism, and anticipates the anti-communist paranoia that would be the downfall of the Living Newspaper Unit. In addition, through highlighting the anti-intellectual association of the left with 'Russians' and other foreigners, *Injunction Granted* introduces a critique of nationalism. This position was gradually eroded as the CPUSA moved to embrace a position of left-nationalism with the 'Democratic Front', and as we shall see in Chapter Three, even the Living Newspaper unit came to embrace a saccharine Americanism as the 1930s wore on.

In the scene 'Jennings vs. Hearst' the network of allegiances between capital, state and the media is depicted through a boxing match between the tycoon William Randolph Hearst and the copywriter Dean Jennings, who had been fired by Hearst for union activity. (Fig. 10) The referee announces Jennings as the 'pride of the Newspaper Guild' and Hearst as the 'Champion of the Non-Collective Bargaining Athletic Association'. The 'Voice of the Living Newspaper' narrates the fight:

> There they go! Hearst leads with a left ... he misses ... Jennings tries an uppercut ... he misses ... Hearst leads with left ... he misses ... Jennings tries an uppercut ... HE SOCKS HIM! HE'S DOWN! The National Labor Board orders Jennings reinstated.[108]

As the referee counts down to Jennings' victory, Richberg appears again on stage, announced by a sign. Though Hearst is out cold, Richberg instructs the referee to hold a re-match that follows the exact choreography of the first. Despite Jennings knocking Hearst out with an uppercut almost immediately, Richberg runs in again with a decision, overriding the referee. Contrary to what the

---

107   Editorial Staff of the Living Newspaper, script of *Injunction Granted*, 1936, scene 24, p. 86.
108   Editorial Staff of the Living Newspaper, script of *Injunction Granted*, scene 25, p. 88.

FIGURE 10 Hearst vs. Jennings, *Injunction Granted*, 1936
PHOTOGRAPHER UNKNOWN. COURTESY OF THE ARNOLD GOLDMAN LIVING NEWSPAPER COLLECTION, SPECIAL COLLECTIONS AND ARCHIVES, GEORGE MASON UNIVERSITY

audience has witnessed, the referee lifts the unconscious Hearst's arm in victory and declares 'The winnah!'[109] This result is a metaphor for real-life events. After Jennings was fired for labour organising at the *San Francisco Call-Bulletin*, the Newspaper Guild petitioned the National Labor Relations Board (NLRB) and National Industrial Recovery Board for his reinstatement. Their initial support for Jennings dissolved when Hearst petitioned President Roosevelt, who nullified the NLRB decision.[110] The lack of justice, as the referee declares 'winnah!' also echoes the repetitive call of the courts – 'Injunction Granted!' – which punctuates the performance whenever a capitalist such as Hearst wins a battle against labour in the legislature.

The Newspaper Guild was founded after Heywood Broun, a journalist and Socialist Party member, published a call for unionisation in his *New York World*

---

109 Editorial Staff of the Living Newspaper, script of *Injunction Granted*, scene 25, p. 89.
110 Bernstein 2010, p. 136.

Telegraph column on 7 August 1933. Broun declared the necessity of a newspaper writers' union, fantasising about how he

> ... could die happy on the opening day of a general strike if I had the privilege of watching Walter Lippman heave half a brick through a *Tribune* window at a non-union operative who had been called in to write the current Today and Tomorrow column on the gold standard.[111]

This image – of the brick going through the window – relates to how the notion of community is wrangled over within *Injunction Granted*. Unlike Johnson's proclamation that the San Francisco general strike was a 'threat to community', for Broun and the workers on stage in *Injunction Granted*, community is formed, affirmed and sustained through the transformative potential of direct action and collective bargaining.

As Lloyd, the actor playing the Clown, emphasised, the cast and production crew for *Injunction Granted* were all on relief, some of the 10,000 unemployed theatre workers who had found employment in the WPA-FTP. Esther Porter Lane, an assistant stage manager on *Injunction Granted*, described how an elderly man called Fuller Mellish played a judge in one scene, a role that had been especially created for him by Losey. Mellish's vulnerability meant he had to be assisted on stage by other members of the cast, and was required only to say 'Injunction Granted!' twice in order to take on this minor role, which assisted in safeguarding him against the growing numbers falling into poverty during the Depression.[112] The actors, therefore, like the audience, formed a bloc which countered Heinz, the demagogue, Rockefeller and the University President as representatives of capital. As with the teenagers and police in *The Roof is on Fire* and *Code 33*, the theatre workers who produced and performed in *Injunction Granted* were directly invested in the drama onstage, frequently adapting the script to bring it up to date with contemporary issues. Like the performances organised by Lacy, we can refer again to Brecht's command that actors draw on their own life and politics to supplement a scripted critique of social conditions.

In the final scene of *Injunction Granted*, over one hundred performers took the stage. (Fig. 6) Staging was used to create the sense of a broad mass through the multi-level assembly of workers onstage, brandishing placards from a variety of unions including the ILGWU, United Auto Workers, United Rubber Work-

---

111   Denning 1997, p. 88. Lippman was a fellow journalist.
112   Brown and O'Connor 1980, p. 81.

ers, Flat Glass Workers and Steel Workers, all newly unified within the CIO. The ultimate drive of *Injunction Granted* was towards full support for the CIO, with gains made through the legislature and state presented as the most viable contemporary path to emancipation. Throughout the second half of the play which focused on the contemporary conjuncture, the merits and failings of different union approaches to the relationship between workers and capitalists was polarised into the 'types' of the AFL and CIO. In line with the politics of the Popular Front, the AFL were criticised as only invested in the upper strata of the labour movement, and as hopelessly disconnected from the rank and file.[113] As *Injunction Granted* celebrated, the formation of the CIO partly fulfilled demands for a union that would represent all workers, skilled or otherwise, an ambition that inherited the IWW's demand of joining up all workers into 'one big union'. In presenting a genealogy of this idea, it is notable that Eugene V. Debs, founder of the IWW and also a Socialist Party candidate at every election from 1904–20, features significantly across the first half of *Injunction Granted* as preferable to Gompers and the AFL during the first two decades of the twentieth century. The IWW organised those who the AFL dismissed: unskilled workers who were frequently African American, recent immigrants or women.[114] The CIO adopted this strategy from the IWW, but in distinction, always worked within the boundaries of the law, moving away from wildcat strikes towards the negotiating table. This was a shift made possible by the 1935 Wagner Act, which protected the right of workers to form and join unions of their own choosing, thus enabling a move away from direct action and the sentiments of Big Bill Haywood (another founder of the IWW) that 'no Socialist can be a law-abiding citizen'.[115]

So unlike the illegal direct action associated with the IWW (as shown in several scenes of *Injunction Granted*), the CIO was affirmed as a lawful means for

---

113 Akin to the criticisms within *Injunction Granted*, Edith Segal's 1935 dance *Sell-Out* saw her donning silk overalls to portray the AFL president William Green. See Graff 1977, p. 38. Segal's dance-polemic replicates the view of the CPUSA towards the AFL as reactionary and 'corrupted by imperialism', particularly during the early years of American Communism. For more details see Zumoff 2014, p. 76.
114 Dubofsky 2000, pp. 5–6.
115 See Dubofsky 2000, p. 90. In addition to the idea of one big union, the CIO also adopted the cultural strategies of the IWW, whose aforementioned Paterson Strike Pageant of 1913 can be seen as a significant precursor to the infamous performance *Pins and Needles*, which was staged by the International Ladies Garment Workers' Union's (ILGWU), and is perhaps the best remembered of the CIO theatrical productions. *Pins and Needles* opened in 1937 and ran until 1940; its skits changed continuously and were entirely acted by garment workers, like the strikers who played themselves in the Paterson Strike Pageant.

workers to gain power. The actors in the final scene were thus subsumed under the specific 'type' of the CIO worker, identifying the newly organised union as a touchstone through which their position in society could be transformed. As Losey explained, this final scene was the only point in which the whole stage was used, whereas preceding scenes were 'spotted' in particular areas. In culminating with this staging, Losey describes how 'The formal point was to create a sense that the earlier scenes were absorbed into the finale, the past related to present'.[116] Like the relationship between the parts of *The Oakland Projects* and its existence as a whole cycle, Losey's intentions, through coalescing the episodic structure of *Injunction Granted* into its final, pageant-like scene, links with Lukács argument that the 'whole' is constantly present in the singular novels that make up Balzac's *Comédie Humaine*.[117]

Injunction Granted's unabashed propaganda for the CIO – positioned in this final scene as the culmination of three centuries of exploitation and struggle – drew strong criticism from Flanagan, wary of the Living Newspaper's vulnerability following the censorship of earlier performances. After the opening night, Flanagan described *Injunction Granted* as 'an editorial, not a news issue', 'bad journalism and hysterical theatre' and stressed that she could not allow Federal funds to play the function of a 'party tool', either Communist or Democratic.[118] Her criticisms were based on legitimate fears about the trouble such a performance could present for herself, the Living Newspaper Unit and WPA-FTP more broadly, and on 6 December 1938, Flanagan was called before the Dies Committee and interrogated by Representative Starnes. Infamously, Starnes quizzed Flanagan on whether 'Mr Euripides' and 'Mr Marlow' were 'communists', ironically attesting to the satire Living Newspapers such as *Injunction Granted* had presented on the anti-intellectualism of anti-communism. Starnes was particularly intent on discovering the propagandistic nature of Federal Theatre Project plays, and Flanagan's response was to stress the pedagogical function of the productions. She was adamant the WPA-FTP had never staged a play that was propaganda for the CPUSA, and when asked specifically about *Injunction Granted* by Representative Thomas, a stockbroker and politician who later served a prison sentence for corruption, Flanagan stated that '*Injunction Granted* is propaganda for fair labor relations and for fairness to labor in the courts', rather than an attack on the legislature.[119] Pressed by Starnes, Flanagan remained con-

---

116 Joseph Losey interview with Arnold Goldman 1972.
117 Lukács 1962, p. 99.
118 Cosgrove 1982, p. 243.
119 Cosgrove 1982, p. 250. Cosgrove's thesis includes an appendix with an extract from Flanagan's testimony.

stant when asked if *Injunction Granted* taught class-consciousness. By stressing the historical nature of *Injunction Granted* as a study of labour in the courts, Flanagan was able to argue that it did not foster 'class hatred', but was simply a documentary record, a position repeated in defence of *One-Third of a Nation*, the Living Newspaper discussed in Chapter Three.[120]

In studying Flanagan's testimony, it is clear that her investigators were particularly fixated on a scene within *Injunction Granted* that showed the Workers' Alliance of America (WAA) occupation of the New Jersey State Assembly in April 1936. Flanagan defended this episode by emphasising that the occupation was 'headline news' and that 'in the Living Newspaper everything is factual'.[121] The WAA arose out of a merger between the CPUSA organised Unemployed Councils and the Socialist Party's Workers' Alliance. It functioned as a political organisation, and resembled something like a union for the unemployed and those employed on relief programmes such as the WPA.[122] During the run of *Injunction Granted*, the WAA caused Flanagan great concern, as they frequently pitched up in the lobby of the Biltmore Theatre in New York, distributing literature among audience members and WPA-FTP workers. Losey and Watson supported them, and the WAA made significant inroads within the Living Newspaper Unit, sanctioning strikes by performers and other WPA-FTP workers.[123]

The episode detailing the activity of the WAA in *Injunction Granted* showed their nine-day occupation of the New Jersey state legislature in response to the depletion of relief funds that over 270,000 New Jersey residents were dependent on. By mid-March 1936, all funds designated for relief purposes that year had already been exhausted and a series of emergency tax measures followed, none of which assisted with the crisis.[124] On 21 April 1936, the Senate reconvened to discuss the critical gap in funding, but only five out of twenty Senate members and a dozen out of 60 Assembly members actually attended the hearing.[125] Enraged by the New Jersey State Assembly's decision to adjourn the meeting until the following week, Ray Cooke and a further nineteen WAA members began to occupy the legislators' chairs after the meeting was halted, announcing they would remain until the crisis was addressed. As the news

---

120 Ibid.
121 Ibid.
122 Despite the initial cross-party alliance, the CPUSA swiftly came to dominate the WAA and undertook much of the legwork of the organisation. See Howe and Coser 1957, p. 197, and Klehr 1984, p. 296.
123 Cosgrove 1985, pp. 241–2. For further details of how Flanagan defended WAA involvement in the WPA-FTP, see Bentley 1988, p. 197.
124 Fuoss 1997, p. 24.
125 Fuoss 1997, p. 25.

spread, dozens of WAA members arrived and eventually occupied fifty out of the sixty seats in the Assembly within a number of hours. Slowly, over the following nine-day occupation, WAA members began to act out the role of legislators, performing their own trial and moving between parodying the actual legislators and enacting idealised self-legislation on behalf of workers and the unemployed.[126]

Injunction Granted represented both the events leading up to the occupation, and the subsequent theatrical experiment with self-legislation by WAA members. I believe the Dies Committee singled out this episode – this play within a play – because of its contemporary reverberations, but moreover for its status as a powerful example of performance as a means to rehearse the transformation and abolition of existing law and order. Akin to the blurring of boundaries between performance and protest that occurred in *Code 33*, the episode showing the WAA is wholly founded on the mobilisation of performance as a means to question the position of performers within a broader social landscape. Consequently, this episode stands as a microcosm of the entire meaning of *Injunction Granted*, a powerful alternative to the fetishisation of law criticised through the drama. Rather than Losey's evaluation of the final scene championing the CIO as the culmination of the overall meaning of *Injunction Granted*, I want to suggest that the episode with the WAA most fully exemplifies the Lukácsean dialectic of meaning as emerging between individual parts and the whole, as well as the Brechtian notion of the rehearsal.

5   Conclusion: Legislation and Rehearsals

Alongside the formation of the CIO, the fortunes of organised labour and the promise of a new type of worker during the New Deal can be measured through the creation of new legislation such as the National Industrial Recovery Act (NIRA) of 1933. Section 7a of the NIRA declared that the federal government must ensure workers are able to form unions and enter into collective bargaining free from interference by their employers. Leading industrialists, supported by members of the Senate, vehemently opposed the NIRA and proposed amendments that would continue to sanction yellow-dog contracts and company unions.[127] In 1935, the NIRA was overturned and replaced by the improved National Labour Relations Act, also known as the Wagner Act. The Wagner Act

---

126   Fuoss 1977, pp. 25–6.
127   Dubofsky 1994, p. 112.

made further gains for organised labour, outlawed yellow-dog contracts and allowed workers the right to form unions of their own choosing. Ultimately, as Melvyn Dubofsky has asserted, the Wagner Act affirmed trade unionism as the preferable path to establishing and maintaining industrial democracy, viewed as a crucial component to economic recovery.[128] However, employers continued to resist the Wagner Act through the commonplace dismissal of militants, and company unions persisted within automobile, rubber, steel and electrical industries.

In 1946, the biggest strike wave in US history took place, developments which were partly enabled by the Wagner Act as well as the socio-political conditions in the immediate aftermath of WWII.[129] This strike wave, alongside the post-war economic realignment of the role of the US state, led to the Taft-Hartley Act in 1947: repressive, anti-labour legislation that enabled the United States Attorney General to obtain an 80-day injunction against threatened strikes.[130] In addition to this attack on the right to strike, Taft Hartley made union contributions to political campaigns illegal, and required union leaders to declare they were not CPUSA members. In response, the labour movement – most prominently the CIO – described the Taft Hartley Act as the 'slave labor act', thus demonstrating the persistence of this metaphor for expressing domination and coercion within the workplace, as well as the continued blindness of white-dominated unions to the relationship between wage labour and slave labour.[131]

In thinking about the rapidity of these legislative developments which had such a profound impact on the fate of US organised labour, it's notable that Alexander Taylor's review of *Injunction Granted* for *New Masses* primarily stressed the limit of bourgeois legislation and capitalist social democracy. Though Taylor affirmed that *Injunction Granted* came 'within spitting distance of being the greatest show on earth', he also had complaints:

> The major dramatic conflict ... was the struggle that arises between workers and the state power as a result of the primary struggle between workers and their employers (a minor dramatic conflict in the play), for better conditions. Now for the play to be artistically integrated (which means, for the audience, that the major conflict is satisfactorily solved), some solution of the *political* question of the workers versus the state power

---

128 Dubofsky 1994, pp. 129–30.
129 See George Lipsitz's *Rainbow at Midnight* for an account of the 1946 strike wave, and its aftermath. Lipsitz 1994.
130 Dubofsky 1994, p. 214.
131 'National Affairs: Barrel No. 2', p. 5.

had to be supplied. It wasn't. Instead, the final 'answer' of the play was a pure-and-simple trade unionism answer of the C.I.O. drive for powerful industrial unions in steel and elsewhere. But that was not an answer which solved the problem of the conflict – the *political* conflict – between the workers and the state power. Consequently the play did not fulfil its own demands.[132]

Taylor's review argues that the formation of the CIO was not quite the victory it was made out to be. To Taylor, the 'answer' of the CIO to the questions of *Injunction Granted* was unsatisfactory, contradicting the condemnation of reformist partnerships between capital and labour, assisted by the state, as derided in the scene with the demagogue. For our own purposes, Taylor's qualms point to the question of how to approach the state from the position of criticising relations of domination and exploitation as they are reproduced by capitalist societies. Beyond the specific histories of the New Deal, we return to the orientation of *Code 33* and the inevitable limits of reform – of creating partnerships between the police – and young people of colour in California during the 1990s.

As an alternative history of how North American performance has sought to rehearse social transformation, this chapter offers one way to move beyond the codification of the medium in the 1960s, as well as a means to historicise the current relationship between social struggles and their negotiation in art practice. The performances discussed here are all built up through episodic staging and marked by the performers being actually invested (within their everyday lives) in the issues they performed. They can be read as developing a mode of realism that attempts to denaturalise social conflict not only for spectators, but also for performers. In addition, they share an emphasis on legislation, with all three performances analysing the use of law as a means of oppression, either via the courts or the police.

Yet, comparing the attention to law in these works also serves to illuminate the divergent state formations of the 1930s and 1990s in the US. The policeman solely embodies the law in *Code 33* and *The Roof is on Fire*, while in *Injunction Granted* the whole legal apparatus is exposed through numerous scenes involving judges, courtrooms and legislators. Within all three performances, the relation of community to the state is contested through struggles against the imposition of law and order. Unlike the frequent proclamations by courts, capitalists and politicians in *Injunction Granted* that strikes and direct action presented a 'threat to community', for the workers on-stage, their portrayal

---

132 Taylor 1936, p. 29.

of community formation was shaped by breaking and transforming the rule of law. The proximity between the episode representing the WAA occupation-performance, the working lives of the performers, and the fate of the Living Newspaper, demonstrates the quality of *Injunction Granted* as a rehearsal for reality. Equally, through conceiving of *The Roof is on Fire* and *Code 33* as rehearsals, we can see the result of these projects as less contained within reform than as acting out, in a Brechtian sense, what many of the youth participating already knew: that as a social group, they were structurally opposed to the police. To restate the importance of the rehearsal, Buchmann and Ruhm note that this concept blends the private and public spheres of production and performance, thus entwining different registers of reality, media representation and fiction, tropes common to *The Roof is on Fire*, *Code 33* and *Injunction Granted*.[133]

As with the contrasting representation of law, there is also a clear difference between the dominant subject-participant of *Injunction Granted* (industrial, unionised workers) and *The Roof is on Fire* and *Code 33* (primarily Black and Latinx youth, who when not in education, were often unemployed). These differences offer some measure of a change in the primary social groups viewed as compatible with the dominant cultural practices that desire a social effect, if we take the Living Newspaper as exemplary of the 1930s, and Lacy's *The Oakland Projects* as exemplary of the way social practice cohered during the 1990s. Evidently, this shift is contingent upon changing class composition in the US, but also the continued blind spots of the left with regards to race. If the 1930s saw the transferral via the New Deal of new responsibilities for the reproduction of workers onto an embryonic welfare state (the Social Security Act, 1935), the 1990s saw continued federal and local reforms of welfare, education and health, alongside the abolition of New Deal era economic reforms. Within a period of mass outsourcing, mass imprisonment, continued de-industrialisation and the domestic militarisation of the police, the reserve army of labour in the 1990s was increasingly reconfigured as a racialised 'surplus population' that may never work. As Michael Denning writes, the impact of financialised neoliberal capitalism has resulted in a situation where 'it is not the child in the sweatshop that is our most characteristic figure, but the child in the streets, alternately predator and prey'.[134] In *The Oakland Projects*, the figure described by Denning forms the primary subject, in contrast with the industrial worker as principal 'type' in *Injunction Granted*.

---

133   Buchmann and Ruhm 2013.
134   Denning 2010. p. 79.

Returning to the racial dynamics of class formation in the US outlined by Roediger, and the assertions by Martinot and Sexton regarding the mass criminalisation of African Americans during the 1990s, I would contend that this transformation should be understood not simply as the gradual loss of gains since a Depression era 'heyday' for the working class. Due to the erosion of Fordism in the US, the financial crisis and the ideological redefinition of the state, the 1970s is frequently described as heralding a new form of capitalism in which the reproduction of the proletariat has been increasingly severed from the valorisation of capital.[135] Of course, the 1970s is also the decade where performance becomes most fiercely codified as a new 'medium' within art history and criticism. By registering the repeated historical separation of African Americans from the promise of 'free labour', as well as the continuity of forms of performance that act as rehearsals for reality, I believe we can attain a more complex view of this trajectory that avoids nostalgia or naïve optimism about the political possibilities of the present.

As Frank Wilderson III writes, Black citizenship in the US can be understood as an oxymoron, a view based upon his recognition of the 'gratuity (as opposed to contingency) of violence that accrues to the blackened position'.[136] For Wilderson, as well as his fellow Afro-Pessimists Martinot and Sexton, this is the current and on-going state of Blackness in the US, a reality inseparable from the historical relationship of slavery to free (white) labour. Yet, unlike the postulation of slavery as a moment of primitive accumulation that is overcome by the arrival of wage labour, as presented in *Injunction Granted*, Wilderson stresses that we witness in late capitalism a 'renaissance' of the 'original desire' of capitalism – the violent '"accumulation" of Black bodies regardless of their utility as laborers' – through the prison-industrial complex.[137]

---

135 This is the picture Denning describes, and this periodisation seems to provide a point of consensus for many on the left. However, different political orientations take the transition to neoliberalism to have different meanings and results. Very briefly, those aligned with a post-autonomist position (with Antonio Negri and Michael Hardt being the most prominent proponents) have described this reconfiguration of the capital/class relation as enabling the revival of revolutionary politics due to new forms of work, technology and social relations. For some socialists and left-liberals, this transformation results in appeals for a return to the post-war consensus. For those within the 'communisation', or other ultra-left, tendencies, there is a stress on the 1970s as the end of a viable politics of 'programmatism', with this being the term used by groups such as Théorie Communiste and Endnotes to describe union centred politics based on affirming, rather than emphasising the self-abolition of, the proletariat.
136 Wilderson 2007, p. 20.
137 Wilderson 2003, pp. 229–30.

For Wilderson, the connection between the slave and racialised incarceration in the twentieth and twenty-first century is founded upon an argument that the prisoner, like the slave, is generative, offering part of the solution to 'late capital's over-accumulation crisis'.[138] The economic and social ramifications of this continuity between the plantation and the prison has been more thoroughly explored by writers and activists including Michelle Alexander, Angela Davis and Ruth Wilson Gilmore.[139] However, for Wilderson, the connection provides the foundation for his assertion that coalitional left politics rooted in the productive worker as the unit of antagonism, will always be severely limited in their battle against capital. For Wilderson, 'the positionality of the slave makes a demand, which is in excess of the demand made by the positionality of the worker'.[140] In this light, we can see the limits of the coalitional scene closing *Injunction Granted*, posited as the final stage of a teleological narrative which does begin with slavery. As with Denning's emphasis on wagelessness and dispossession as the structuring logic of capital rather than the wage, Wilderson exposes the limit point of Popular Front era communist politics that solely stresses an identity politics of productive labour, as exemplified in the climax of *Injunction Granted*. As we shall see in the next chapter, through another work by Lacy alongside dances by Edith Segal, the insertion of gender into this equation is also necessary if we wish to intensify and extend the antagonism.

Equally, by following the argument that there is an unbreakable link between the slave system and the criminal justice system in the US, we can also identify severe limitations of ambition in the attempt by *The Oakland Projects* to ameliorate the relation between police and young people of colour. As I write, the list of names of unarmed Black people killed with impunity by US police forces continues to grow, as too does the resistance against this violence. As one writer expresses, 'The endless stream of young Black men shot by police borders on excess, demonstrating the pure interchangeability of such names as equivalents, meaning that such seemingly particular empirical cases are in actuality a general condition'.[141] This is the meaning of the 'type' in its most brutal form, and by setting these works in relation to one another, we arrive at an expanded understanding of its meaning. Discussing Lukács's realism, Alex Potts emphasises that his

---

138   Wilderson 2003, p. 30.
139   See Davis 2003 and Wilson Gilmore 2006.
140   Wilderson 2007, p. 22.
141   R.L.

analysis of typology and perspective is grounded in ideas of organic wholeness that at some level are incompatible with the imperatives informing most modern art. This incompatibility derives in part from his assumption that a properly communist outlook on the modern world can resist being subsumed within the fragmenting and abstracting realities of the modern capitalist world.[142]

By comparing this evaluation of Lukács with the way I have suggested types work in *The Roof is on Fire*, *Code 33* and *Injunction Granted*, we can arrive at the meaning of the type as a real abstraction, rather than as in the Lukácsean desire for a mode of realism *resistant* to the fragmentation of the modern world.[143] Equal to the limitations of Lukács's type is Brecht's command that the alienation effect should 'show the world in such a way that it becomes manageable'.[144] Brecht saw this aspect of the alienation effect as enabling his epic theatre to become 'natural and earthy', thus overcoming the 'mystical' qualities of bourgeois theatre.[145] While this may be the case for the presentation of certain types in *Injunction Granted* (Heinz, the judges, the Professor, etc.) the particular anxieties prompted for the Dies Committee by the WAA scene exceeds this in its unruly militancy. Similarly, the utter failure of the police to become 'manageable' in *Code 33* comes to represent nothing but the brutal reality of their existence along lines that exceed the reformist orientation of the performance. All of these works present stunted attempts to use performance as a means to re-imagine and propose solutions to the domination and exploitation of poor and working-class people. But rather than describing their attempts as failures, or stressing their residual power in constructing social groups that stepped beyond existing communities, I suggest that their nature as performances – that is, where they are rehearsing – tells us a great deal more about the world they emerge from, and how it might be transformed.

142 Potts 2013, p. 54.
143 By real abstraction, I mean 'abstraction not as a mere mask, fantasy, or diversion, but as a force operative in the world'. See Toscano 2008, p. 274.
144 Brecht 1964, p. 140.
145 Ibid.

CHAPTER 2

Social Practice / Social Reproduction

1   Introduction

Despite their shared episodic structure, use of types and strategies of realism, I want to stress again that the significant difference between Lacy's *The Roof is on Fire* and *Code 33*, and the Living Newspaper *Injunction Granted*, lies in the distance between their subject-participants. While the subject and makers of *Injunction Granted* were articulated as workers – whether industrial or theatrical – Lacy's subjects were primarily youth of colour, struggling against a culture that systemically positioned them as part of the surplus population. As I argue towards the end of Chapter One, this disparity clarifies shifts in the primary social groups viewed as compatible with exemplary cultural practices that seek to work 'socially' in the United States. This is contingent upon changing class composition, but also registers the continued blind spots of the left with regards to race and sections of the population that do not match up with dominant white representations of a proletarian, vanguard subject.

If, partly as a corrective to the limits of that traditional subject, Michael Denning writes that it is actually wagelessness rather than the wage that structures the reproduction of capitalism, this chapter takes up that cue and addresses works which thematise and enact gendered processes of mostly unwaged social reproduction.[1] The chapter begins by discussing a selection of works by the communist dancer Edith Segal and the way that these formed part of the New York City proletarian dance scene of the 1930, a world which in comparison with other leftist cultural groupings discussed in this book was overwhelmingly dominated by women. In the second half of the chapter, I turn to Lacy's *Expectations* (1997), an element of *The Oakland Projects* which involved collaborating with pregnant and parenting teenagers on the production of a summer school and an installation at the Capp Street Project Gallery in San Francisco. By drawing on Marxist and feminist theories of social reproduction, I ask how these practices encountered and challenged the obstacles to human life and sociality encountered in capitalist societies. Moreover, debates within social reproduction theory about invisible and unrecognised labour are relevant to both Segal's dance works and Lacy's *Expectations* due to their contested status as cultural work. Segal was frequently criticised for producing merely 'agit-prop',

---

1   Denning 2010, p. 79.

even by communist commentators such as Edna Ocko, whilst Lacy's work – despite more recent mainstream success and the shifts in nomenclature discussed in the introduction – has been linked to the historically marginalised community arts tradition.[2] Theories concerning social reproduction therefore assist in building a sharper analysis of the growth in social practice over the last 20 years, and of what this means in relation to state formation.[3]

Notably, Lacy's *Expectations* responded to the repeal of Aid to Families with Dependent Children Program (AFDC), a federal assistance programme that had been established in 1935 via the Social Security Act. As Carole Pateman explains, unlike social insurance and other claims on the public purse such as tax allowances for mortgages or business subsidies, by the 1990s welfare had a very narrow meaning in the US and had purely come to designate AFDC.[4] Its abolition therefore meant the removal of a welfare system established during the Depression, the period in which Segal's collective dances about housework and domestic labour were created. The comparison between Segal's and Lacy's practices is therefore not only taken up to examine how social reproduction often forms the assumed, yet unspoken logic of social practice, but also to clarify how changes in state formation impacts upon the cultural and artistic status of these works.

2   Cells in Organisms/Cogs in Machines

Born in 1902, Edith Segal grew up on the Lower East Side of Manhattan in a fairly orthodox, working-class Jewish family. She first took dance classes at the Henry Street Settlement House, which was founded by Lillian Wald in 1893 and

---

2 Edna Ocko criticised Segal's *Black and White* and the Segal-led Red Dancers as only appealing to 'undeveloped' dance audiences. See Ocko, February 1935, p. 25. Segal's response was to argue that the particular form of a dance, whether it be agit-prop, dramatic or concert (with concert meaning bourgeois standards) should be determined by the workers (dancers and audience) as a class. See letter (undated, presumed 1935) in the Edith Segal papers (Box 2), Dance Collection, The New York Public Library, Astor, Lenox and Tilden Foundations. Lacy's prominence has increased following the purchase and subsequent display of *The Crystal Quilt* (1985–87) by Tate Modern in 2012. In spring 2013, Tate Modern staged a large performance by Lacy entitled *Silver Action* and in the autumn of that year, Creative Time produced a major commission by Lacy in New York entitled *Between the Door and the Street*. In 2019, Lacy had a solo retrospective at SF MOMA, and in 2021–2022, a solo exhibition at the Whitworth Gallery, Manchester.
3 The development of social reproduction theory as a method for feminist art historians and theorists has grown in recent years, as marked by a special issue of *Third Text*. See Dimitrakaki and Lloyd 2017.
4 Pateman 2005, p. 34.

inspired by Jane Addams's Hull House in Chicago. Like Addams' Hull House, Henry Street is paradigmatic of the settlement movement as female-led with strong links to the arts, which were often posited as providing a good moral influence on the poor. Similar to how the pageant was affirmed as a means to cultivate a shared sense of history among immigrants in the US during the early years of the twentieth century, the settlement house movement also sought to create cohesion and assimilation within an ethnically divided working class.[5] Through her involvement with the Henry Street Settlement, Segal joined dance classes at the newly formed Neighborhood Playhouse. In 1915, the Neighborhood Playhouse was established with support from the philanthropist sisters Alice and Irene Lewisohn as one of the first 'little theatres' in New York City that mixed professional and amateur drama to produce experimental, modernist productions.[6] At the Neighbourhood Playhouse, Segal learned ethnic styles with visiting teachers such as the Anglo-Indian dancer Roshanara, and studied interpretive dance in the manner of Isadora Duncan, whose influence continued to loom large throughout Segal's life.[7] Segal attended the Neighbourhood Playhouse for around twelve years, and during the 1920s became radicalised by attending courses in socialism and dance at the Rand School of Social Sciences. A few years later, she gravitated towards the Workers' Party of America USA, an organisation that formed the legal front for the illegal and still underground CPUSA and in 1924 she performed a solo dance to the *Internationale* at the Lenin Memorial Pageant in Chicago.[8] That same year, Segal also became the Social Director for the International Ladies Garment Workers' Union (ILGWU) summer camp, Unity House.[9]

Images of the workshops organised by Segal at Unity House clearly display the influence of Duncan in the poses and movement of the participants, their

---

5 Carson 1998, pp. 526–8.
6 Henderson 1991, p. 235.
7 Graff 1997, p. 27.
8 Draper 1960, p. 174. It is unclear whether Segal was a Socialist Party member during the 1920s. However, the ILGWU was a Socialist Party union, and as Segal worked at their camp, Unity House, between 1924–7, it seems likely. In 1923 the underground Communist Party was dissolved, and the Workers' Party (openly called the CPUSA from 1929) emerged as the sole American Communist Party. It seems that Segal's trajectory involved her in both SP and Workers' Party events and organisations during the 1920s, before she joined the Workers' Party (CPUSA) in 1927, the same point at which she left Unity House. For more on the SP, see Shannon 1955 and Weinstein 1967.
9 Brian Dolber has described the ILGWU as fostering a 'hegemonic Jewishness' that was centred on socialism up until the latter half of the 1920s. As the Social Director of Unity House, Segal played a vital part in continuing the radical programming begun by Fania Cohn, the Executive Secretary of the ILGWU's Education Department. Beginning in 1915, Cohn initiated an edu-

FIGURE 11   Edith Segal and ILGWU members at Unity House, 1924
PHOTOGRAPHER UNKNOWN. COURTESY OF THE JEROME ROBBINS DANCE
DIVISION, NEW YORK LIBRARY FOR THE PERFORMING ARTS

flowing garments and the setting among nature. (Fig. 11) Segal's work at Unity House forms an important precedent to the proletarian dance movement during the 1930s, and foregrounds the idea that dance could assist in building a radical community among women workers, signalling her particular formation in a female dominated climate where close connections existed between experimental modernism, radical politics and amateur artistic activity.

In 1927, Segal joined the CPUSA, and her membership of the Party was marked not only by her political commitment but also by a belief that the Party was 'a very positive influence ... not only in my work, but I believe in the whole cultural movement in our country'.[10] Part of the communist cultural movement in the US involved the formation of amateur proletarian dance groups.

---

      cation programme in Local 25 of the ILGWU, intended to boost the self-confidence of young, immigrant needle workers, as well as a sense of community and 'sisterhood'. See Dolber 2008, p. 188.

10   Edith Segal, 'Music and dance and the Left in the 1930s'. Interview with B. Lemisch, February 1981. Oral Histories of the American Left 1920–80, Tamiment Library/Robert F. Wagner Labor Archives, New York University Libraries.

In 1932, the Workers' Dance League was organised, which in 1935 became the New Dance League (hereafter WDL/NDL), signalling the CPUSA's adoption of the Popular Front strategy through the neutralising change of name.[11] Under the umbrella of the WDL/NDL, the Needle Trades Workers' Industrial Union Dance Group (NTWIUDG) was organised by Segal and joined by women working in all aspects of the needle trades from milliners to dressmakers, furriers to machinists. Like the ILGWU dance group pictured at Unity House almost a decade earlier, the NTWIUDG also involved reaching out to women in their workplaces and unions, encouraging them to join a dance group and contribute to the development of a militant proletarian culture. In line with the ambitions of much communist culture during the Third Period, Segal's work with amateur dance groups was at the forefront of the WDL/NDL's drive to use dance as a 'weapon in the class struggle'.[12] Alongside adult amateur groups such as the NTWIUDG, Segal also taught dance to workers' children. These sessions sought to develop children's class consciousness and strengthen the radical communities they were growing up in: a typical Segal-led children's group included exercises such as 'Are you a Worker or are you a Banker?' and simple versions of her 'On the Barricades' composition.[13]

Figure 12 is an image of the NTWIUDG that was reproduced in the Workers' Dance League Sparatkiade programme for 1933, accompanied by a note written by Bella Hurst, secretary of the Union. Hurst affirmed the aims of Segal and the wider proletarian dance community as follows –

> At first we did not realise how much of our daily struggles could be utilized as thematic material for the dance, and how effective a medium it can be in helping workers to better understand and fight against their conditions. We approach our theme work thru (sic) discussions and group improvisations, choosing our themes from our daily struggles.[14]

---

11 The WDL/NDL served as an umbrella for numerous other groups during the 1930s such as the New Dance Group, the Theatre Union Dance Group, the Jack London Rebel Dancers of Newark, the Red Dancers, the Nature Friends Dance Group, the Modern Negro Dance Group and the New Duncan Dancers, among others. It was likely formed in response to the establishment of the Workers' Cultural Federation (WCF) in 1931. See Hemingway 2002, pp. 21–2 for details of the WCF.

12 Hemingway 2002, p. 29.

13 'On the Barricades' was first performed by adult members of the League at the 1931 Lenin Memorial Pageant. For details of children's classes see Edith Segal, 'Children's Work', in *New Dance*, March 1935, p. 13. Courtesy of the Edith Segal papers (Box 2), Dance Collection, The New York Public Library, Astor, Lenox and Tilden Foundations.

14 Bella Hurst, programme for the *Workers' Dance League Spartakiade*, 4 June 1933. Edith Segal papers (Box 4), Dance Collection, The New York Public Library, Astor, Lenox and Tilden Foundations.

FIGURE 12   Dance Group of the Needle Trades Workers' Industrial Union, page from the Workers Dance League Spartakiade program, Sunday June 4th 1933
PHOTOGRAPHER UNKNOWN. COURTESY OF THE JEROME ROBBINS DANCE DIVISION, NEW YORK LIBRARY FOR THE PERFORMING ARTS

Segal confirmed Hurst's affirmation of collective organisation in a 1935 article in *New Theatre*, writing that 'The subject matter is social and is the concern of all the participants in the dance ... therefore not the private property of the director, or even of the group, but that of the audience and society'.[15] In relation to Hurst's and Segal's accounts, we can glean that the amateur adult groups and children's groups alike formed a means of expanding and reproducing the communities through which revolutionary struggles could be organised, forming part of a counter-hegemonic culture. Like the Living Newspaper and *The*

---

15   Edith Segal, 'Directing the New Dance', *New Theatre*, May 1935, p. 23.

Oakland Projects, the quality of the dance groups as both entertainment and outreach mechanism should be understood as applicable to performer and audience, with the boundary between these categories deliberately blurred.

That collective decision-making structured Segal's proletarian dance classes, rather than the transferral of technical knowledge from teacher to student, or of Communist Party doctrine from field organiser to worker, appears to follow Denning's argument that US communist culture did not always conform to Party orthodoxies.[16] However, in attempting to unpick the relational quality of these groups, Denning's view needs to be set in relation to Theodore Draper's argument that American communism was a movement that always exceeded the party, instead made up of 'auxiliary organizations', 'mass organizations', 'fronts', 'fellow-travellers' and so on.[17] The ecology that Draper points towards is defined in relation to the concept of a 'front' and its use as a Leninist strategy. As Draper describes, the 'front' operated as a means towards 'mediating between the politically pure sect and the politically impure mass movement' through a highly bureaucratic and 'complicated system of transmission belts'.[18] Perhaps we can think of Segal's workshops (and the wider proletarian dance scene) as existing between these two analyses of American communism. Though they were unorthodox in their incipiently anti-Leninist challenge to hierarchical structures, the dance workshops nevertheless acted as a 'transmission belt' to the Party, with their pedagogical orientation directing members of the group towards class struggle as part of the communist movement.[19] As Ellen Graff notes, 'one purpose of such groups was to get workers moving politically and to prime them for actual strike action and picketing. Workers' classes made up scenarios that they danced in a kind of rehearsal for the real thing', a quality connecting back to the argument I made for reading *The Roof is on Fire*, *Code 33* and *Injunction Granted* as rehearsals.[20]

Ruth Allerhand, another proletarian dancer, echoed Hurst's and Segal's emphasis on collective dance as an aesthetic process towards communism, stating

---

16 Denning 1997.
17 Draper 1960, pp. 172–3. As James Weinstein has explained, the formation of the Workers' Party (the front for the underground CPUSA) involved a return to the SP position of 1919; calling for a mass movement with transitional demands as opposed to violent revolution organised through cells. See Weinstein 1967, pp. 258–9.
18 Draper 1960, p. 182.
19 As mentioned, this approach to cultural pedagogy inherits the type of workers' education pioneered by Fannia Cohn within the ILGWU, beginning in 1915. Cohn's classes drew on the thought of progressive educator John Dewey alongside the peer education techniques of shop-floor study groups. See Chapter 5 in Orleck 1995.
20 Graff 1997, p. 42.

that the experience of performing in a worker mass-dance was one in which 'The individual no longer feels that he is the whole, he now sees that he represents the substance. He is not so much a link in a chain, a cog in a machine, as a very alive, very productive cell within a body'.[21] Here, Allerhand's contrasting of the organic with the mechanical, as well as her interpretation of the individual's role in the mass dance, is strikingly reminiscent of Siegfried Kracauer's 1926 description of the popular dance troupe the Tiller Girls in 'The Mass Ornament' –

> The bearer of the ornaments is the *mass* and not the people [*Volk*], for whenever the people form figures, the latter do not hover in mid-air but arise out of a community. A current of organic life surges from these communal groups ... Only as parts of a mass, not as individuals who believe themselves to be formed from within, do people become fractions of a figure.[22]

As Frederic Schwartz explains, Kracauer's description of the Tiller Girls presents a troubled version of the notion that ornament expresses organic community spirit. Unlike the accounts of ornament by art historians such as Alois Riegl and Heinrich Wölfflin that influenced Kracauer, as Schwartz explains, Kracauer 'uses the mass ornament to posit the arrival of a post-hermeneutic age, employing the postulate of the unmediated interrelatedness of all aspects of a culture to show that it *no longer obtained* ... since there is no more community ... there is no more spirit in ornament'.[23] Despite Kracauer's initial statement that a 'current of organic life surges from these communal groups', by the end of his description the Tiller Girls are positioned negatively, as 'not part of a *whole community* but fragments of an alienated mass'.[24] Therefore, Kracauer's final analysis of the Tiller Girls poses them as a capitalist perversion of the way in which ornament stood for organic community in Riegl and Wölfflin. With their mechanical movements analysed as Taylorist, the Tiller Girls's coherence is ushered in by reification. They are ciphers for the technological innovations of high capitalism, and instead of organic community, they represent the living, breathing 'social hieroglyphic' of the commodity form described by Marx.[25]

---

21   Allerhand 1935, p. 26.
22   Kracauer 1995, p. 76.
23   Schwartz 2005, p. 142.
24   Ibid. (My emphasis).
25   'Value ... does not have its description branded on its forehead; it rather transforms every product of labour into a social hieroglyphic' (Marx, 1990, p. 164). As Mark Franko has

The aesthetic form of community espoused by Allerhand in describing the proletarian mass dance stands in sharp contrast to Kracauer's take on the Tiller Girls. For Allerhand, the proletarian mass dancer is emphatically *not* a Taylorist 'link in a chain' or 'a cog in a machine' but 'a very alive, very productive cell within a body'.[26] This presents an organic vision of the proletarian mass dance that works against the mechanics of industrial capitalism, thus connecting with the pervasive notion that community is something more naturally obtained in rural settings, and that human sociality is disrupted or damaged by urban and industrial environments, qualities already conjured up in the pastoral, Duncan-esque scene of Segal's workshop at Unity House. However, in contrast to this romantic anti-capitalism, Marx and Engels notoriously argued that growth of industrial capitalism had 'rescued a considerable part of the population from the idiocy of rural life' in *The Communist Manifesto*.[27] Furthermore, in his writing on the 'Housing Question', Engels wrote that the subsumption of the countryside under industrial capitalism would save 'the rural population from the isolation and stupor in which it has vegetated almost unchanged for thousands of years', while in *Capital* Volume I, Marx argued that more developed countries were destined to show the less developed an image of their own future.[28] By the 1880s, however, Marx rejected this view, particularly when approaching the Russian context, and instead found himself reconciled with the notion of a 'multiplicity of roads of social transformation'.[29]

Within the Soviet Union during the 1920s, it was posited that the advanced capitalism of Taylorism formed a valuable science that could be appropriated for communism. This view was propagated through the work of the Proletkult poet and leading Soviet Taylorist, Alexei K. Gastev, who became the founder and director of the Central Institute of Labor in 1920. Within the early Soviet Union, the influence of Taylorism extended into theatre, acting and dance, and Meyerhold was particularly influenced by the analysis of the mechanics of labouring in scientific management. As Rose Whyman explains, the appeal of Taylorism within the Soviet Union was founded on the notion that the 'system' must come before the individual, and this assisted in founding a new approach to mass performance.[30] Despite their proximity to the CPUSA, then, it is not-

emphasised, the Tiller Girl herself as a worker reliant on selling her labour power was also *actually* commodified; a realisation of the allegories she performed of productivity and the circulation of commodities. See Franko 2002, p. 33.

26   Allerhand 1935.
27   Karl Marx and Friedrich Engels 1998, p. 40.
28   Marx 1990, p. 88 and Engels, *The Housing Question* (1872) cited in Draper 2004, p. 220.
29   Shanin 1983, pp. 17–18.
30   Whyman 2008, pp. 223–6.

able that for Allerhand and Segal, the notion of a system was foundational to the workings of proletarian dance, but an organic, bodily metaphor carried this meaning, rather than a mechanical one.

The polarisation between valorising and negating organic and pre-industrial notions of community can be mitigated through recourse to Bloch's theory of non-simultaneity, which suggests that the collision of different temporalities within capitalism is a necessary facet of its reproduction. Non-simultaneity enabled Bloch to analyse the rise of German fascism, with its rhetoric of blood and soil, as well as to imagine its overthrow, posited as communist. To distinguish between these two forms of non-simultaneity which are expressed as reactionary or revolutionary, Bloch wrote that

> The revolutionary knotted line, in which contradiction finally tangles up at a single point and rapidly presses for the revolutionary unravelling, can accordingly occur only in contemporaneous contradictions which are themselves the growing child Future or differentness, not in non-contemporaneous ones whose greatness is long past ...[31]

Revolutionary non-simultaneity is crucially *not* anachronism or nostalgia, as Bloch insists that any valorisation of the past over the present depends on the false notion that the past is dead. Instead, he points towards where congealed forms of earlier society, unsubsumed by capital and contradictory to our present, can conjure up 'sentimentally or romantically, that wholeness and liveliness from which communism draws genuine material against alienation'.[32]

Having in mind the present-moment liberation of 'the still possible future' from the past, Bloch viewed the class-conscious revolutionary proletariat as drawing on experiences of non-simultaneity to understand themselves as the subjects of history.[33] This is how we can understand the organic metaphors in Allerhand's descriptions of the proletarian dance as expressive of a revolutionary politics, rather than as a nostalgic fantasy of a lost idyll. By drawing on an imagined idea of lost sociality – even if only metaphorically – this assisted proletarian dance in its mission to produce a consciousness amongst participants of their subjective position within the class struggle. Allerhand's description of the dancer as a 'productive cell' and not a 'cog in a machine' points towards the conception of the individual dancer's relation to the collective as organic, rather than as comparable to the mechanised 'system' of Taylorist production.

---

31 Bloch 1991, p. 110.
32 Bloch 1991, p. 112.
33 Bloch 1991, pp. 110–11.

The primacy attached to the dancer as 'productive cell' connects to Marx's characterisation of human labour as a 'productive expenditure of human brains, muscles, nerves, hands', with the dances that rehearsed being on a picket line offering one example of how the body could be diverted from wage labour, and instead, 'primed for action' as part of the communist movement.[34]

Finally, and perhaps most importantly, Allerhand's deployment of an organic metaphor as productive over and above 'cogs in machinery' hints towards the uneven quality of the work most of the women in the NTWIUDG were doing. During this period, the textile industry encompassed factory labour as well as a large percentage of women workers toiling at home. Sweated labour, contracting and sub-contracting meant that the garment industries were chaotic, with homework often seasonal and based on intense periods of labour to increase output.[35] Despite their location within an 'industrial union', Allerhand and the members of the NTWIUDG would have likely encountered the supposedly 'pre-capitalist' working conditions of homework, meaning they directly experienced the forces of non-simultaneity described by Bloch, with collective dancing standing as a method to explore such contradictions.

Furthermore, the metaphors of the organic and the mechanical in Allerhand's description also resonate with how processes of racialisation interact with gender and class struggle. Roediger's analysis of the formation of a 'popular sense of whiteness' in America poses this as dependent on a nationally diverse white working class reaching consensus around the notion 'that blackness could be made permanently to embody the pre-industrial past that they scorned and missed'.[36] The ideological positioning of African Americans as pre-industrial operated as a racist means towards primitivising individuals and communities and thereby legitimising their subjugation. Roediger describes how this characterisation partly emerged through a popular understanding of slave labour as something that wage labourers affirmatively identified themselves *against*, forming 'a wretched touchstone' against which white workers measured their 'fears of un-freedom' and 'a friendly reminder that they were by comparison not so badly off'.[37] The formation of whiteness was thus dependent on racialising the negative connotations of not having internalised capitalist work discipline. The transitioning of slang such as coon, buck and mose from being descriptions for white men perceived as virile, dashing dandies, to racial slurs against Black people exemplifies this process. Each of these terms

---

34   Marx 1990, p. 134.
35   Gugliemo 2002, pp. 253–4.
36   Roediger, p. 97.
37   Roediger 1999, p. 49.

'went from describing particular kinds of whites who had not internalized capitalist work discipline and whose places in the new world of wage labor were problematic, to stereotyping Blacks'.[38] However, the imagining of Black people as having supposedly eluded the industrial disciplining of the individual worker was simultaneously configured as attractive, with popular entertainment cementing this dynamic. As Roediger writes, in racist street theatre and minstrelsy, 'resistance to the new industrial morality' was expressed through whites playing Black people, offering whites an opportunity to act 'wild' or irrational.[39]

As with the reality of homework, sub-contracted out to female garment workers by industrial firms, the process of consigning Black people to a different mode of production and temporality underpins forms of domination often figured as excessive to the capital-labour relation. These inevitably intersect, as in Angela Davis' description of how Black female domestic workers were employed via open markets that congregated in the Bronx, akin to a 'modern version of slavery's auction block' throughout the 1930s and 1940s, where, as with the slave auction at the beginning of *Injunction Granted*, the selection of servants was often based on physical appearance.[40] In discussing this history, Davis hones in on a 1938 article in *The Nation* outlining the exploitation of these women, highlighting the title of 'Our Feudal Housewives'.[41] Through this headline we get a sense of the overwhelmingly negative reality of the continued existence of supposedly 'pre-capitalist' labour relations. Writing a few years earlier, the Harlem communists Ella Baker and Marvel Cooke described the 'Bronx Slave Market' in the NAACP's newspaper, *The Crisis*, and in 1934, another communist, Grace Hutchins, characterised domestic work as feudal, stressing that the depression-era unemployment crisis meant many domestics were employed without wages and only provided with room and board.[42] That African Americans and women were popularly posited during the 1930s as nonsynchronous with the dominant mode of production complicates the deployment of organic metaphors against industry in the descriptions of Segal's dances due to their gendered, and as I shall turn to now more fully, racialised qualities.

---

38 Roediger 1999, p. 100.
39 Roediger 1999, p. 109.
40 Davis 1983, p. 95.
41 Ibid.
42 Baker and Cooke 1935, and Hutchins 1934, p. 100.

3 *Black and White* at the Rockland Palace: The Body against the Belt

On Saturday 22 March 1930, Edith Segal and African American dancer Alison Burroughs performed *Black and White* at the Second Annual Inter-Racial Dance at the Rockland Palace in Harlem. Burroughs's mother was the prominent Harlem Communist organiser Williana Burroughs, and her father Charles Burroughs had directed W.E.B. DuBois's 1913 pageant *The Star of Ethiopia*. Prior to becoming involved in the proletarian dance scene, Burroughs had studied at the Dalcroze dance institute in Geneva.[43] Figure 13 shows a rehearsal photograph of *Black and White* from 1928; here Segal and Burrough's naked bodies are positioned in front of a backdrop painted with factory machinery, a chimney billowing smoke, a cog encircling their arms which are raised at right angles. In Segal's choreography for *Black and White*, the bodies of the dancers – playing workers – were positioned against such machinery, again raising the relation of the mechanical to the organic.

Black and White begins with a Black and a white worker heading into the factory, their movements inflected with drudgery. The dance is accompanied throughout by a regular drumbeat, symbolising the temporality of the factory. A rattle or piano interrupts the drum at various points, signalling the authoritarian call of the 'boss', and at other points a 'positive call', which stands for communism. The dance begins with hammering motions, indicating 'primitive methods of work'. In this phase, the dancers gesture towards each other, showing a 'natural desire for class solidarity'.[44] However, in each instance where they begin to come together, they fall apart, demonstrating, as Segal wrote, the 'prejudices instilled in them by their common exploiter: the capitalist class'.[45]

The second phase involves more automated motions intended to reflect industrialisation, with the dancers mimicking mechanisation through a 'double saw' motion. A rattle is then sounded and the workers 'look at each other with hatred'.[46] They shuffle into position at the belt and begin to work, repeating for 32 measures a movement based on belt-based factory work that was intended to show 'the inter-relationship of workers under the most advanced system of capitalist production'.[47] Halfway through this sequence, the white worker falls and remains on the ground as a result of the 'speed-up' process; the Black worker also falls at the end of this phase. Following their fall,

---

43 Manning 2004, p. 74.
44 Segal, March 1935, p. 19.
45 Ibid.
46 Ibid.
47 Ibid.

FIGURE 13   Trui H. Uruma, Edith Segal and Allison Burrough's in rehearsal for *Black & White* 1928
COURTESY OF THE JEROME ROBBINS DANCE DIVISION, NEW YORK LIBRARY FOR THE PERFORMING ARTS

both dancers try to rise without looking at each other and fall again. They then rise to their knees simultaneously, and gaze at each other's fists as if readying to strike each other. They pause, a 'disruptive voice' (the rattle representing the boss again) rings out and they strike each other, one after another, fall again, and look down at their own fists. The two workers return to the belt and repeat the earlier movement based on assembly-line work, speed up and look at their hands 'wonderingly'. Then the rattle rings out a 'positive' call (the call of communism), and they lean towards each other, trying to come together whilst looking at their own fists. They clasp hands, conveying a 'feeling of tremendous difficulty in rising with clasped hands, from kneeling to standing position'. The sequence ends with a call to other workers, and each dancer walking diagonally with arms outstretched. The dance ends with workers pointing at the audience 'challengingly'.[48] As Segal wrote in *New Dance*, 'the enemy, the exploiting class, is not shown but *felt* through the quality of work movements, which are forced, inhuman, mechanized', and by the end of the dance, the workers have united against this common enemy.[49] Critic Deborah Jowitt's review of the 1984 re-staging of *Black and White* with Serge St Juste and Gary Onsum at PS1 in New York City described how initially the two workers maintain separate kinespheres, coming together and merging at the point at which the 'positive' call rings out (the voice of communism).[50]

The representation of industrial labour in *Black and White*, as well as of Black and white unity as only possible through communism, is strongly tied with the CPUSA's drive to recruit Black members during the Third Period, an ambition that would gain pace during the Popular Front.[51] The dance was first performed in the Spring of 1930 by Segal and Burroughs at three CPUSA organised events. Firstly on 8 March at an International Women's Day mass meeting, then at the Interracial Ball (which is my focus here), and finally on 1 April at the Gastonia Strike memorial event at the Manhattan Lyceum.[52] The performance of *Black and White* at the Rockland Palace Interracial Dance formed part of an evening of entertainment chaired by Joseph Brodsky of the International Labor Defence. William Z. Foster, one of the three-person secretariat of the CPUSA in 1930, gave a speech, as did Herbert Newton, a prominent African American organiser and staff member of the Harlem Communist paper, *The Liberator*. (Fig. 14) However, the main portion of the night's entertainment and surely the biggest draw for most of the audience was the performance by Duke Ellington and his Orchestra who played from the opening of the evening until 1 a.m. On the closing of their set, Segal played the piano as the 1,600 attendees joined in a

---

48 Score for *Black and White* in the Edith Segal papers (Box 2), Dance Collection, The New York Public Library, Astor, Lenox and Tilden Foundations.
49 Edith Segal, 'Mayday Script', p. 19 (my emphasis – it seems the counter-posing of 'feeling' to 'showing' is intended to demonstrate the meaning of the dance for the performers as well as the audience, and relates back to the collective, rather than didactic mode of pedagogy Segal emphasised with the NTWIUDG).
50 Jowitt 1984, p. 71 Kinesphere is a concept drawn from Rudolf Laban and simply means the sphere around the body, the periphery of which can be reached by the dancer extending her limbs. See Laban, p. 10.
51 For a comprehensive overview of how the CPUSA responded to the so-called 'negro question' during the Third Period, see Zumoff 2014, and for details of this during the Popular Front, see Klehr 1984.
52 Graff 1997, pp. 37–8.

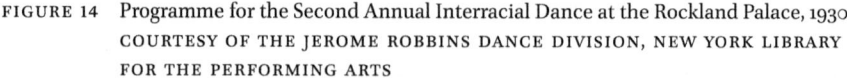

FIGURE 14 Programme for the Second Annual Interracial Dance at the Rockland Palace, 1930
COURTESY OF THE JEROME ROBBINS DANCE DIVISION, NEW YORK LIBRARY FOR THE PERFORMING ARTS

recital of *The Internationale*. The evening's entertainment continued with Segal and Burroughs's performance of *Black and White* and concluded with speeches from Brodsky, Foster and Newton.[53]

In terms of Duke Ellington's role in this event and the cultural position of jazz during this period, it is worth noting that during the early years of the 1930s, big band jazz remained a mostly Black activity. As Lewis Erenberg writes, it was only later in the 1930s that jazz would move from the margins to the centre of American popular culture, a development associated with the whitening of the genre though prominent players and bandleaders such as Benny Goodman and Paul Whiteman.[54] Ellington himself described this process in 1939, noting prominent events such as Goodman's performance with the Budapest String Quartet. While he does not disparage individual musicians, he clarifies that their activities do not concern him, or his group, 'personally'. Instead, he explains that 'Our music is always intended to be definitely and purely racial. We try to complete a cycle'.[55]

This idea of a cycle was grounded in the possibilities of reconstructing an African tradition of musical forms such as call and response, improvisation and polyrhythm, a quest that was embedded in the necessity of invoking a history that predated slavery – or to use a Blochian phrase, of liberating 'the still possible future' from the past. For Ellington, adherence to these musical forms assisted in the collaborative work between bandleader and players, and as Ellington's trumpeter Cootie Williams noted, 'everyone in the band would pitch in and help write songs', a statement which relates to Segal's affirmation of collective organisation within the NTWIUDG.[56] The organicism of Ellington's sound and practice within the band ('completing a cycle') was grounded in appeals to the universal; as he described in a 1930 interview, the same year as his performance at the Interracial Ball, 'I am not playing jazz. I am trying to play the natural feelings of a people'.[57] But in thinking about the place of organic, universal metaphors here, it is crucial that Ellington's non-simultaneity came through his desire to 'complete a cycle' – or as he described *Tone Parallel to Harlem* – to weave 'a musical thread which runs parallel to the history of the American Negro'.[58]

---

53 Manning 2004, p. 72 and Naison 1983, p. 36.
54 Erenberg 1999.
55 Ellington 1930, p. 135.
56 Erenberg 1999, p. 9.
57 Florence Zunser interview with Duke Ellington 1993, p. 45.
58 Oakley 1993, p. 156.

Fred Moten describes the importance of Ellington's 'people' as denoting an eruptive, lyrical universalism –

> This influence of my people to which Ellington refers, in what it hopes for (a genuinely new universal) and in what it disrupts (that which has heretofore been given as the universal) is the sound of love. But this drive of and for 'my people' – who are, for Ellington and according to Ellington, 'the people' – is complicated; it continually erupts out of its own categorization ...[59]

As Moten describes, the eruptive quality within Ellington can be understood as the disruption of a dominant universal. The emphasis Moten places on the relationship between the universal and the 'sound of love' moves beyond Ellington's own description of his music as being a 'real reflector' of the nation's feelings, and towards the (re)production of *feeling* – a new kind of 'universal' – that I think is also captured in Segal's hopes that in *Black and White* 'the enemy, the exploiting class, is not shown but *felt*'.[60] Thinking about this emphasis on 'feeling' at the Interracial Ball, we could also consider Ellington's 1930 description of the effect his Orchestra had, saying that 'You only have to watch a dance floor full of dancing couples to realize that music is the most vital thing in swaying the emotions of a multitude'.[61] Yet, rather than the relationship between music and dance standing solely as emotional manipulation, Ellington would stress just a year later that 'When we dance it is not a mere diversion or social accomplishment'.[62]

That Ellington's performance and Segal and Burroughs' *Black and White* both make appeals to universalism and 'natural feeling' must be read in relation to the other aspects of the Interracial Ball. The fact Segal and Burroughs performed *after* Duke Ellington and the singing of the *Internationale* but crucially *before* the political speeches, means their performance of conflict and reconciliation set within the space of production (the factory) acted as the meeting point between the social and the political during the process of the evening, or between what Bloch called the 'totally synchronous' 'language of communism' and the non-synchronous contradictions and subjective experiences of capital which had surely led many of the communist and fellow-travelling dancers and

---

59 Moten 2003, p. 26.
60 Segal, 'Mayday Script', p. 19.
61 Zunser interview with Ellington 1993, p. 45.
62 Ellington 1931.

musicians to the ball.⁶³ The experience of singing the *Internationale* and witnessing Segal and Burroughs dance – after dancing to Duke Ellington (never a 'mere diversion') – laid the ground for the speeches and *Black and White* thus served as a kind of mediating point between the heterodox, eruptive politics of the social, and the orthodoxy of Party politics.⁶⁴

Vitally, Segal and Burroughs's dance at the Interracial Ball transplanted the lived politics of the interracial dance *back* into the industrial workplace, declaring that black and white bodies could only dance together against their 'forced, inhuman, mechanized' work once they stood together, opposed to capital. In order to illustrate this, the body was figured in *Black and White* as against industrial machinery and posited as espousing a similar form of organic universalism that had been conjured earlier in the evening by Ellington's orchestra. In the rehearsal photographs for *Black and White*, Burroughs and Segal's nude bodies are intertwined in hard poses that mimic mechanised labour. Yet, the softness of their bodies clashes with the stiffness of their gestures as well as the factory painted on the backdrop, posing them, and all the dancers at the Rockland Palace, not as links in chains, or cogs in machinery, but in a manner more akin to Allerhand's description of the proletarian dancer as 'a very alive, very productive cell within a body'.⁶⁵ That their bodies were female and black and white also inflects this dance, in which dancers break away from machinery, with an anti-industrial sentiment that complements its obviously anti-capitalist overtures.

4   Dance and Domestic Labour

Looking beyond industry, Segal also organised dances that specifically addressed domestic labour during the period of the Popular Front. Taking its title from the Nazi programme for women, *Kinder, Küche, Kirche* (Children, Kitchen, Church) was an anti-fascist critique of the role reserved for women by the Nazis, and was performed by two amateur groups: the predominantly German

---

63   Bloch saw orthodox 'communist language' as 'totally contemporaneous and precisely orientated to the most advanced economy', aspects that he viewed as difficult for 'nonsynchronous' people to understand, meaning National Socialism had more successfully captured their 'subjective' experience of non-simultaneous contradictions. Bloch 1991, p. 105. I have addressed the subject of feeling and communism elsewhere, in a collaborative essay with Hannah Proctor. See Abse Gogarty and Proctor 2019.
64   For a sense of contemporary party debates on race relations and labour see Kelley, 1990, Naison 1983 and Zumoff 2014.
65   Allerhand 1935.

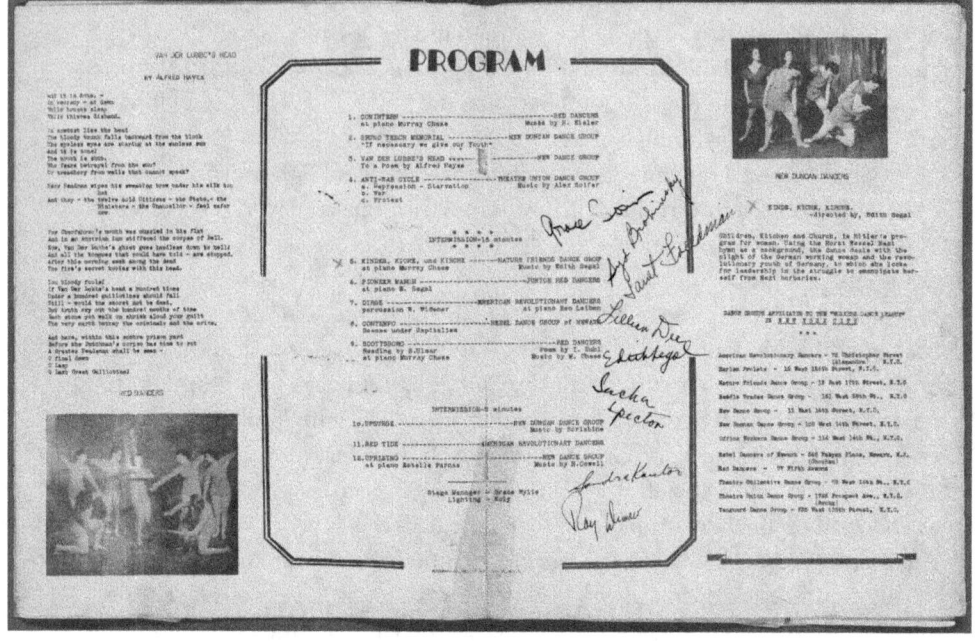

FIGURE 15   Photograph of the New Duncan Dancers performing Kinder Küche Kirche printed in the New Dance League Bulletin, summer issue, 1936
COURTESY OF THE JEROME ROBBINS DANCE DIVISION, NEW YORK LIBRARY FOR THE PERFORMING ARTS

'Nature Friends' dance group, and also the New Duncan Dancers (Fig. 15) (in 1935 and 1936 respectively).[66] In addition, Segal also choreographed *Dance of the Washerwomen*, which was performed by the Red Dancers in 1935. (Fig. 16) The choreography of this was based on domestic work, and inspired by watching Polish and Ukrainian women travel together at night, going in groups to

---

66   Nature Friends is an international movement that emerged out of Austria; it was initially founded in 1895 as a labour organization that combined ecology with progressive sympathies. In the USA, Nature Friends groups cropped up in German-speaking communities from the 1910s. Camp Midvale, their camp in New Jersey, was founded in 1930 and served as the centre for their East Coast activities, which included sponsored hikes for causes such as the Scotsboro Boys and the Abraham Lincoln Brigade. The relationship between modern dance, nature and the left has an interesting precedent in the towering figure of Isadora Duncan, who was outspokenly radical, had an idealised notion of nature and flirted with paganism. As mentioned, Duncan's influence on Segal is clear in the photographs of the ILGWU at their summer camp, adorned with Duncan-esque flowing scarves and surrounded by nature.

FIGURE 16   Red Dancers, *Dance of the Washerwomen*, 1935
PHOTOGRAPHER UNKNOWN. COURTESY OF THE JEROME ROBBINS DANCE
DIVISION, NEW YORK LIBRARY FOR THE PERFORMING ARTS

clean office buildings.[67] In the photograph of *Dance of the Washerwomen*, this group dynamic is manifested through two trios that flank a seventh woman dancer lying prone on the ground. The trios appear as a kind of chorus, watching over their comrade who has fallen with exhaustion. Read from left to right, the photograph of the New Duncan Dancers performing *Kinder, Küche, Kirche* (Fig. 15) shows a reverse-evolutionary movement with each figure falling a little closer to the ground.[68] The falling motion and proximity to the ground in both these dances repeats aspects of *Black and White*, where both workers were shown to fall as a result of the speed-up of the belt. In *Kinder, Küche, Kirche* and *Dance of the Washerwomen* we gain a dual representation of domestic labour as waged work (the 'feudal housewife') and unwaged work, demonstrating that

---

67   Leslie Farlow, oral history interview with Edith Segal, 1991, audiotape, Dance Collection, New York Public Library for the Performing Arts.
68   Thanks to Richard Braude for his suggestions on how to read elements of the choreography through this photograph.

this was labour largely undertaken by women, across both spheres. There is much less information about these dances than there is about Segal's work with industrial unions, but they are revealing as counterpoints to the woman-as-industrial worker presented in her choreography for the union dance groups, and in *Black and White*.

The critical representation of domestic work in Segal's dances sharply contradicts Michael Denning's assertion that the Popular Front representation of motherhood was overwhelmingly characterised by 'sentimental maternalism', which he exemplifies through the reception of Dorothea Lange's *Migrant Mother*.[69] Denning describes the Popular Front politics of motherhood during the depression as a 'pro-natalist crusade', a drive that is arguably inextricable from forms of nationalism.[70] In contrast, Segal's work, particularly *Kinder, Küche, Kirche*, underscored the relationship between repressive gender roles, social reproduction and nationalism. By taking this into account, alongside histories of militancy amongst proletarian housewives, we get a different picture to Denning's view of depression-era politics around social reproduction. For example, Annelise Orleck has detailed how African American mothers left their babies on caseworkers' desks at the Cleveland Emergency Relief Association in 1932, refusing to collect them until free milk was provided.[71] Similar struggles include Polish housewives setting thousands of pounds worth of meat on fire at meatpacking warehouses in Chicago to highlight that high prices were not the result of shortages.[72] These struggles may have predated the Popular Front, but I don't believe they disappeared after that transition.[73]

Before the Popular Front, from the late 1920s to the mid-1930s, the CPUSA closely aligned with these struggles, primarily through their affiliation with the United Council of Working-Class Housewives (UCWCH), which had been established in 1926 by Clara Lemlich Shavelson. Like Segal, Shavelson had attended the Rand School of Social Sciences in the 1920s and had also been a prominent

---

69 Denning 1997, p. 137.
70 Ibid.
71 Orleck 1993, p. 149.
72 Ibid.
73 Rosalyn Baxandall presents a rich history of the heterogeneity of gender politics in the CPUSA from the 1930s–40s, emphasising that the Party not only provided an arena for political action, but also supported a rich social life that permitted more sexual freedom than was available in the mainstream. In thinking about periodisation and the relation between Party and rank and file, Baxandall stresses that the 'bohemianism of the 1910–1917 period lingered in the ranks, if not in the ruling party circles'. See Baxandall 1993, p. 151.

member of the ILGWU.⁷⁴ In 1933 and 1938, Shavelson ran on the CPUSA ticket for the New York State Assembly. Within the UCWCH, women from Communist and non-Communist organisations regularly worked together across Party lines to organise consumer protests and lobby for regulation in the years from 1930–6. As Orleck emphasises, such alliances were possible because their politics concerned the very reproduction of life, and interestingly, the one other area of pan-leftist alliances during this period was around unemployment, notably through the CPUSA's support for the Socialist Party led Workers' Alliance of America, which organised Unemployment Councils and led the occupation of the New Jersey State Assembly which featured in *Injunction Granted*, as discussed in Chapter One.⁷⁵

Kinder, Küche, Kirche and *Dance of the Washerwomen* formed part of a leftist culture where the response to women's oppression was being avidly discussed. During the late 1930s, Mary Inman, the primary theorist of women's oppression within the CPUSA, forcefully argued against the dominant view within the Party that women's oppression would be overcome as increasing numbers of women joined the workforce and became unionised. As she wrote, domestic work did not disappear, and instead female wage labourers frequently found themselves doing a 'second shift' in the home. In 1938–9, Inman's writing was serialised in the *People's Daily World* (the West Coast organ of the CPUSA), and her book *In Woman's Defense* was published as a whole volume in 1940, which led to her being regarded as the CPUSA's leading authority on women's oppression.⁷⁶ Denning has described this book as the most 'ambitious Marxist analysis of women's oppression of the period', a statement that complicates his summary of Popular Front gender politics as dominated by 'sentimental maternalism'.⁷⁷ Due to the influence of the book, Inman's writing formed the basis for a nationwide course on the woman question in CPUSA-affiliated workers' schools.⁷⁸ However, this swiftly changed after California party leaders Eva

---

74 Orleck 1993, p. 153 and p. 163.
75 See Orleck 1993, p. 156. As discussed in the previous chapter, the WAA had a strong footing within the WPA-FTP, and whilst working for the WPA-FTP in Detroit as an actor and choreographer, Segal had been a member and organiser. It is also notable that reproductive labour and unemployment became the categories through which broader organisation could occur in the 1930s. This highlights the limits to how the far left has historically oriented itself too one-dimensionally towards productive labour, an issue that has returned to the fore in recent years.
76 Inman 1940.
77 Denning 1997, p. 145.
78 Its publication had been delayed due to WWII, but in 1940 alone *In Woman's Defense* went into three printings.

Shafran and Al Bryan came to Inman's classroom on 24 March 1941 to inform the students that, despite Inman's conclusions, housework cannot be described as productive labour. Shafran followed up on this judgement by cancelling the course.[79] Inman experienced a harsh response from the Party bureaucracy for her pursuit of a Marxian analysis of how women's unwaged activities in the home contributed to the accumulation of surplus value and the maintenance of class relations.

Inman reasoned that housewives form the greatest reserve army of labour-power in the US, called upon during wartime and moments of crisis, and argued that by encouraging women to become wage labourers, the CPUSA overwhelmingly led women towards the exploitation experienced by male proletarians, rather than emancipation. Moreover, in thinking about the position of proletarian women, Inman recognised that they carried the double burden of waged *and* domestic labour. The shortcomings of the Party's approach thus led her to analyse the structural relation of domestic work performed by women to the reproduction of capitalism, marking her writing as a significant precursor to materialist feminist analysis from the 1970s onwards.[80]

In *Woman Power*, Inman claims that two forms of production underpin capitalism:
1) The production and reproduction of life (home)
2) The production of the means of existence (fields, factories)[81]

For the sake of convenience, I will refer to the first 'system' simply as reproduction. Inman's argument for reproduction as productive of value was argued most clearly in reaction to the outlining of the 'official Marxist-Leninist line on housework' published in *The Communist* by 'Professor X', a pseudonym for Avram Landy, educational director of the CPUSA.[82] In 1943 Landy went on to publish 'Marxism and the Woman Question', where he accused Inman of economic illiteracy, of not having read Engels properly and of 'glorifying' housework.[83]

---

79 Inman taught a course at the Los Angeles Workers' School entitled 'Women's status under capitalism and its relation to the Labor Movement'. Weigand 2001, p. 37.
80 A good summary of these debates can be found in Arruza 2013.
81 Inman 1942, p. 28.
82 Weigand 2001, p. 40.
83 Landy 1943, pp. 8–10. Landy's *Marxism and the Woman Question* was the final nail in the coffin of what could have been a fruitful debate over housework and women's oppression, a subject particularly relevant during and in the aftermath of the war as women entered, and then left, wage labour. However, as Weigand has demonstrated, despite Inman's acrimonious exit from the Party in 1941, her theories continued to be implemented within CPUSA strategy on the Woman Question. This included the formation of the National

Writing against Inman's earlier *In Woman's Defense*, Landy identified the economic character of domestic labour as solely consumptive, stating that the housewife simply consumes the wages brought home by her husband, and that housework is 'only work for one's own family'.[84] Inman railed against this, quoting Marx from *Capital* Volume I to make her point: 'This incessant reproduction, this perpetuation of the laborer, is the sine qua non of capitalist production'.[85] Inman argued that for Landy to truly believe that the housewife and mother are solely engaged in consumption, he would '... have to hide the laborer's navel. For labor-power can no more exist independent of the laborer than steam-power can exist independent of the steam engine'.[86] In addition, responding to the accusation that housewives only work for their families, Inman added that this obscuration of their 'useful role in social production' and the viewing of housework as a labour of love allows for the mystification of the 'whole relationship between the 222,000,000 housewives and their husbands' employers, who in reality are also the wives' employers'.[87]

Inman solidified her argument by demonstrating the necessity of reproductive labour to the perpetuation of that 'peculiar commodity', labour power, explaining that the raising of women to be 'cooks, nurses and housekeepers is as necessary to capitalist production as the raising and educating of the laborers themselves'.[88] Inman not only clarified the integral role of reproductive labour to capitalism in this discussion, but also theorised the push for women's entry into the labour force as constitutive of the financial crisis which erupted in 1929:

> The theory that the working class housewife is doing nothing useful, nor socially necessary, in the work she does in the home in the creation of labor-power, was popularized during the depression era in the United

---

Women's Congress in 1946 and the National Nursery Movement; Inman's former comrade, Susan B. Anthony, led both initiatives. See Weigand 2001, pp. 52–4.

84   Landy 1943, p. 58.
85   Marx quoted in Inman 1942, p. 34.
86   Inman 1942, p. 37. Inman in this respect follows Marx directly: 'The labor-power withdrawn from the market by wear and tear and by death, must be continually replaced by, at the very least, an equal amount of fresh labor-power. Hence the sum of means of subsistence necessary for the production of labour-power must include the means necessary for the worker's replacements, i.e. his children, in order that this race of peculiar commodity-owners may perpetuate its presence on the market'. Marx 1990, p. 275.
87   Inman 1942, p. 72.
88   Inman 1942, pp. 51–2.

States, when, in order to restore the falling rate of profit, the 'economic royalists' dreamed of drawing women and children out of the homes into industry, cutting the wages of men, and smashing the rising trade union movement.[89]

Clearly, Inman was ambivalent about the emancipatory possibilities of waged work for women. Whilst she emphasised that women were less isolated when working as wage labourers, she also acknowledged that their entry into the labour force was frequently part of an attack on other workers when they were employed as strike-breakers or hired at lower wage rates than men. Inman's solution, like that of many Marxist-feminists since, was the socialisation of domestic work.

Excessively rosy accounts of the position of Soviet women such as those published earlier in the 1930s in *Working Woman* probably informed Inman's faith in this solution.[90] However, as Wendy Goldman has outlined, there were stark transformations in the official position on women in the Soviet Union between the revolution in 1917 and the 1930s, with the Zhenotdel, the women's department of the central committee, eliminated in 1930 because it was viewed as interfering with the Five Year Plan.[91] As Goldman emphasises, the 'mania for production' at the heart of Stalinist ideology eventually obliterated any ambitions of transforming gender relations through re-arranging domestic work.[92] Rather, during the Stalinist era, housework was designated as an anachronistic remnant from pre-communist or even pre-capitalist times, a variant on Lenin's view that housework was partly gendered as female through capitalist social relations, but was additionally a remnant from the peasantry's 'century-old traditions of patriarchal life'.[93] Lenin also used the metaphor of slavery to describe housework in 1919:

> Notwithstanding all the laws emancipating woman, she continues to be a domestic slave, because petty housework crushes, strangles, stultifies and

---

89 Inman 1942, p. 61. It is interesting to note here that Inman uses the term 'economic royalists'. As Maurice Isserman has noted, members of the Browder-era CPUSA blunted 'their criticisms of capitalism, substituting such fuzzy, Rooseveltian categories as "economic royalism" for the more explicit and starker dichotomies of Marxist class analysis'. See Isserman 1982, p. 9.
90 Goldman 1993, pp. 1–4.
91 Goldman 1996, p. 52.
92 Goldman 1996, p. 46.
93 Lenin quoted in Vogel 1983, p. 118.

degrades her, chains her to the kitchen and the nursery, and she wastes her labor on barbarously unproductive, petty, nerve-racking, stultifying and crushing drudgery.[94]

Here, we can see that Lenin viewed housework as petty, nerve-racking, stultifying, and crushing precisely *because* it is unproductive. As with the CIO's denunciation of the Taft Hartley act as the 'slave labor bill', discussed in the previous chapter, this category is intended to distinguish between labour relations and barbarity. In Lenin's argument, no distinction is made between wage labour and socialised labour, rather it is slavery which stands as external to both capitalism and communism, and slavery which forms the appropriate metaphor for housework. The conception of housework as unproductive was evidently central to Soviet discussions on women's oppression from Lenin onwards, which perhaps indicates why the CPUSA were so swift to denounce Inman. Indeed, the tone of debate between Inman and Landy was infused with value judgments that denoted 'unproductivity' (women) as equivalent to uselessness, laziness, irrelevance, and 'productivity' (men) as progressive, useful and essential to the historical advance of society. As already indicated, this emphasis on hyperproductivity was related to attempts within the Soviet Union to repurpose Taylorism for a communist society, guided by Lenin's belief that the 'rational distribution of social labour' had enormous potential to maintain productivity whilst shortening the working day under communism.[95]

In the teleological vision of the CPUSA, women joining the workforce formed part of a programmatic, productivist path to communism, much divorced from revolutionary goals. In this respect, the over-attention paid to the question of whether housework was productive or unproductive is a red herring, suggestive only of the conceptual limitations of the party and much orthodox Marxist thinking when it comes to the question of gender. Though the Inman debate demonstrates the limits of imagining, or proposing a transition to, a communist society solely in terms of transforming the ownership of the means of production, it focuses too heavily on women's oppression as resulting from particular activities – housework, sex, childbirth and care – rather than the relations which ensure they repeatedly fall under a gendered division of labour. In moving towards Lacy's *Expectations*, we will start to see some of the limits of this approach, and the necessity of integrating Lise Vogel's analysis of

---

94   Lenin 1919.
95   Lenin 1914.

women's oppression in capitalist society as situated within the framework of overall social reproduction, a view that can also assist in building an analysis of racial oppression within capitalism.

Vogel outlines how the reproduction of the labour force is shaped by a number of processes, including the generational replacement of workers by childbirth and the maintenance of labour power via tasks normally performed by women. However, following Marx, Vogel also explains that new immigrants and the incorporation of other forms of labour into the wage relation, such as slavery and other forms of bonded labour, may also replenish labour power. Furthermore, certain segments of the population may not access the reproduction of their labour power within the family unit but in prisons, workers' dormitories and migrant labour camps. By reminding the reader of these other methods and sites of the reproduction of labour power, Vogel highlights how class, race and gender are interlinked, and how the state mediates these relations. For example, public education and health care have historically transferred some reproductive responsibilities onto the state. Or, as Vogel explains 'society's total domestic labor can also be reduced by employing migrants and prison populations', processes legitimised by state policy.[96] Conversely, as we will see in the discussion of Lacy's *Expectations*, the state may also withdraw support, pushing forms of work back into the (female), unwaged domestic sphere, issues taken up in an article entitled 'The Logic of Gender' in the journal *Endnotes*. *Endnotes* analyse what they describe as the re-naturalisation of gender within moments of crisis and austerity, described as a process of 'abjection' wherein activities that were previously waged or carried out via the state, are returned to the unwaged, female-gendered sphere.[97] This analysis approaches the crisis in social reproduction since the beginning of the neoliberal era, and the changing role and responsibilities of the state in reproducing the working class. As in the comparison I made in Chapter One, the change in the dominant subject-participant between Segal's dance works and Lacy's project is one that partially registers the decline of the industrial working class in the US. In addition, we can again see this shift as marking a transformation in the social groups that politicised art practices have sought to address and collaborate with across both periods. Because both Segal and Lacy worked primarily with women, the

---

96   Vogel 1983, p. 154.
97   *Endnotes* call these spheres the 'directly market mediated' and 'indirectly market mediated', and they account for a grey area between these, which primarily designates state-supported institutions and services.

distinct demographics of the groups they collaborated with reveals transformations in the management of social reproduction by two divergent state formations.

In the second half of this chapter, we will return to Denning's description of 'the child in the streets, alternately predator and prey' as the most characteristic figure of neoliberal capitalism, and the relevance of this assessment to the women that Lacy worked with in *Expectations*.[98] By examining the gendering of these women's experiences in relation to the subject-participants of *The Roof is on Fire* and *Code 33*, as well as by contrasting this group to the women in Segal's proletarian mass dances, we get a powerful snapshot of how community-based, collective art practices intersect with, and seek to repair, the damages done to sociality in capitalist societies. Through these practices, I believe we can see how fully social reproduction lies at the heart of this dynamic.

5   Expectations and Welfare Reform

> Other than the scary young male teenager, another potent symbol in public culture was the image of the female pregnant African American teenager ... that carried the weight of the stigma of 'welfare mom'. The young women would tell us that when they rode on the bus, for instance, strangers thought they could touch and talk about their bellies, often negatively: 'Oh, there is one of them'. This was at the same time that welfare was being dismantled, both in California, and later, nationally.
>
> SUZANNE LACY, 2007[99]

In 1997, Suzanne Lacy began a project called *Expectations* with a group of 32 pregnant and parenting teenage high school students from the Bay Area in California, creating a series of collaborative artworks and pedagogical encounters. The project emerged as a coherent sub-project within *The Oakland Projects* through Lacy's relationship with Sheila Jordan, an educator who had become

---

98   Denning claims that the classical Marxist designation of a reserve army of labour, or *lumpenproletariat*, is not adequate to describing the current crisis of employment. However, neither is Giorgio Agamben's 'bare life', nor descriptions of 'precarious life', due to their tendency to suggest a world in which there actually *are* disposable people. Denning worries that Agamben's theory can result in a neo-Malthusianism rather than a critique of capitalism as the system that renders human beings disposable. See Denning 2010, pp. 79–80.

99   Suzanne Lacy, speaking at the 'Working in Public' seminar series at Robert Gordon University in 2007.

a City politician. Jordan worked for the Alameda County Office of Education, which had a small programme called Comprehensive Team Pregnancy and Parenting Program. The programme had a very high dropout rate and was perceived to be failing the young people it was supposed to benefit. Lacy suggested to Jordan that alongside youth and adult collaborators from *The Oakland Projects*, she could coordinate an education programme within this scheme that would also be a work of art.[100] The first stage of *Expectations* involved an art-centred summer school programme for pregnant and parenting teen girls who had dropped out of high school, or were deemed to be at risk of dropping out of formal education. I will discuss this part of the project in brief, before focusing on the Capp Street exhibition, which opened in September 1997 and followed the summer school, exploring how this distinguishes *Expectations* from other public outcomes within *The Oakland Projects*, which were primarily performance-based.

Many of the young women participating in *Expectations* had been involved in other aspects of *The Oakland Projects*, and the issue of teen pregnancy first arose during *The Roof is on Fire* performance (1994). *Expectations* responded directly to government policy, like other aspects of *The Oakland Projects* such as *No Blood No Foul*, specifically the 1996 abolition of the federal Aid to Families with Dependent Children Program (AFDC).[101] In tandem with this attack made by the state, the media also pursued a widespread scapegoating of teen mothers, with the ABC *Prime Time Live* anchor-executive Diane Sawyer waging a campaign on behalf of 'mad as hell' 'taxpayers' to personally 'shame' teenage mothers as 'Public Enemy No. 1'.[102]

In 1996, the Personal Responsibility and Work Opportunity Reconciliation Act (PRWORA) was passed, a piece of welfare legislation that eliminated AFDC, a federal assistance programme that had been established in 1935 via the Social Security Act. Two key political factors made possible the legislation of the PRWORA and the reversal of a welfare structure that had existed since the New Deal. Firstly, President Clinton's declared goal of transforming 'welfare as we know it', and secondly, the pressure put on his administration by the so-called 'Republican Revolution' of 1994. In 1994, a year into Clinton's first term as President, the GOP gained control of a large number of state legislatures, and then-

---

100   Suzanne Lacy, speaking at the 'Working in Public' seminar series. The team Lacy worked with on *Expectations* included teens Leuckessia Hirsh and Unique Holland, who had also been involved in *The Roof is on Fire*.
101   Chappell 2010, p. 10. *No Blood No Foul* was a performance organised in 1996 in response to the Oakland-based *Kids First!* policy.
102   Males 1996, pp. 27–8.

leader Newt Gingrich became speaker of the House of Representatives following congressional elections. In 1994, the GOP released the *Contract with America* policy document that pledged to transform welfare, reduce 'illegitimate' births, enforce work, and save taxpayer money via the 'Personal Responsibility Act'. The PRWORA was a milder, modified version of this policy, rewritten following initial vetoes of the more extreme proposals the GOP had put forth, which included the proposal to entirely prohibit welfare to mothers below 18 years of age.[103]

Despite these modifications, the PRWORA was an openly ideological piece of legislation, as demonstrated by the preamble to the bill which stated that 'Marriage is the foundation of a successful society', an 'essential institution ... that promotes the interests of children'.[104] Within the bill, out of wedlock births were presented as a pathological blight, with teenage mothers positioned as the cause of poverty.[105] The abolition of AFDC was replaced with block grants for 'Temporary Assistance to Needy Families' (TANF) that were to be administered at state level. Though this devolved some power from the Federal government, restrictions were enforced to prohibit individual states from weakening the PRWORA regulations, and a five-year limit on all TANF claims was imposed. However, although states were disallowed from extending this limit, they were permitted to enforce shorter limits on claimants. The federal government also implemented work programmes (such as workfare) for the long-term unemployed, and states that failed to meet quotas to get claimants off welfare were penalised. Following the pattern of decentralisation from central government, states were also encouraged to outsource the administration of the block grants for TANF to private firms, religious organisations or charities.[106]

Though the PRWORA had seemingly relaxed the initial proposals within the Personal Responsibility Act prohibiting welfare to mothers below 18 years of age, the devolution of the legislation meant that individual states could deny benefits to unmarried teenage mothers wholesale. Teenage mothers were also mandated to attend school or participate in a work programme (with which the *Expectations* summer school complied), and in a number of states, their claim for TANF payments was dependent on them living with a parent or guardian. Within popular opinion and the media, the PRWORA amplified a moral

---

103 O'Connor 2001, p. 4.
104 Personal Responsibility and Work Opportunity Reconciliation Act of 1996, *Public Law* 104/193, Aug. 22, 1996, United States Statutes at Large.
105 O'Connor 2001, p. 13, and *Personal Responsibility and Work Opportunity Reconciliation Act of 1996*.
106 O'Connor 2001, pp. 15–16.

panic against out-of-wedlock births, with Gingrich in particular stirring up outrage towards 'illegitimacy' and targeting welfare as the cause behind 'children having children'. As Brendan O'Connor has noted, such questions of welfare, illegitimacy and teenage pregnancy have been politically sensitive in the US since the Moynihan Report of 1965, and are inflected by issues of race, religion, gender and sexuality alongside class.[107]

The PRWORA, as opposed to earlier welfare legislation, was almost entirely oriented towards inculcating better work habits amongst recipients. Workfare programmes and tax credits for employers who employed long-term welfare claimants were two such strategies within this crusade and the ultimate drive of the PRWORA was to make claimants work for their benefits. This move suggested full 'citizenship', and the respect due to citizens, could only be gained through employment.[108] Yet, unlike the New Deal creation of government agencies such as the WPA as solutions to mass unemployment, the PRWORA instrumentalised the long-term unemployed as a more highly exploitable labour force, as evidenced by the Republican argument that those on work programmes should receive below minimum wage because of the additional benefits they claimed. A number of unions opposed workfare schemes vociferously, viewing them as a dirty tactic to undercut wages and undermine the stability of those already within the workforce, an echo of union complaints in the 1930s about federal programmes undercutting union wage rates.[109]

Pateman argues that the introduction of PRWORA specifically brings women within the logic of the poor law. Prior to the abolition of AFDC, single mothers were the only remaining group of able-bodied adults whose non-participation in the labour market did not prohibit their receipt of welfare in the US.[110] Yet, rather than seeing the New Deal era as the golden age of an American welfare state, it is worth stressing the gendered and racialised dynamics that were inherent to the introduction of the Social Security Act in 1935. From its inception, the Social Security Act intertwined with the proliferation and maintenance of very low wages and thus second-class citizenship for certain segments of the workforce in the US. Southern politicians opposed the introduction of the Act in Congress and this led to agricultural, domestic, educational and hospital workers not being included within the Act, thus excluding the workforces with the highest number of Black and Latinx workers. From its inception

---

107 O'Connor 2001, p. 20.
108 Pateman 2005, p. 35.
109 O'Connor 2001, p. 23.
110 Pateman 2005, p. 40.

until 1960, Aid to Dependent Children (ADC was the earlier name for AFDC) frequently excluded African American, other minority women and unmarried mothers, as these women were considered 'employable mothers'.[111] By recognising this history, the introduction of the repressive PRWORA can be set within a more complex view that acknowledges how welfare provision in the US has continually intertwined with the disciplining function of wage labour, and the differential levels of citizenship offered to women and people of colour.[112]

As Marx explained, 'Political economy ... does not recognize the unemployed worker ... insofar as he happens to be outside this labour relationship'.[113] Marx described the spectre-like qualities of the unemployed for bourgeois economists, the heightened visibility of this part of the populace to 'the doctor, the judge, the grave-digger, and bum bailiff'.[114] I find this helpful when thinking what the PRWORA sought to achieve with regard to the surplus population in the US. It is no coincidence that the ideological foundations of the legislation involved the affirmation of the nuclear family as the 'foundations of a successful society'. As Megan Weinstein has noted, the focus on 'unwed' pregnancy in the PRWORA – with unwed teenage pregnancy positioned as the apex of moral turpitude – was based on the idea that marriage is both a moral and practical solution to poverty. Not only does this make the short-sighted assumption that replacing women's dependence on the state with women's dependence on men is a feasible resolution for the economically vulnerable, but, as Weinstein has emphasised, 'research suggests that marrying men in poor communities to escape poverty is also not a practical answer'.[115] In particular, the high rates of death, incarceration and unemployment among Black males, as discussed in Chapter One – factors consistently reproduced by the US legal system – concretely undermine the economic autonomy of Black families, should heterosexual partnerships be desirable. As Lacy said of teenage girls – the primary subject of *Expectations* – in relation to the rest of the *Oakland Projects*, 'the issue of looking at the trajectory of teen pregnancy and its relation to policy was not a lot different than what happens to the bodies of young men as they're beaten up and imprisoned'.[116]

---

111   Pateman 2005, pp. 46–7.
112   Pateman 2005, p. 49.
113   Marx 1988, p. 86.
114   Ibid.
115   Weinstein, p. 124.
116   Interview conducted with Suzanne Lacy on 26th May 2013. Lacy also makes the observation that youth first appear in the criminal justice system as victims, with parity across boys and girls. Often, their second appearance in the system is as perpetrators of minor

When thinking about transformations in welfare and family life, it is important to remember that the value of labour power differs from other commodities because a 'historical and moral element' must be acknowledged.[117] Between the post-war years and the 1980s, the 'historical and moral element' frequently resulted in the payment of a 'family wage', typically Fordist, and respondent to trade union demands. The decomposition of the labour movement and onset of neoliberalism effectively obliterated the possibilities of a family wage in the US for much of the workforce. From the outset then, the socially conservative vision of Clintonite welfare reformers, which situated heterosexual marriage as a solution to the crisis and replacement for the minimal social safety net previously provided by the state, was stunted. This is not to mention the absurdity of such proposals following decades of struggles against women's isolation in the domestic sphere. Thinking through the material contradictions of the PRWORA highlights that teenage pregnancy acted as a cipher for the direction of welfare reform in two ways. Firstly, teenage pregnancy provided an easy scapegoat for social anxieties about unwed motherhood leading to a fundamental shift in social demographics. Secondly, and most importantly, the vilification of teenage pregnancy in the PRWORA and welfare reform debate ultimately stands for a covert continuation of a state-led offensive against the rights of poor women – in particular poor Black women – to reproduce.[118]

6 'Each Week We Started with the Body'

Having detailed the political and ideological stakes within which *Expectations* began, we can see the project had a real urgency in addressing teenage pregnancy and parenting through the voices of those who had been demonised by the state and the media. Alongside Lacy, Leuckessia Hirsh and Unique Holland, various artists, architects and poets assisted as guests within the summer programme. There was always a team of six teaching and supporting the 36 women attending, 32 of which completed the course.[119] The young mothers who joined

---

crimes, mostly committed by males in their mid-teens. However, by adulthood, it is disproportionately young men who were victims of crime as children that appear within the criminal justice system, while young women who were victims of crime as children become users of the health care system. Also see Lacy, 2013, p. 83.

117   Marx, 1990, p. 275.
118   Weinstein 1998, pp. 127–8. For more on the attacks on reproductive rights for the poor, and how this is racialised within the US, see Davis 1983.
119   Lacy notes this was a 'remarkably high rate' for completion. See Suzanne Lacy, speaking at the 'Working in public' seminar series at Robert Gordon University in 2007.

the programme had been nominated by adults within partnering organisations and schools, and were required to fill out an application from which they were selected.[120] The classes took place at the YWCA, and the women participating had free meals and childcare during the course. In terms of the content Lacy developed for this 'curriculum as artwork', the focus was on the body and this drew strongly upon Lacy's earlier experiences in all-female, feminist art environments in California during the 1970s. In *Expectations*, Lacy prioritised the young women's relationships to their body, 'because we found that young women did not talk about their bodies and the changes that were happening to their bodies'.[121]

This involved talking about sexuality, alongside the social conditions the women lived in and that their babies would soon enter. The young women also read, wrote, did life size drawings of their bodies, made timelines of their relationships, video diaries and worked with a poet. (Fig. 17) Within the focus on the body, specific themes emerged including the women's relationships with their baby's father, family, social services, politics and the public, and throughout they made drawings that were subsequently included in the exhibition at Capp Street Gallery. Participants also discussed the PRWORA and though Lacy notes that the teenagers 'did not necessarily put the whole thing together' –

> The young women came with a lot of sophisticated experience and observations ... they certainly did understand when people turned around and looked at a girl with a big belly on a bus. They understood the permission that members of the public gave themselves to touch the young woman's belly or to comment on her state. Those people would often be white and the girl often, though not exclusively, would be Black. That was something that they talked about repeatedly. It shows an awareness of the way their image operated on a local level.[122]

With Lacy, Unique Holland and the other coordinators, the young women also did physical exercise and developed dances. The group also worked with a graphic designer to produce a document that was sent to legislators and politicians across the state. Like the rest of *The Oakland Projects*, *Expectations* sought to work with public policy, both through the document and a symposium held at the close of the exhibition.

---

120 Suzanne Lacy, personal interview, 26 May 2013.
121 Ibid.
122 Ibid.

FIGURE 17   Suzanne Lacy with Leslie Becker, Lisa Findley, Amana Harris, Leuckessia Hirsh, Unique Holland, Annice Jacoby, Sheila Jordan and Maxine Wyman, Image of summer school workshop within the *Expectations* project, 1996–97
PHOTO BY SUZANNE LACY. COURTESY OF SUZANNE LACY

While the structuring of the summer school around the immediate experiences of the young women connects with the principals behind worker education that formed the foundations of Segal's dance projects, Lacy's pedagogy was in fact formed within the West Coast feminist art scene of the 1970s. As a teacher within the Feminist Studio Workshop in the early 1970s, Lacy had also introduced the topic of welfare.[123] Going back a little further to the beginnings of the West Coast feminist art scene, in 1968 Lacy began a graduate programme in psychology at Fresno State College in California, following her work as a community organiser for the Volunteers in Service to America programme (VISTA). At that time, Fresno had a department called the 'Experimental College' within which Lacy ran a course in feminist psychology; other courses included Chicano studies, African American studies, Marxism and anarchist theory. With Faith Wilding, Lacy coordinated a feminist reading group and consciousness-raising group and these projects, alongside her background in psychology, informed the development of Lacy's practice as based upon processes of social interaction.[124]

In 1970, Judy Chicago joined Fresno to run the first Feminist Art Program, intent on creating an alternative structure for women artists and her own artistic development. After some lobbying, Wilding, an English literature student, and Lacy, a psychology student, were admitted to the Feminist Art Program, which at the outset met off-site in order to establish its autonomy from the College.[125] In the autumn of 1971, the Feminist Art Program moved from Fresno to the recently founded California Institute of the Arts (CalArts). Although Lacy also transferred to CalArts, she joined the Women's Design Program (directed by Sheila de Bretteville) rather than the Feminist Art Program, meaning she was not directly involved with Womanhouse, perhaps the most renowned feminist art experiment of the early 1970s. Through the design programme, Lacy encountered Allan Kaprow, who was teaching there. Alongside Judy Chicago, he had a formative influence on Lacy, with real congruence existing between Kaprow's Happenings and the development of early feminist performance.[126] As Lacy writes, Kaprow's interest in secular, daily 'rituals' such as sweeping the floor or brushing your teeth was closely linked with contemporaneous feminist practice, such as Mierle Laderman Ukeles' Maintenance Art. Lacy also describes the differentiated art-world reception of this form of performance when done by women: whilst Kaprow's work was read as a formal investigation into repetitive movement, work by women was read almost solely through its political content.[127]

---

123 Lacy 1994, pp. 267–8.
124 Like so many educational institutions across the US, the last years of the 1960s at Fresno State College were full of political ferment, and Lacy was involved in struggles supporting the United Farm Workers, demonstrations against the Vietnam War, and protests against the dismissal of radical faculty members.
125 Irish 2010, pp. 25–6.
126 Wilding 1994.
127 Lacy and. Lippard 2010, pp. 156–7.

The reception of 1970s feminist art has gone through a number of battles, including what Helen Molesworth describes as the essentialism vs. post-structuralism debate, which took up Judy Chicago as exemplary of the former, and Mary Kelly as representing the latter.[128] In a convincing leap, Molesworth opens up this dichotomy through the work of Laderman Ukeles and Martha Rosler in order to demonstrate that all four of these artists were criticising the naturalisation of domestic labour as female, and questioning the split between the private and public sphere.[129] Laderman Ukeles' *Maintenance Art Manifesto* (1969) follows the same logic as many Marxist-feminist investigations into domestic labour and can therefore assist in analysing the thematic of social reproduction within Segal's work and Lacy's *Expectations*. Like Inman, Laderman Ukeles divides human labour into two categories, development and maintenance, which stand for production and reproduction. In her account, these categories take on an aesthetic content, with development meaning 'pure individual creation; the new; change; progress; advance; excitement; flight or fleeing' and maintenance described in the following terms: 'Keep the dust off the pure individual creation; preserve the new; sustain the change; protect progress; defend and prolong the advance; renew the excitement; repeat the flight'.[130] The manifesto insists that the progress, change and individual creation typically associated with modernity (capitalist production) are reliant on the hidden and unglamorous labour of maintenance (reproductive labour). Laderman Ukeles extended this dichotomy beyond the household into the art institution, where she made visible the work of professional cleaners. Sent to art institutions, the manifesto was essentially a project proposal that Ukeles would live in the museum and perform her maintenance activities. She proposed that she would 'sweep and wax the floors, dust everything, wash the walls', creating 'floor paintings, dust works, soap-sculpture, wall-paintings'.[131]

Laderman Ukeles's *Maintenance Art* illuminated the private sphere in order to reconsider the public, an endeavour common to Kelly's *Post-Partum Document*, which represented two forms of labour undertaken by Kelly; artwork and domestic work. By staging the two forms of work together, Molesworth convin-

---

128 Molesworth's article opens with a discussion of the late 1990s revival of 1970s feminism, which was articulated in a number of exhibitions and publications. Like the 1930s and 1990s, Molesworth's analysis suggests that the 1970s form another point during which there was a proliferation of collective, community art works staged in relation to political crisis in the US, an issue that is regrettably beyond the scope of this book. Molesworth 2010, p. 72. See also Stakemeier and Vishmidt 2016, pp. 85–91 for a related discussion.
129 Molesworth 2000, p. 77.
130 Molesworth 2000, p. 78 and Mierle Laderman Ukeles, 'Maintenance Art Manifesto'.
131 Laderman Ukeles.

cingly argues that *Post-Partum Document* debunks 'the myth of nonwork that surround both forms of re-production (artist as genius, mother as natural)'.[132] Set within the aesthetic parameters of conceptual art – the populist critique of which is usually along the lines of 'anyone can do it' – *Post-Partum Document* 'suggests that the same is true of the labor of mothering, for to de-naturalize such labor is to make it non-gender-specific'.[133] *Post-Partum Document* and *Maintenance Art* make domestic work visible, but as Molesworth emphasises, by doing art work as domestic work, and domestic work as art work, both works problematise these activities as similarly un-subjected to the laws of value (as opposed to wage labour).[134]

In connection with this, the Californian collective Mother Art that grew out of the Woman's Building in Los Angeles offer a prescient example of how similar moral controversies began to emerge over state spending for welfare and funding for the arts at the onset of the neoliberal American state. In their 1977 *Laundryworks*, Mother Art produced Laundromat performances timed to wash and dry cycles. These involved doing actual laundry, pinning up washing lines and hanging artworks across them. Alongside performances and temporary exhibitions, a pamphlet was available in English and Spanish explaining that *Laundryworks* was intended to 'transform the tedium and drudgery of the work by providing fresh visions in an effort to bring about an awareness of ourselves as human beings sharing a common task with the community'.[135] Yet, despite *Laundryworks* being based on re-imagining the split between public/private spheres, the project is difficult to compare with Inman's visions of professionalising domestic labour. Instead, Mother Art *affirmed* the tasks carried out in these spaces along moral lines, and sought to transform the alienation and boredom of the commercial laundries by designating the activities carried out within them as art. Therefore, unlike the conceptual nominalism of Laderman Ukeles' earlier *Maintenance Art*, the aesthetic of *Laundryworks* was compensatory, with its place as an artwork valorised as the means by which certain tasks might become less stifling. This aspect, alongside the fact that Mother Art had been awarded a $700 grant from the California Art Council, set up particular stakes for the public reception of *Laundryworks*, which bear upon the status of *Expectations* as a social practice artwork is inseparable from its direct engagement in social reproduction.

---

132   Molesworth 2000, p. 87.
133   Ibid.
134   Although of course the difference is that in the popular imaginary, housework is seen as primitive, and art is often positioned as an escape from wage labour.
135   Moravec 2003, p. 72.

In 1978, a year after the project was over, *Laundryworks* became a controversial example of supposedly wasteful government spending following the passage of Proposition 13, a piece of legislation that lowered property taxes in California and limited increases.[136] As discussed in the introduction and previous chapter, one of the primary effects of Proposition 13 was a drastic reduction in public revenue that caused California's public schools to fall from fifth in the country in per-pupil spending to 45th by the 1990s. Proposition 13 therefore had a drastic impact upon the educational opportunities offered to the youth participating in *The Oakland Projects*.[137] In the wake of this legislation and the constriction of public spending, an article in the *Los Angeles Times* ridiculed Mother Art and *Laundryworks* as an absurd waste of public funds that attempted to bring culture to housewives. Following this 'exposé', Mother Art briefly became the poster girls for right-wing attacks on public spending and none other than Ronald Reagan waded into the debate, laying into the collective on air whilst doing a stint as a talk show host in between being Governor of California and President of the United States. With the legislation of Proposition 13 forming an important backdrop to the reception of *Laundryworks*, we can see how the New Deal consensus over the necessity for welfare and public spending was largely diminished by the end of the 1970s, with art positioned as especially wasteful when it sought to address social need.[138] Yet, by the 1990s, and the emergence of *The Oakland Projects*, art was being positioned as a salve to the crisis prompted by reductions in public spending on welfare and education.

These works from the 1970s illuminate the political stakes surrounding my argument that we consider both Segal's practice and *Expectations* through the lens of social reproduction, because across each example, the representation and staging of motherhood and domestic labour *as art* shift our conception of these activities. Yet, in observing the trajectory from Segal's dances

---

136   McLaughlin et. al. 2009, pp. 42–3.
137   Meyerson 2009.
138   Enraged by how politicians and the press were adamant that women doing laundry did not want or deserve access to culture, Mother Art organised a series of protests/performances in response. *Mother Art Cleans Up City Hall* and *Mother Art Cleans Up the Banks* (1978) involved scrubbing and dusting the exterior of these buildings as a gesture highlighting the 'real source of waste and corruption of public interest'. See Liss 2009, p. 2. Unlike Laderman Ukeles, then, Mother Art performed an affirmation of art and domestic labour as 'useful' and the state and banks as 'useless', a form of moral opposition that foreshadows recent developments in social practice such as Tania Bruguera's establishment of a manifesto for '*Arte Útil*' (Useful Art). These connections are discussed further in the coda to the book.

through the works dating to the 1970s to *Expectations*, my contention is that the aesthetic dimension of this work becomes compromised, as affective and caring labour becomes increasingly inseparable from artistic labour.[139] In contrast with Segal's dance works, the attention to reproduction in *Expectations* is less about the maintenance and growth of an oppositional culture, and more about the very reproduction of life. Further, unlike Laderman Ukeles and Kelly, *Expectations* cannot be assessed as a conceptual investigation into the content and form of particular activities. Rather, the character of *Expectations* can be seen as foreshadowed by the moral affirmation of *Laundryworks*, and the increased proximity therein between art and social care within the context of a shrinking state.

The extreme investment demanded by the *Expectations* summer school from Lacy and her collaborators is illuminating in this respect. Lacy recalls that by the midpoint of the programme, all involved were exhausted. She stresses that the producers faced the 'overwhelming reality of working with youth' in a more acute way than other aspects of *The Oakland Projects*, and closely experienced the systems that perpetually fail young people.[140] The artists, designers and choreographers teaching on the project constantly faced obstacles to making art, as the 'sheer effort to provide personal support and social services' was overwhelming. Lacy stresses that only Amana Harris, who had worked locally as a high school teacher, was remotely prepared for the work the project demanded.[141] Clearly, inserting questions of reproduction into the public sphere at the point of conflict (an education programme for teen mothers) is different from staging the relation between art and reproduction in the art institution (as with Kelly and Laderman Ukeles). In this sense, it becomes important to analyse the appearance of *Expectations* within the Capp Street Gallery, and how this related to the summer school programme. Namely, what aesthetic emerged within the installation, and how did it visually mediate the 1970s inflected feminist pedagogy of the programme?

---

139 Helena Reckitt describes the work of Ukeles as the forgotten, or perhaps ignored history behind much of the work promoted by Bourriaud as Relational Aesthetics. Through this, Reckitt also provides a persuasive, feminist argument against a clear-cut periodisation of 'immaterial' production within art and the broader economy. She suggests that curators such as Bourriaud and social practice more generally often focus upon activities previously denigrated as reproductive or affective labour, identifying this turn as linked with the broader 'feminisation of labour', i.e. a rise in precarious, service-oriented jobs. See Reckitt 2013, p. 151.
140 Lacy, PhD thesis, 2013, p. 88.
141 Ibid.

FIGURE 18   Suzanne Lacy with Leslie Becker, Lisa Findley, Amana Harris, Leuckessia Hirsh, Unique Holland, Annice Jacoby, Sheila Jordan and Maxine Wyman, Image of drawing made by summer school programme participant within the *Expectations* project, 1996–97
PHOTO BY JEFF MCLANE. COURTESY OF SUZANNE LACY

7   *Expectations* at Capp Street Gallery

In the *Expectations* exhibition at Capp Street Gallery, the viewer was immediately confronted with an oversized, 12-foot high crib, so enormous that it is difficult from the images of the installation to determine what this object represents. The audience had to squeeze through the limited space between the crib and wall of the gallery, meaning the number of viewers at any one time was limited by the spatial constraints imposed by the crib. Affixed to the wall facing the side of the crib through which the audience passed were small-scale reproductions of the drawings made by the teenagers, documenting the progress of their relationships and childbirth. (Fig. 18) The scale of these diaristic images contrasted with the crib imply that the narrative leading up to the birth was squashed by the presence of a child, and because of the size of the crib, viewers encountered the drawings at very close range.

At the end of the narrow passage, the crib was open, and the audience could climb a set of stairs to enter. A disordered arrangement of school desks, chairs,

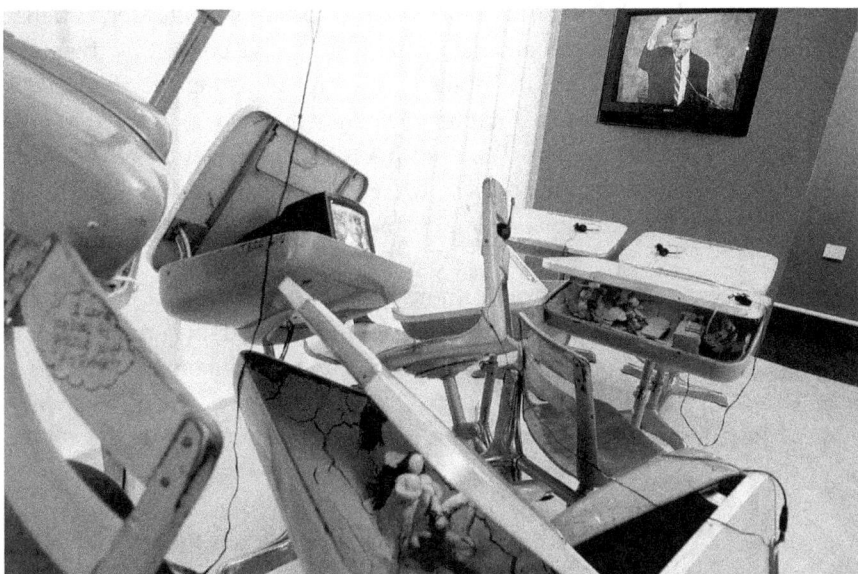

FIGURE 19   Suzanne Lacy with Leslie Becker, Lisa Findley, Amana Harris, Leuckessia Hirsh, Unique Holland, Annice Jacoby, Sheila Jordan and Maxine Wyman, *Expectations*, 1996–97, installation at Capp Street Gallery, San Francisco, California
PHOTO BY SUZANNE LACY

and televisions concealed smaller elements like the clay figurines created by the young women during the summer school. The desks and chairs were standard issue school furniture and arranged to appear as if they had been knocked over, or lifted up. (Fig. 19) Pushed together and piled on top of each other, some of the furniture was also suspended from the ceiling. The backs of the chairs and desktops were inscribed with graffiti written in curved, adolescent script normally associated with affirmations of high school crushes or a favourite sports team. Here, the scrawl declares instead 'I want my baby to grow up with his Father!!' Inside the desks, amateurish small clay sculptures represented the process of birth, or scenarios tracking the reactions and social expectations they confronted as pregnant and parenting teenagers.

Expectations was the only aspect of *The Oakland Projects* which had its 'public' component exhibited within an art institution. Unlike all the other public acts within *The Oakland Projects*, which were manifested as performances or video works, *Expectations* involved the production of an installation and presentation of objects. It is somewhat ironic, then, that given the appearance of *Expectations* within an art institution and its use of more orthodox mediums, it has received far less attention than the performance works from *The Oakland Projects*. One reason for this might be that the installation in some ways repeated the then unfashionable visual tropes of so-called 'essentialist' 1970s feminist art. In their scale and content, the works created by the participants and installed within the desks by Lacy relate strongly to works such as Sherry Brody and Miriam Schapiro's *The Dollhouse* (1972) Created for the Womanhouse exhibition, this displayed many of the tendencies that would become clichés of the feminist art movement. The overall effect of *The Dollshouse* was to make feminine décor monstrous. As Schapiro describes –

> As you peer inside each sumptuous and ordered room, the organic harmony implicit in nesting becomes evident. Real and imaginary invading creatures, however, disturb the serenity ... Outside the nursery window, a giant grizzly bear sits nearby in an alabaster egg, menaced by a scorpion ... Ten men stare in at the kitchen window ... a mysterious menace from the outside.[142]

The aesthetic combination of the monstrous and the feminine, particularly when produced by women artists, has frequently been analysed through Julia Kristeva's theory of the abject.[143] This refers to a phenomenological experience in which the boundaries of the body and the integrity of the self are unsettled: death, sex, defecation, vomiting, menstruation, childbirth and pregnancy are all states Kristeva associates with the affective qualities of abjection.[144] As already mentioned, *Endnotes* mobilise Kristeva's concept of abjection to describe how domestic work may be attached to or cast off from women at various points, but nevertheless always forms part of their existence within capitalism. In many ways the overall content of the Womanhouse exhibition was marked by the repeated appearance of that which could be termed abject, including Judy Chicago's *Menstruation Bathroom* and Robbin Schiff's *Nightmare Bathroom*. Formally similar to these works, the small clay figurines that the young women from the summer school had made and concealed in the installation of *Expectations* represented birth, a bodily state normally hidden from view.

---

142 Schapiro, quoted in the online archive of content from Womanhouse http://womanhouse.refugia.net/.
143 The popularity of Kristeva's theory of abjection for a reading of art works seems to have reached an apex in the mid-1990s, spurred on by the exhibition 'Abject Art: Repulsion and Desire in American Art', which took place at the Whitney Museum of Art in 1993. See the catalogue Houser, Jones et al. (eds.) 1993. Hal Foster also gives an account of Cindy Sherman and Kiki Smith's work in terms of the abject as specifically feminine.
144 Kristeva 1982.

My description of this imagery as clichéd rests on Martha Rosler's criticism of the work around Womanhouse. As she wrote

> [V]alorizing, in the name of 'women's culture', traditional handicrafts developed under conditions oppressive to women (or under preindustrial relations of production) is liable, at the least, to be misunderstood. Even more, valorizing fantasies of the self and the world born of these conditions may wind up serving repressive ends.[145]

Within the installation of *Expectations*, the small clay figurines as well as the drawings could potentially be seen as uncritically inheriting the tendency to affirm 'natural' qualities of 'womanhood', characteristic of aspects of 1970s feminist art. Furthermore, following Rosler, the naïve amateurism – even primitivism – of their form could be viewed as creating a feedback loop with the ideological positioning of women, particularly women of colour, as in need of authoritative paternalism (in this case, the 1996 welfare reform). Yet, the process of ideology critique introduced by the summer school, drawing on the methods of 1970s feminist pedagogy but foregrounding a critique of contemporary political economy, destabilises this effect. Furthermore, within the installation, the style of the small sculptures was forcefully undercut by the audio-visual component, demonstrating that despite a proximity of style and process, the thematisation of social reproduction within *Expectations* involved forms of oppositional analysis perhaps absent in the 'cultural feminism' criticised by Rosler.

At the back of the crib, next to the desks concealing the figurines, a monitor was installed which played a short video. This looped together imagery of a speech by the then Republican Governor of California Pete Wilson alongside a video of Asha Zitani, one of the young women who participated in *Expectations*, reading a letter in response to Wilson. Interspersed between these two dialogues are shots of the California legislators to whom Wilson delivered his 1997 State of the State Address, and shots of the group that participated in the *Expectations* summer school. The contrast between the bodies of Wilson and Zitani, and the legislature and *Expectations* group is, of course, stark. The video opens with Wilson declaring that the reform introduced by Clinton, demanding that three-quarters of a million welfare recipients find work, had hammered home the need to transform welfare in California. Wilson states that 'if we fail

---

145 Rosler 1977, p. 68.

to meet that requirement ... the new law imposes substantial penalties on us. But greater than any financial cost, is the human cost to people, who stay on welfare rather than work'. Going on to describe welfare as 'incentivising' out-of-wedlock birth, Wilson's punitive, ideological rhetoric makes a causative link between dependency on state funds and 'pathological blight' amongst poor communities. In his speech, fatherless boys are 'overwhelmingly more likely to end up behind bars' and 'illegitimacy hatches social pathology'. Fading in and out of the audio track is the sound of the legislature applauding. Wilson's words are played out of synch with the picture, his image appearing more like a puppet, or a badly dubbed film.[146]

Clapping acts as a constant low-lying backing track to Wilson's out-of-synch address, swelling into a wave of applause and increasing in volume as the camera pans across the members of the legislature in slow motion. The effect of a delay on the image in relation to the sound contradicts Wilson's authoritative tone and muddies the speech he delivers. The final part of this section erases Wilson's voice entirely and leaves only the backing track of applause, which plays over Wilson delivering his now silenced speech and more shots of the legislature. The screen then fades to black, before a shot of a Black toddler appears on screen, and here the image quality becomes that of a home video as opposed to the mass media produced camera angles and slow pans across the legislature that characterised the shots of Wilson. The toddler appears on screen for a number of seconds before Zitani faces the camera and reads aloud her response to Wilson. Zitani begins by stating that she found Wilson's speech 'very disrespectful and ignorant'. The video of Zitani reading her letter is interspersed with shots of a room of young, mostly Black and Latinx women gathered together. As the legislature stands for the community Wilson represents, Zitani here stands for the community of *Expectations*. These representations coalesce into types, as in *The Oakland Projects* performances discussed in the previous chapter, with Zitani positioned as powerfully capable of counteracting the ideology spouted by Wilson. Zitani's speech goes on to state that she works 'extremely hard, as do other poor welfare families, because I have the biggest responsibility of raising the future ... Being a mother takes so much strength and energy ... I am a teacher, nurturer, doctor, provider, protector, cooker, cleaner'.[147] This rhetoric of 'working hard' at being a mother as the justification against cutting welfare of course links back strongly to those

---

146 These quotes are all drawn from the film, courtesy of Suzanne Lacy.
147 Ibid.

arguments made in the 1930s by housewives' organisations that articulated the care of families and reproductive labour *as work*, as well as 1970s campaigns such as Wages for Housework.

The video work is counterposed or played off against the small sculptures and drawings of birth, family and their placement on the interior and exterior of the giant crib. The contrast between the public 'political' sphere of Pete Wilson's speech and other elements of the installation creates a dynamic that avoids romanticising birth or pregnancy but instead disrupts the cliché that the domestic sphere operates at arms-length from the social or the public. In situating these very 'feminine', crafty and amateurish sculptures and drawings in relation to the video's representation of the public sphere, the installation at Capp Street laid bare the function and necessity for capitalism of the spheres' separation. The installation also problematised the split between 'essentialist' and 'post-structural' feminism along the lines identified by Molesworth in Laderman Ukeles and Rosler's work from the 1970s. By revealing how the private labour of birth, mothering and reproduction is *always* politicised, especially in relation to ideological shifts which manifest in the material structures of welfare reform, the installation firmly de-naturalised the idea that reproductive labour is outside the political sphere and immanent to the category woman.

8 Conclusion: Reproducing Culture, Reproducing Life

Segal's dance works and Lacy's *Expectations* illuminate the stakes of social reproduction as a paradigm for thinking through these periods that saw increased activity among artists working 'socially'. The projects examined here involved work by women who were not primarily dancers or artists that allowed for an exploration of their broader living conditions. However, there are crucial differences that allow us to understand the changing stakes for artists working in this way. Segal's and Lacy's practices are of course reflective of the different circumstances of production in the 1930s and the 1990s and are sharply distinguished by the reconfiguration of the arena in which they enact or address social change, as well as by the subject-participant at their forefront. Segal worked primarily with unionised female industrial workers and the infrastructure for her projects was drawn from the communist movement. In contrast, Lacy worked with pregnant and parenting teenagers, mostly unemployed and not participating in formal education outside of the *Expectations* summer school, which was supported by Alameda County Office for Education, the Capp Street Gallery and other public and third sector partners. The relationship between the subject-participant of these works and the institutions that supported their making is telling. It marks the caesura between these two periods as one linked to the dissolution of the forms of organisation that supported an oppositional culture centred on affirming the worker against capital. By paying attention to debates on gender, and how they frequently fell outside this affirmation within leftist circles during the 1930s–40s, as the case of Inman attests, we get a hint towards the current impossibility of a comparably work-centric, anti-capitalist movement. Considering *Expectations* in relation to Segal's dances clarifies the changes in class formation along gendered and racialised lines, but also enables us to see these intersecting forms of oppression as ever-present, rather than as resulting from a clean historical break.

In order to analyse this transformation in relation to *Expectations* and Segal's dances, I discussed works from the canon of 1970s feminist art to emphasise the changes and growth in artistic engagements with social reproduction and 'women's work'. As those examples highlight, the thematisation of social reproduction within art has hugely expanded since the 1930s, with its formal qualities and status as art provoking on the one hand a de-naturalisation of domestic labour, and on the other, a moral and political affirmation of staging 'women's work' as capable of leading transformations in social relations within the sphere of art and culture. To be sure, the ideology of 1970s West Coast feminist art frequently valorised 'women's culture', and as Rosler emphasised, 'fantasies of the self and the world born of these conditions'.[148] Yet, contra poststructuralist critiques from the 1990s, the affirmation of 'woman' during the 1970s should not be hermetically sealed and dismissed as a hopelessly 'essentialist' strategy. Rather, I argue that the affirmation of womanhood as a political identity was a step within the trajectory of the feminist movement, just as the workers' movement historically affirmed a 'worker' identity as emancipatory, with this characteristic strongly present in much of Segal's work.

By situating Segal's and Lacy's work together, we gain a dialectical view of aesthetic engagements with class and gender, and the ability to think beyond the total affirmation or negation of those identities as political strategy, or aesthetic experience. As my discussion has demonstrated, the diminishing of the ideal type of the worker, affected by the transformations in the state's management of labour and social reproduction, must also be understood through the limitations of that type. Yet, in approaching the somewhat reduced or austere quality of *Expectations* – in that the project demonstrates the pressure for socially engaged art to provide forms of social care abandoned by the state – we

---

148   Rosler 1977.

can reflect on the continued resonance of Segal's dance works, centred instead on the reproduction of a revolutionary politics. My concern is not with a nostalgic valorisation of Segal's dances over *Expectations* as a method of collaborative cultural work, but rather to question how we can re-actualise earlier forms of struggle in the present.

CHAPTER 3

Housing, Homelessness and Documentary

In this chapter, I address two projects that sought to challenge the perpetual housing crisis in the United States through the aesthetics of social documentary, albeit in the expanded form of an exhibition and a performance. The chapter begins with an analysis of Martha Rosler's *If You Lived Here ...* (1989–90) in order to foreground questions about the relationship between social documentary and social practice. *If You Lived Here ...* (1989–90) attempted to reckon with the limits of a representational approach to dispossession, long a preoccupation within Rosler's practice. The project revolved around three exhibitions at the Dia Art Foundation in SoHo, New York City, which displayed work on housing and urban development by numerous artists and activists. Alongside the exhibitions, public programmes opened up discussion and the project also incorporated the work of existing support groups for the homeless into its structure. I approach *If You Lived Here ...* in relation to Rosler's engagement with Depression-era documentary photography in order to emphasise how social practice in the 1990s frequently attempted to sidestep the burden of representation, whilst addressing similar social issues as those concerning the documentarians of the 1930s. The chapter then turns to *One-Third of a Nation* (1938), a Living Newspaper produced by the WPA-FTP that responded to the Wagner-Steagall Housing Act of 1937. Similar to *If You Lived Here ... One-Third of a Nation* was preoccupied with the role of development and financial speculation in the housing crisis and took this up through a performative, expanded social documentary. Through this chapter, two central questions emerge. Firstly, what kind of historical models are available within cultural work of the 1930s and 1990s and how do these shape the morals and politics of social documentary and social practice? Secondly, if both projects indexed the past in order to propose solutions in the present, what limitations emerge from this emphasis on historical facts?

A crucial route in exploring these questions rests upon interrogating the frequent yet differing invocations of a usable past within *If You Lived Here ...* and *One-Third of a Nation*. As described in this book's introduction, the concept of a usable past gained particular force during the Depression years, when the interrogation of American history took shape across a broad range of cultural initiatives, from the WPA Index of American Design to the seventeen-volume collection *Slave Narratives: A Folk History of Slavery in the United States from Interviews with Former Slaves conducted by the WPA Federal Writers Project*. As

Alfred Haworth Jones writes, the search for a usable past during the 1930s was situated both as an effort to summarise and close a chapter – with 1929 posited as a historical break – and conversely as a means to shape the future by studying the successes and failures of the past.[1] It is largely the latter approach that informs the works discussed in this chapter, with their expanded documentary indexing a history from which conclusions for the present might be drawn. In this chapter, I not only seek to illuminate the stakes of invoking a usable past during the 1930s, but stress how the internalisation of that idea within social documentary provides a seed-bed for some founding tenets within the formation of social practice in the 1990s, within which *If You Lived Here ...* stands as exemplary.

The politics of home, community and nation are embedded into these works and shaped by the way that the American state has consistently yoked its housing policy to the private sector. Since President Hoover and the first formation of a Federal housing policy, home ownership has been emphasised as preferable to the collective provision of affordable mass housing.[2] In 1931, the Hoover Administration responded to the Depression by issuing the Hoover commission report on Home Building and Home Ownership that led to the development of 50 million single-family homes.[3] Citizens were given state assistance to purchase these properties through the Federal Home Loan Bank Act of 1932, which established a reserve banking institution for home mortgage lending. In 1933, the Home Owners Loan Act provided further funds to help individuals and families re-mortgage their homes.[4] Despite the welfare policies instigated by the 1937 Housing Act, which forms an important legislative backdrop to this chapter, the majority of the New Deal housing programmes continued this pattern, aimed at resuscitating the private housing system.[5] Quangos created during the New Deal such as the Federal Home Loan Bank Board, the Federal Housing Authority (FHA), the Home Owners' Loan Corporation, and the Federal National Mortgage Association, (better known by the colloquial 'Fannie Mae') have subsequently been at the forefront of innovations in mortgage lending throughout the twentieth century.[6] The extension of credit to the working class was enabled through a variety of financial mechanisms including the

---

1 Haworth Jones 1971, pp. 710–11.
2 Marcuse and Keating 2006, p. 144.
3 Hayden 1981, p. 8.
4 Marcuse and Keating 2006, p. 141.
5 Marcus and Keating 2006, p. 144.
6 Hays 1985, p. 84.

securitisation of mortgages and collateralised mortgage obligations.[7] By the 1990s, what we now call the subprime mortgage bubble began to grow, with the introduction of credit default swaps and other financial instruments.[8] The steady growth of lending for home ownership forms part of the present normalisation of debt as a means of maintaining the daily needs of social reproduction, especially for low-income groups, women and people of colour.[9] This individualisation of social reproduction through debt has certainly become more extreme since the advent of neoliberalism, but it is by no means a break from the past. Comparing the imbrication of debt, housing and social reproduction during these two periods shows us that as the working class has apparently waned from view within American political discourse, it remains ever structurally reinforced as a subject position.

Through grasping the interdependency of fictitious capital, production and reproduction that underpins the history of housing policy in the US, we gain a more dialectical view of the relationship between the 1930s and 1990s, free from nostalgia for a golden era of 'real', industrial labour and a minimal welfare state as a more moral or palatable form of capitalism. By recognising that land value and finance capital – despite its 'fictitious' status – always involves a claim on future labour in the form of rent, we can also avoid falling for the idea that labour in the west under neoliberal governance is 'immaterial', a buzzword which continues to recur in the analysis of social practice as a 'dematerialised' art form.[10] As mentioned in the introduction, the growth of this type of art practice is frequently viewed as simply reflecting de-industrialisation and finance capital.[11] It is worth repeating my central claim within this book that a comparative history that takes up the interaction of state, nation and community presents the best case against such a truncated sense of the contemporary

---

7   Bellamy Foster and Magdoff 2009, p. 94.
8   Schwartz 2009, p. 191.
9   Roberts 2013, p. 22.
10   By drawing on Marx's unfinished work, David Harvey asserts that the categories of ground rent and land value must be understood as part of the overall dynamic of capital, despite their appearance as contradictory to the value form. Unlike production, labour is not the source of value when we look at land and this is why Marx includes it in his analysis of 'fictitious capital'. Harvey writes that within capitalism, 'Fictitious capital in land makes its claim upon future labor indirectly (as in the case of housing purchase with the aid of a mortgage) through the future circulation of wages and other forms of revenue'. The way land as fictitious capital mobilises a claim on future labour means that members of the working class are compelled to sell their labour power at a price appropriate to the fluctuating cost of housing. This becomes particularly important where state provision of housing is slight, as in the US. See Harvey 1989, p. 102 and Harvey 1982, p. 347.
11   See Bishop 2012, pp. 216 and 231 and Fraser 1997, pp. 111–16.

stakes of social practice, allowing us to think more carefully about how particular artworks mediate the social.

1   *If You Lived Here ...*

Between 1974–5, the artist Martha Rosler photographed scenes on the Bowery, a street in New York that has long been mythologised within literature, art and cinema. These photographs, paired with text, comprise the series entitled *The Bowery in two inadequate descriptive systems* (completed 1976), a critical response to the histories of documentary photography in the US. As she wrote, the Bowery had become the archetypal New York 'skid row', with this designation reinforced by the proliferation of documentarians detailing the strip through the twentieth century. The photographic representation of The Bowery's inhabitants express a range of sentiments, from outrage to moralism to 'slumming spectacle', existing as 'concerned photography', exposé or even surveillance.[12] Within these images, the homeless person often comes to exist as a kind of 'end game' with that individual judged as having made a 'miserable *choice*'.[13] In contrast to this history, Rosler rendered her subject absent, with the black and white photographs of the shop fronts and detritus signifying the denizens of the street through discarded liquor bottles and cigarette packets. The absent figures here are of course those members of the surplus population that Marx viewed as impossible for political economy to acknowledge, and Rosler's reluctance to capture their image dramatises this lack of recognition, refusing the role of the documentarian as camera-eye for the judge, bailiff or policeman.[14]

In 1981, Rosler wrote the following, which helps to frame her intentions in *The Bowery*, and the continued valences of documentary photography within the conception and structure of *If You Lived Here ...*:

> Let us consider the Bowery again, the site of victim photography in which the victims, insofar as they are now victims of the camera – that is, of the photographer – are often docile, whether through mental confusion or because they are just lying there, unconscious ... Especially now, the

---

12   Rosler 1990, p. 303.
13   Rosler 1990, p. 322.
14   Marx 1988, p. 86. This also returns to the argument made by Denning in 'Wageless Life', as discussed in the previous two chapters. For a closer discussion of *The Bowery in two inadequate descriptive systems*, see Edwards 2010.

meaning of all such work, past and present, has changed: the liberal New Deal state has been dismantled piece by piece. The War on Poverty has been called off. Utopia has been abandoned, and liberalism itself has been deserted.[15]

Rosler's statement in the above quote that *the meaning of all such work* – classic representations of the homeless – had changed with the onset of neoliberalism foregrounds her return to social documentary as a method for analysing dispossession during the turn of the 1980s with *If You Lived Here ...* As she explains, *The Bowery in two inadequate descriptive systems* was emphatically not a dismissive or ironic quotation of classic documentary photography, but rather an attempt to look at a 'history that was decrepit' but in need of revision.[16] This notion underpins Rosler's continued mobilisation of social documentary as a usable past. However, if *The Bowery in two inadequate descriptive systems* interrogated documentary photography's frequent didacticism, *If You Lived Here ...* necessarily took on an agitational tone towards the subject of homelessness following the abandonment of utopia, and even the desertion of liberalism.

In the late 1980s, the subject of homelessness took on new urgency in the US. The numbers of people sleeping rough rose exponentially in cities like New York, which Rosalyn Deutsche ties to the 60 percent decline from 1975–81 in single room occupancy dwellings.[17] Single room occupancies were often part of hotels, or 'old-law' tenements that sheltered formerly homeless individuals; the absent subjects of Rosler's *The Bowery in two inadequate descriptive systems* would have typically resided in these buildings. The decline of single room occupancies also meant that the category of the 'bum' was replaced by the term 'homeless', as large sections of this population were evicted. With that transition, the stereotypical image of alcoholic single males was expanded to include 'bag ladies' and people suffering from mental illness. Throughout the 1980s, the category of the homeless broadened further to include war veterans, inner-city mothers and children as well as 'refugees from the rust belt and the foreclosed family farm'.[18] Homelessness became increasingly racialised, and the media's disproportionate focus on white homeless families was attached to the novelty of their dispossession.[19] Amidst this climate, Rosler returned to the question of

---

15   Rosler 1990, p. 307.
16   Buchloh 1999, p. 42. See also Rosler 2004 for a discussion of her return to questions of documentary within *If You Lived Here ...*
17   Deutsche 1996, p. 47.
18   Rosler, 'Fragments of a Metropolitan Viewpoint', p. 20.
19   Ibid.

housing, homelessness and the city, this time transforming the deconstructed documentary of *The Bowery in two inadequate descriptive systems* into a durational work grounded in collaborative production across a range of media. *If You Lived Here ...* was centred less on the politics of representation, and instead attempted to activate a social formation capable of analysing and practically responding to contemporary urban dispossession.

Rosler began the project in 1989 following an invitation from the Dia Foundation, which had been encouraged by board member Yvonne Rainer to broaden its public programming. At the time, Dia was well known for publishing book projects that were frequently politicised, but their public programme and exhibitions were far more conservative. Rainer also pushed for Group Material to be given a commission, and the two projects subsequently took place at a storefront space on Wooster Street in SoHo, making this a rare moment of explicitly political art in Dia's programming. Both commissions were framed under the umbrella of a 'Town Meeting' project that gained funding from the National Endowment for the Arts (NEA) and the New York State Council on the Arts. In applying to the NEA, Dia stated that the aim of the Town Meeting project was to 'bridge the disparate communities within the art world and between the art world and other communities and publics'.[20] The funding of this project coincided with the Culture Wars, discussed in the introduction, and its support by the NEA anticipates the institutional transformations that would follow in the 1990s and the prioritisation of funding for 'socially useful' projects. The location of Group Material's and Rosler's projects at Dia also chimed with the recuperation of alternative art practices within high-art institutions that took place in New York during the 1980s. Other examples include the emphasis on politicised work by artists including David Wojnarowicz and Group Material at the Whitney Biennale of 1985, or the 'Committed to Print' exhibition in 1988 at the Museum of Modern Art that displayed hundreds of radical-leaning works on paper.

Following on from Rosler's critique of liberal representations of the dispossessed with *The Bowery in two inadequate descriptive systems*, it is unsurprising that her impulse to do a project around housing in 1989–90 within a mainstream art institution was qualified by fears that it might end up as a 'pity show'.[21] Going beyond the contemporaneous co-opting of radical practices by mainstream institutions, Rosler's qualms were further complicated by the contradiction between Dia's sponsorship of the project and its implication in what

---

20 Rounthwaite 2017, p. 227.
21 Rosler personal interview, 3 October 2013.

she describes as the 'real estate/art institution nexus'.[22] As part of their expansion in the 1980s, Dia had acquired a significant amount of property in Tribeca and SoHo, thereby becoming deeply entangled in the forms of urban development Rosler's project criticised. The title of the project – styled with ellipses as *If You Lived Here ...* – referred to a real estate campaign slogan which read 'If You Lived Here ... You'd be home now' designed to advertise downtown condominiums to suburban commuters, a marketing strategy drawn from the logic that views poor areas as an urban frontier, ripe for pioneers. By 1989, when the project began, the instrumentalising of artists as urban pioneers was solidifying as a redevelopment strategy, with Mayor Ed Koch's initiation of the Artists Home Ownership Program in the earlier part of the 1980s standing as exemplary. By providing low interest loans, this programme enabled artists to buy units within 16 abandoned buildings in a dilapidated zone of the Lower East Side. Applying artists were requested to form groups and prepare architectural plans for the rehabilitation of the buildings into live/work units at a low cost.[23] The Program was eventually defeated in 1983 by local outrage at the city's desire to funnel three million dollars of public funds towards artists' housing, yet these plans remained an important point of reference during the public forums which took place as part of *If You Lived Here ...*[24]

While *If You Lived Here ...* is the first major project by an artist that sought to grapple directly with the instrumentalising of artists as a gentrifying force, Rosalyn Deutsche and Cara Gendel Ryan's 'The Fine Art of Gentrification' (1984) was foundational to Rosler's critique. In this article, Deutsche and Gendel Ryan argued that the art world played a 'crucial role' in the drastic transformation of SoHo and the Lower East Side.[25] Viewing gentrification as a form of neo-colonialism, Deutsche and Gendel Ryan highlight the racial dimensions of the 'reclaiming' of primarily working-class, black and Latinx neighbourhoods as a 'frontier' of urban renewal.[26] This forms an early contribution to the now significant and diverse body of literature on the role of artists and art institutions in urban gentrification that by 2002, more than a decade after *If You Lived Here ...*, resulted in Richard Florida's notorious affirmation of the 'creative class' and art as a tool of urban regeneration.[27] In response to Florida, and to the instrumentalising of art as a regenerating force by civic bodies and

---

22   Rosler, 'Fragments of a Metropolitan Viewpoint', p. 40.
23   Rosler, 'The Artists Home Ownership Program', p. 151.
24   Deutsche and Gendel Ryan 1984, pp. 101–2.
25   Deutsche and Gendel Ryan 1984, p. 94.
26   Ibid. See also Smith 1996.
27   Florida 2002.

corporations, Harvey, Gregory Sholette and many others have authored important critiques.[28] Yet, despite over three decades of discussion on the subject, hand-wringing self-criticism continues to dominate discussion among well-intentioned artists, critics and curators, with not enough attention being paid to race and class, despite the centrality of these categories to Gendel Ryan and Deutsche's pathbreaking analysis.[29] The frequent over-emphasis on 'cultural capital' tends to favour a myopic focus on the extent to which artists propel, and are complicit with, gentrification, always situating individual consumption and lifestyle choices as the agents of change rather than engaging in a materialist analysis of property markets and land speculation.[30]

It is of course no accident that the urban renewal of New York City via gentrification took place following the fiscal crisis of 1975. As Joshua Freeman argues, the fiscal crisis can now be viewed as a critical turning point in the history of privatisation, paving the way for New York City to become an early test-site for the 'fall of social democracy in America'.[31] This drastic re-alignment was bolstered by the addition of over 215,000 business, service and financial sector jobs to New York City's economy over the years 1977 to 1984, while over 100,000 blue-collar jobs were eliminated.[32] The transformation of labour markets gathered apace as the 1980s waned, and between January 1989 and December 1992 the nationwide recession hit New York harder than most of the country. Even the mid-1990s economic boom did not aid matters, and in 1998, fewer New York City residents held jobs than in 1989. During the 1990s, those New Yorkers employed outside the upper ranks of finance, real estate and business services continued to live in a recession.[33] Where they lived – and how they were able to defend their homes and communities – formed the focus of *If You Lived Here …*

Unfolding over a full year, Rosler's project encompassed exhibitions, screenings, public forums and events related to housing, organised into three sub-

---

28 Harvey 2002; Sholette 2011.
29 Responding to the depiction of artists as the shock troops of gentrification, Daniel José Older emphasises that the unspoken word in this debate is all too often 'white'. As he argues – 'there have always been artists in the hood. They aren't necessarily recognized by the academy or using trust funds supplementing coffee shop tips to fund their artistic careers, but they are still, in fact, artists. The presumptive, unspoken "white" in the first round of artists' gentrification narrative is itself an erasure of these artists of color'.
30 For an overview of some of these debates, as well as Rosler's most recent take on the relationship between art and gentrification, see Rosler 2014.
31 Freeman 2000, p. 272.
32 Deutsche and Gendel Ryan 1984, p. 94.
33 Freeman 2000, p. 332.

FIGURE 20 Martha Rosler, Installation view of "Home Front" in Martha Rosler, *If You Lived Here ...*, Dia Art Foundation, (photograph © Martha Rosler, provided by the artist)
COURTESY OF MARTHA ROSLER

projects and exhibitions. The first was entitled *Home Front* and thematised contested housing and addressed the relation between art and gentrification directly. Printed on the wall of that exhibition was a statement by Mayor Ed Koch stating 'If you can't afford to live here, mo-o-ve!', which summed up the city's attitude to community disruption and displacement by gentrification. (Fig. 20) The second was entitled *Homeless: The Street and Other Venues* and focused on homelessness. Here, an aphoristic quote from Peter Marcuse – 'Homelessness exists not because the system is not working but because this is the way it works' (Fig. 21) – replaced Koch's bootstrapping epithet that had confronted viewers in *Home Front*. Drawn from the perspective of a geographer invested in viewing homelessness through the overall dynamic of capital, this view dovetailed with the frontline activities of Homeward Bound, a self-organised coalition of homeless people who set up an office within Wooster Street during that exhibition. As a group, Homeward Bound had formed in 1988 through an encampment in front of City Hall in protest against the Koch administration's woeful record in addressing homelessness. The final exhibition, *City: Visions and Revisions*, explored possible solutions to the housing crisis. The Situationist slogan 'Under the Cobblestones, the Beach' was painted on the wall of the gallery, a phrase that sought out radical visions for social transformation. (Fig. 22) Across all three phases of *If You Lived Here ...* there was an engagement with documentary, domesticity, and the possibility of art providing practical solu-

FIGURE 21   Martha Rosler, Installation view of "Homeless: The Street and Other Venues" in Martha Rosler, *If You Lived Here ...*, Dia Art Foundation, New York 1989
PHOTOGRAPH © MARTHA ROSLER, PROVIDED BY THE ARTIST

FIGURE 22
Martha Rosler, Installation view of "City: Visions and Revisions" in Martha Rosler, *If You Lived Here ...*, Dia Art Foundation, New York 1989
PHOTOGRAPH © MARTHA ROSLER, PROVIDED BY THE ARTIST

tions to social crisis, with public forums ensuring a sustained conversation throughout the year.

Among other issues, Koch's support for artists' housing was discussed in the public forum entitled 'Artists' Life/Work' which took place as part of *Home Front*. The transcript of this event reveals a heated debate between artists, housing activists and those involved in urban studies. Jero Nesson, an artist who established a cooperative live/work space in Boston, argued that artists should professionalise their need for housing and studio space and work alongside local government. In contrast, Adrienne Leban, an artist from Manhattan alongside Marilyn Nance, a photographer from Brooklyn, self-critically asked how artists could participate in struggles against displacement whilst knowing they form part of the problem. Joe Giordano, a painter employed in the Department of Cultural Affairs, advocated that artists form alliances and lobby for their interests as a group often marginalised by property speculation, despite their implication within this process.[34] Anticipating the lack of a common political touchstone for artists around the issue of housing, in 1980 Rosler had already observed that

> As artists' incomes shrink, except for the relative few, and as urban real estate in most cities continues to escalate in value, artists, who have functioned as pioneers in 'reclaiming' decayed urban areas, will find themselves displaced, and the stability of artists' communities, so essential to the creation of art, will be seriously threatened.[35]

In response to this contradiction and the divergent positions evidenced within the Artists' Life/Work forum, *If You Lived Here ...* sought to establish a collective formation which would recognise artists' need for housing whilst opposing their instrumentalisation within processes of urban regeneration.

This ambition affected the style of the storefront space on Wooster Street. The phrase 'Come on in – We're home' was stencilled in large red letters on the door, and ACT UP (AIDS Coalition to Unleash Power) displayed posters on the exterior of the building. The curation sought to undermine the usual style of Dia exhibitions, and Rosler notes that many art world visitors 'seemed to miss the pristine quality of the modernist space, feeling intimidated by the volume of work and the reading room'.[36] Despite this, Rosler is adamant that descriptions of the exhibition as chaotic are inaccurate. There were clear medium-based distinctions, with TV monitors playing films, photographs and paintings displayed on the walls, and paper-based materials stored in filing cabinets and on pin-boards. Rosler stresses a logic to the way the displays were organised: some of the work was salon-hung, other parts tacked up more casually, but the overall aim was for an accretion of meaning throughout the three instalments of *If You Lived Here ...*[37] The space sought to counter the standards of mainstream art world displays, and because of the project's purported function as a temporary site for analysing and responding to the housing crisis, the

---

34   Artists' Life/Work: Housing and Community for Artists.
35   Rosler 2004, p. 328.
36   Ibid.
37   Ibid.

install appeared more like a community centre or infoshop. Once inside, the viewer might spend an extended period of time browsing the library installed in each phase of the project, watching films or sifting through the leaflets that offered services, advice and notifications about housing struggles. The sign on the front door was the first signal that visitors were less positioned as viewers, and instead situated as ideally entering a space where they could interact with the material in multiple ways, opening up the possibility of having an activist, aesthetic or research encounter with the subject.[38] Different aspects of the exhibitions were also clearly targeted towards different demographics, perhaps most notably in how Homeward Bound, a self-organised coalition of homeless people, took up residence at Wooster Street for the second phase of the project, offering counselling as well as information about shelters, employment services and soup kitchens.[39]

Two central aesthetic coordinates underpinned *If You Lived Here ...* The project foregrounded the domestic and emphasised the home as a site of social reproduction. This was situated alongside Rosler's continued engagement with the history of documentary as a genre that has been used both to naturalise and denaturalise dispossession. Yet, the majority of writers have emphasised the exhibition strategy of *If You Lived Here ...* as the most significant aspect of the project. Marion Von Osten describes it as crucial to the emergence of 'New Institutionalism' and the 'project exhibition'.[40] Nina Möntmann situates *If You Lived Here ...* as anticipating the turn towards research-based and discursive practices in the early 2000s, locating it as standing between the alternative art scene of the 1970s, and the subsumption of those aesthetics into the art world where they rest as an 'internalized critique within the institutions themselves'.[41] Although valid, these analyses exemplify Rosler's claim that the primary reception of *If You Lived Here ...* in its afterlife has been among curators, whilst the accompanying book has gained significance within urban studies. The limitations of this derive from the challenges of writing about the ephemeral, process-driven nature of social practice, yet by analysing *If You Lived Here ...* in relation to Rosler's oeuvre, we can begin to clarify the stakes of mobilising documentary and the domestic as the primary formal coordinates for the project.

Each exhibition within *If You Lived Here ...* was marked by the repeated appearance of everyday objects. These included the kitchen installed in the

---

38   Ibid.
39   Rosler, 'Fragments of a Metropolitan Viewpoint', 1991, p. 36.
40   Von Osten 2010, p. 58.
41   Möntmann 2009.

FIGURE 23 Martha Rosler, Installation view of "Home Front" in Martha Rosler, *If You Lived Here ...*, Dia Art Foundation, New York 1989
PHOTOGRAPH © MARTHA ROSLER, PROVIDED BY THE ARTIST

first part of the project, *Home Front*, which stored food and domestic appliances, set up alongside a small TV monitor. (Fig. 23) In the second exhibition, *Homeless: The Street and Other Venues*, beds were set up opposite wall-hung exhibits. Initially these were installed so members of Homeward Bound could sleep in the gallery; however, due to building regulations, Dia foreclosed this possibility, meaning the six beds remained neatly made up and lined up against the wall, their serial placement recalling the institutionalised environment of a homeless shelter, yet here unused for the intended purpose of rest. Visitors to the gallery were left uninformed as to whether the space was being used as a shelter or not, and although the beds remained unused, in Adair Rounthwaite's analysis their presence echoed the strategy of 'tactical visibility' that Homeward Bound had sought to cultivate through their encampment at city hall – it allowed them to establish a headquarters within the Wooster Street gallery.[42] Across all the exhibitions, sofas and rugs faced TV monitors instead of the usual hard-edged seating in galleries, and the overall effect of these details blurred the visual characteristics of public and private space. Signs of domesticity also cropped up elsewhere; a small white picket fence surrounded some of the dis-

---

42   Rounthwaite 2017, p. 128.

plays in the third exhibition, *City: Visions and Revisions*, symbolising middle-American clichés of the home. Coffee tables, rugs and pot plants appeared in all the shows, resting alongside artworks, notices and information boards, again situating the environment of the Wooster Street space somewhere between gallery, home and community centre. All these signs of domesticity within *If You Lived Here ...* signal the home – whether in the form of a homeless shelter or a bourgeois fortress – as a site of social reproduction, a theme coursing through much of Rosler's practice.

In earlier works such as *Bringing the War Home: House Beautiful* (1967–72), *Semiotics of the Kitchen* (1976) and *Service: A Trilogy on Colonization* (1978), Rosler addresses how gendered, raced and classed forms of violence and social domination are produced and inscribed within the domestic sphere. A series of photomontages, *Bringing the War Home: House Beautiful* seamlessly inserts photographs from the Vietnam War into middle-class homes. In the short video piece *Semiotics of the Kitchen*, Rosler recites an alphabetised list of kitchen equipment, combined with increasingly aggressive gestures demonstrating the use of various appliances. With *Service: A Trilogy on Colonization*, Rosler addresses the classed and racialised culture of food. Encompassing three short novels printed on postcard-sized pages, the project was initially conceived as a piece of mail-art organized into a tripartite structure, like the three exhibitions comprising *If You Lived Here ...* The first story, *A Budding Gourmet*, is written in the voice of a bourgeois housewife, who mindlessly enthuses about her ability to cook foreign cuisines, complete with patronising, racist affirmations that 'Indians are extremely spiritual'. The second story, *McTowers Maid*, tells the story of a young fast-food worker and her tussles with colleagues and management. The final story, *Tijuana Maid*, written in Spanish, relates the harassment and exploitation of a Mexican domestic worker after migrating to the US.[43] In all these works, Rosler explores how violence seeps into social reproduction through the various paid and unpaid activities of women. While *Bringing the War Home* renders this formally through photomontage and *Semiotics of the Kitchen* engages the building blocks of language to speak to patriarchal structures, the playing with different voices and modes of narrative in *Service: A Trilogy on Colonization* foreshadows the collaborative practice of *If You Lived Here ...* by introducing multiple perspectives in order to map the classed, gendered and racialised structures underpinning everyday experiences of food and cooking.

---

43   Rosler, 1978.

Several of the documentary works displayed as part of *If You Lived Here ...* drew on and expanded the histories of photographic representation of homelessness that Rosler had earlier addressed in *The Bowery in two inadequate descriptive systems*.[44] The Stryker's Bay tenants group in Upper Manhattan screened their agit-prop documentary film entitled *Don't Move, Fight Back*, whereas George Corsetti's *Poletown Lives!* details the history of the Polish quarter in Detroit, destroyed in 1981 to make way for a new Cadillac plant. Rosler describes Bob McKeown as utilising traditional social-documentary strategies to photograph the formation of the Homeless Union in Wayne County, Michigan, several of which were displayed. In the accompanying book to *If You Lived Here ...* two of these photographs are reproduced, both of which were included in the exhibition. One shows the first convention of the union, with elected officers and the steering committee posing in front of a church altar and a banner in the background that reads 'National Homeless Union: Homeless not Helpless'. The predominantly black members of the union pose in front of the banner, and are mostly looking away from the camera, arms crossed, forming a line that signals their collective strength. The second photograph shows a black family, with the mother and father either side of two young girls who look directly towards the camera while the gaze of their parents is directed towards their right, attentive perhaps to the discussion taking place off-camera, as this photograph captures the formation of the Union. McKeown's other contribution to *If You Lived Here ...* was made in collaboration with the Urban Center for Photography and directly intervened into the landscape of dispossession by flyposting enlarged photographs on rotten buildings, stencilled over with the statement 'Demolished by Neglect', a strategy that sought to denaturalise the crisis of homelessness. (Fig. 24)

Rosler emphasises that her sustained engagement with social documentary rests upon a refusal of art-world snobbery towards politicised or populist forms as well as a continued belief in the possibility of those strategies for building solidarity with a wide range of audiences. Social documentary, and its New Deal era heyday, forms a usable past for *If You Lived Here ...* in a manner that exceeds the more formal exploration of *The Bowery in two inadequate descriptive systems*. It forms the foundation for a collective political formation in a period marked by – in Rosler's words – the final dismantling of the New Deal state and the abandonment of utopia. Yet the mobilisation of the genre as usable past within the exhibitions of *If You Lived Here ...* did not mean it was posed as a uniformly positive source. Rosler's 'In, around and afterthoughts (on documentary

---

44   Rosler, 'Fragments from a Metropolitan Viewpoint' 1991, p. 36.

FIGURE 24 Installation by the The Urban Centre for Photography, *Demolished by Neglect*, on display in Martha Rosler, *If You Lived Here ...*, Dia Art Foundation, New York 1989
PHOTOGRAPH © MARTHA ROSLER, PROVIDED BY THE ARTIST

photography)' essay, which criticises the reformist tendencies of classic documentary photography, was pasted alongside photographer Mel Rosenthal's text 'On Photographing the Homeless' in order to establish a debate between two positions which diverged on the politics and ethics of photographing the dispossessed. As Rosler emphasises, a primary difference between her position and Rosenthal's lies in the fact that while she has largely produced work within the circuits of the artworld, Rosenthal's photographing of the homeless formed part of a broader project that represented Bathgate, the South Bronx neighbourhood where he worked at a health clinic, with the images circulated in activist publications or made for the people he photographed, who often did not own any images of themselves.[45] This contradictory relationship between the art world and activism was brought to the fore in *If You Lived Here ...*, embedded within the project's aim of criticising gentrification whilst being hosted at Dia. Rosler's ethical and political qualms over this parallels her critique of the repressive dimensions within reformist documentary photography in *The Bowery in two inadequate descriptive systems*. More broadly, in thinking back to the discussion of Lacy's collaboration with the police in *The Oakland Projects* in Chapter One, the relationship between Rosler's position in *The Bowery in two inadequate descriptive systems*, and the orientation of *If You Lived Here ...* links with debates over the ethics of the typically reformist collaborations that have increasingly become central within social practice's drive towards usefulness. Here, we can begin to see how the logics, contradictions and fault lines within the histories of New Deal era social documentary act as a seedbed for the ambitions of social practice, and yet also establish its limitations.

Moving beyond the primary aesthetic coordinates of domesticity and social documentary, and thinking through how the latter formed a usable past, each exhibition within *If You Lived Here ...* also included works we might categorise as social practice, in their attempt to shift analysis into solutions by offering provisional salves to homelessness. Polish artist Krzysztof Wodiczko's *Homeless Vehicle Project* (1988) was presented within *If You Lived Here ...* through photographs and plans. Based on a supermarket trolley, the *Homeless Vehicle* was designed in collaboration with homeless people and provided the space for some rudimentary needs; shelter, sleep and washing, with the lower part designed for storing belongings. The top compartment expands into a basic bed and the aluminium nose of the vehicle folds down into a washbasin. Emphasising that the *Homeless Vehicle* is obviously not a solution to the housing crisis, the geographer Neil Smith nevertheless argues that it serves to make the homeless visible, while offering greater mobility and thus resistance to laws against begging and sleeping rough.[46] Rather like Rounthwaite's analysis of the function of the beds within *Homeless: The Street and other Venues*, Wodiczko's *Homeless Vehicle* enacts tactical visibility. Similarly, the Atlanta-based architectural collective the Mad Housers attempted temporary solutions to homeless-

---

45   Rosler, 'Fragments from a Metropolitan Viewpoint' 1991, p. 34.
46   Smith 1992, p. 58.

FIGURE 25   The Mad Housers erecting shelter in Brooklyn
PHOTOGRAPH © MARTHA ROSLER, PROVIDED BY THE ARTIST

ness by building small shelters. (Fig. 25) One of these shelters was displayed within *Homeless: The Street and Other Venues*, but they were usually erected without planning permission in order to intrude into a regulated urban landscape.[47] (Fig. 26) Other practical solutions came in the shape of a project entitled 'Homes for People with AIDS', a collaboration between the architectural designers Gustavo Bonevardi and Lee Ledbetter, the urban planner Linda Baldwin, the principal of a construction management-design firm (Morgan Hare) and Joe Lay, a clinical psychologist. The project came about as a way to target the development of infill housing in vacant lots towards the needs of homeless people with AIDS. The proposal was intended for a city-owned vacant lot in the South Bronx which would include living units as well as communal spaces, offices for nursing services, counselling, alternative treatments and a central kitchen for on-site food preparation.

In thinking back to *The Bowery in two inadequate descriptive systems*, and Rosler's investment in the critical purchase of social documentary as a usable past, *If You Lived Here ...* must be understood as a re-appraisal of the genre for the turn of the 1980s into the 1990s, its strategies expanded beyond repres-

---

47   The Mad Housers 1991, p. 228.

FIGURE 26 The Mad Housers shelter installation at "Homeless: The Street and Other Venues" in Martha Rosler, *If You Lived Here ...*, Dia Art Foundation, New York 1989
PHOTOGRAPH © MARTHA ROSLER, PROVIDED BY THE ARTIST

entation into the growing field of social practice. Akin to the mobilisation of different voices in *Service: A Trilogy on Colonization, If You Lived Here ...* involved working through the different positions of groups and individuals in order to create a collective formation that could contest the dominant ideology which individualised homelessness as a mark of social dysfunction, a view perhaps best encapsulated during that period by President Reagan's comment in 1988 that some people slept on grates as a personal preference.[48] My understanding of the project in this way relates to how the domestic sphere was positioned as a visual and dialogical connector between the various collaborators working on the project, from Rosler and other artists, to groups providing front-line services for the homeless. Appearing at a moment marked by the retrenchment of social welfare, growing homelessness and the emerging discourse of artists' role in gentrification, *If You Lived Here ...* took a somewhat utilitarian approach to these issues, and thus risked re-inscribing the instrumentalising aspects of social documentary earlier criticised by Rosler. If the project fulfilled Rosler's ambition that '[t]here has to be room for an interested art practice that does not simply merge itself into its object',[49] perhaps it did so through an internalised auto-critique that rested upon the project's relationship to classic, Depression era documentary photography as a compromised, but nevertheless usable past.

By thinking through Fredric Jameson's concept of 'cognitive mapping', we might deepen this analysis in relation to the appearance of the project at the apparent apex of 'postmodernism'. For Jameson, cognitive mapping is an aesthetic form capable of manifesting an adequate reply to the distinct historical phase of late capitalism, and its cultural form in postmodernism. Jameson views postmodernism and late capitalism as marked by a unique explosion of culture through the social realm, and thus an increased dissolution of culture's 'relative autonomy'.[50] On the one hand, this dissolution of autonomy has been taken to reduce the possibility of an effective oppositional culture, as art merges with the social realm, a view already established in 1944 by Theodor Adorno and Max Horkheimer in *Dialectic of Enlightenment*.[51] On the other hand, the dissolution of culture's autonomy has also been repeatedly read as underpinning the emergence of 'creative' or 'cognitive' capitalism as a regime of accumulation that produces a new vanguard, anti-capitalist collective subject.[52] These opposing views on the relation of culture to capitalism also under-

---

48 Associated Press 1988.
49 Rosler, 'Fragments of a Metropolitan Viewpoint' 1991, p. 35.
50 Jameson 1991, p. 48.
51 Adorno and Horkheimer 1998.
52 Maurizio Lazzarato and Franco 'Bifo' Beradi are the most prominent voices in the debate

pin both criticisms *and* affirmations of social practice as an art form that in its dematerialised, affective and relational form has been taken to reflect de-industrialisation and the move towards a service economy. Yet, if art practices that take social relations as their material have often been read as a merely passive reflection of economic shifts, for Jameson, cognitive mapping offers an active response to the expansion of culture, as well as the abstractions of late capitalism. In this light, he describes cognitive mapping as an updating of Lukácsian and Brechtian aesthetics, which seeks to stress their shared interest in art as a de-reifying force, despite divergences over form and style, as discussed in Chapter One. Cognitive mapping updates the writing of the 1930s by emphasising the spatial as its organising principle in order to enable a critique of trans-national 'late capitalism', and a 'situational representation on the part of the individual subject to that vaster and properly unrepresentable totality which is the ensemble of society's structures as a whole'.[53] Although cognitive mapping clearly raises issues of representation, Jameson stresses that this aesthetic is not mimetic, but rather poses a simultaneous *analysis* of representation so as to adequately respond to the deepening abstraction that Jameson views as characteristic of late capitalism. Jameson partly follows Louis Althusser's 'scientific' notion of ideology in his concept of cognitive mapping, as well as Althusser's argument that authentic artworks allow us to '"perceive" (but not know) in some sense *from the inside*, by an *internal distance*, the very ideology in which they are held'.[54] As related to such formulations, Jameson proposes cognitive mapping as the privileged means to access the general sense of totality produced by neoliberal capitalism.

Whilst stressing that classic social documentary in its 1930s guise was not wholly adequate to the political climate of neoliberalism, Rosler was nevertheless unwilling to completely abandon those forms, despite her criticisms as they were articulated in *The Bowery in two inadequate descriptive systems* and the 'In, around and afterthoughts ...' essay. This is comparable with Jameson's revival and transformation of Brecht and Lukács' aesthetics. The investment in the forms and aesthetics of the 1930s, at the point where capitalism has supposedly entered a drastic new historical stage (as Jameson claims), is striking. If we follow a non-teleological line of thinking and stick with Bloch's criticism of the notion that cultural forms become obsolete, as discussed in previous chapters, the historical assumptions undergirding the cognitive map must be

---

that has sought to valorise the 'cognitariat' as a vanguardist subject. See Lazzarato 1996 and Beradi 2009.
53   Jameson 1991, p. 51.
54   Althusser 1971, p. 204.

supplemented. In particular, there are limits to Jameson's analysis of postmodernism as a 'break' marked by 'hyper-abstraction' due to the machinations of finance capital. As discussed in the introduction to this chapter, one of the primary manifestations of fictitious capital is in land, where in the case of rent or a mortgage, there is a continuous claim on future wages and therefore on labour in order for that form of capital, as well as the proletariat, to survive. Fictitious capital is not unique to neoliberalism – as we shall see directly in the narrative of *One-Third of a Nation* – and as Gail Day stresses, Jameson's view fetishises finance capital as capable of surviving on its own internal metabolism. This is a fantasy which, as Day explains, has been 'long characteristic of capital's very own utopias and dreamworlds'.[55] In contrast, *If You Lived Here ...* disallows the possibility of inadvertently endorsing capital's own dearly held fantasies of having broken from labour. It does so by stressing the domestic sphere as not only the site from which capitalism is reproduced, but also the place from which forms of life that exceed its grasp might spring.

In this respect, it is also notable that *If You Lived Here ...* contrasted the aesthetics of domesticity and social documentary with the genres of representation that most regularly mark out the naturalisation of wealth and dispossession. In *Home Front*, statistical graphs and planning documents for housing were arranged at eye-level, interspersed with real estate advertisements that offered luxury lifestyles. Neither the abstractions of the state in the form of city planning, nor the dreamworlds of high capital can convey the reality of dispossession and the ploughing of wages into rent each month, and here the image register of the graph and planning document functioned, as Rosler describes, to 'crystallise' 'a blurred social picture' and produce a form of realism that emerges through the work of the viewer making connections, a process which looks rather like the ambitions of Jameson's cognitive map.[56] By thinking through *If You Lived Here ...* as centred on the possibility of producing and reproducing new social relations within the midst of a housing crisis, the return to social documentary should be understood as an attempt to critically examine a history, indeed, to source a usable past in confronting the specificities of dispossession at that moment when, as Rosler had already written eight years prior, utopia had been 'abandoned' and liberalism 'deserted'. By turning to the expanded, performative *One-Third of a Nation*, we can examine the valences of how New Deal era social documentary forms a usable past for Rosler. Through this comparison, we might begin to ask how

---

55 Day 2011, pp. 222–3.
56 Rosler, 'Fragments of a Metropolitan Viewpoint', p. 32.

the cognitive map of neoliberalism contrasts with the social documentary of the Depression. Secondly, in addressing the play's focus on dispossession and fictitious capital, we can complicate the notion that neoliberalism is marked by a decisive historical break from capital's reliance on labour.

2   *One-Third of a Nation*

One-Third of a Nation opened in New York on 17 January 1938 and was seen by over 200,000 people during its run. It was also staged with local casts in Cincinnati, New Orleans, Seattle, Detroit, Portland, Philadelphia and San Francisco throughout that year. The play was the most successful production of the Living Newspaper Unit, and was described by Lorraine Brown and John O'Connor as the most memorable production from the WPA-FTP overall.[57] Like *Injunction Granted*, the Living Newspaper discussed in Chapter One, *One-Third of a Nation* used that theatrical form to index a chronology of social struggles. If the drama of *Injunction Granted* culminated in the formation of the Congress of Industrial Organizations as the apex of contemporary labour struggles in the US, *One-Third of a Nation* dramatised the accumulation of profits through land and the housing crisis during the Depression. Bringing viewers up to the present day, the narrative culminated in 1938, and directly responded to the success and limits of the Wagner-Steagall Housing Act of 1937. In contrast to *Injunction Granted*, the use of documentary conventions within *One-Third of a Nation* were largely disconnected from satire and experimental theatrical devices. These formal differences were not incidental but, as I shall argue, contingent upon the decline of the Popular Front during the late 1930s. As we shall see, *One-Third of a Nation* is suggestive of the move towards a sentimental nationalism within the Cultural Front, a problem also taken up in the final chapter.

In 1937, the Wagner-Steagall Act introduced the United States Housing Authority (USHA), which created government subsidies for the provision and improvement of housing for those on a low income. The Act was intended to eradicate slums and replace them with new, sanitary housing developments. Nathan Straus, the head of the USHA from 1937–42, was a staunch advocate of public housing who battled the many politicians and legislators reluctant to allocate sufficient funds to his agency. In a speech made to the Chamber of Commerce in 1937, Straus outlined his hopes for the housing programme the Act would enable. Revealingly, his emphasis that bad housing created cit-

---

57   Brown and O'Connor 1980, p. 161.

izens lacking in the correct morals and manners to succeed in 'civilized society' couched the struggle for state provision of housing as necessary for the monitoring and betterment of the poor.[58] Straus also assured right-wing Chamber of Commerce members that decent housing would act as a bulwark against revolt, stating that 'The slums must go or the society that tolerates them will'.[59] At the same time, he affirmed that the new homes would be built at the 'minimum' standard compatible with 'decency and comfort' in order to avoid creating a sense of 'entitlement' amongst the poor.[60] Such sentiments sought to position state-funded housing provision as in the interest of the bourgeoisie, with Straus stressing that private industry could not be relied on to provide decent housing.[61] Pre-empting the inevitable accusations of socialism from right-wing politicians and legislators leery towards all forms of public funding, Straus guaranteed that the Wagner-Steagall Act would not interfere with the business of private landlords, or affect the profits of private construction. To the contrary, he emphasised that the USHA would boost growth in construction across the private sector. Though the Wagner-Steagall Act created the USHA and granted a portion of public money for the building of new 'decent' homes, it followed on from, and did not interfere with, the previous New Deal housing policy of slum clearance begun with the Public Works Administration (PWA).[62] Yet, Straus's difficulties in promoting the cause of public housing only increased after the US entered World War II, when the USHA was increasingly accused of wasting money on 'socialistic' projects that could be better spent on defence.[63]

The Wagner-Steagall Act ultimately had to cohere with the drive of New Deal housing policy as primarily targeted towards the recovery of property markets, whether through slum clearance or through initiatives such as the Federal National Mortgage Association (Fannie Mae), which was founded a year later in 1938.[64] Fannie Mae was ushered in to purchase mortgages from lenders whose borrowers were defaulting, and also involved the creation of a secondary mortgage market. Alongside other initiatives such as the GI Bill, which provided loans for returning soldiers, Fannie Mae was instrumental in rescuing a housing

---

58 Straus 1966, pp. 159–160.
59 Straus 1966, p. 160.
60 Straus 1966, p. 164.
61 Straus 1966, p. 161.
62 This policy was criticised by many housing reformers such as Lewis Mumford and Catherine Bauer, who argued that slum clearance prior to the building of affordable housing simply provided a favour to private developers, razing the ground for new speculation on prime real-estate locations in the heart of cities. See Biles 1990, p. 34.
63 Biles 1990, p. 42.
64 Hays 1985, p. 84.

market that had catastrophically slumped during the Depression. The ensuing expansion in homeownership through mortgage loans in turn stimulated the economy through the growing market for associated commodities such as cars and domestic appliances, with the suburban homeowner lifestyle coming to characterise the transformation of the domestic sphere during the boom years and Fordist heyday of the 1950s. In thinking through how this expansion in homeownership relates to Straus's arguments for broader public housing, it seems evident that they share an ideological tendency to position welfare and government provision as an investment that would produce a compliant and docile working class.

Just as Straus was concerned with how the slums undermined morals, *One-Third of a Nation* was similarly invested in showing how tenement living corrupted sexual, social and domestic norms within communities. The play matched Straus's belief in the necessity of a state-run housing authority, demonstrating through multiple scenes the degeneration of living conditions when housing provision was left to the impulses of private capital. The title of *One-Third of a Nation* was taken from Roosevelt's second inaugural address, which, like Straus's appeals, sought to emphasise that the excesses of private interest were not only dubious *morally*, but also economically. Stating that he still saw 'one-third of a nation ill-housed, ill-clad, ill-nourished', Roosevelt stressed that green shoots of economic recovery did not mean the affairs of big business should return to pre-Depression norms, and insisted the state should remain active in public spending.[65] As with *Injunction Granted*, *One-Third of a Nation* guided the audience through the thicket of history with the aid of the Voice of the Living Newspaper, or Loudspeaker, who provided background information and introduced scenes. The everyman character of the 'Little Man', or Mr. Buttonkooper, also held the drama together, often asking questions of the other players on stage. However, if the Clown figure in *Injunction Granted* often contradicted the Loudspeaker and ridiculed other characters, the Little Man replaced satire with faux-naïve musings. His role was to ask questions, and slowly learn from the drama along with the audience. Gaining knowledge through the unfolding of a litany of historical scenes, the Little Man would by the end of the play be able to challenge the conditions he witnessed and propose solutions, in other words, to learn from this usable past. Unlike the biting satire the Clown directed towards capitalists and corrupt judges, the Little Man lacked rage, instead forming a moderate, wholesome guide for the audience.

---

65 Roosevelt quoted in Browder 1998, p. 157.

One-Third of a Nation achieved a documentary objectivity by building up its narrative through a range of source materials including newspapers, police reports and academic articles. The set design by Howard Bay was done in two different ways, with the final version evidencing a stress on realism that harmonised with the documentary emphasis on 'facts'. For the dry run of the play at Vassar College in 1937, where the WPA-FTP director Hallie Flanagan had studied and taught, Bay drew on Expressionist theatre design by erecting symbols of tenement life – an oversized leaky tap, a roach, a toilet seat and broken fire escape – above a bare stage. As Mardi Valgemäe writes, this enlargement and distortion typifies Expressionist stage design, and in *One-Third of a Nation*, their use was intended to convey life in the slums as stark and nightmarish.[66] Yet, by the time *One-Third of a Nation* appeared in New York in 1938, the staging revolved around a real tenement house rising to 70 feet high, cut through so the audience could view the drama inside. (Fig. 27) In preparing the set, Bay joined Langdon Post, then head of the NYCHA, on demolition trips to rotting tenement buildings so he could request parts of the building, such as balustrades or cornices.[67] Post would instruct the demolition workers to set those parts aside, and once they were deloused and sent over to the WPA-FTP, Bay and his team would graft them onto the set.[68] The final staging, and the transition from an expressionist aesthetic, was intended to appeal more closely to documentary 'facts' about housing, with the use of elements from real tenements lending authenticity.[69]

One-Third of a Nation opens with the chaos of a tenement fire and shows the bureaucratic corruption of City officials and the fire department in assisting with this disaster. We also see the landlord, Mr. Schulz's negligence of his property as responsible for the fire, through a conversation between Schulz and his tenant Mr. Rosen, mediated by the Loudspeaker. The landlord, Schulz, affirms that in a 'big city like this' land never goes down in value, and because he paid more than the land was worth when he bought it, his debts mean he cannot fix the apartments or lower the rent. Instead, because of the steady inflation in land across the city, the rents must 'go up, up, up' without any money to spare

---

66   Valgemäe 1972, p. 114.
67   Brown and O'Connor 1980, p. 172.
68   Ibid.
69   *One-Third of a Nation* also attempted to reflect local conditions through the set. Two days before *One-Third of a Nation* opened in Philadelphia, a tenement in that city had caved in, so instead of the play beginning with the household fire described in the script, it opened with a portion of the set collapsing. See Brown and O'Connor 1980, p. 173.

FIGURE 27 Staging *One-Third of a Nation*, Seattle, 1938
COURTESY OF THE FEDERAL THEATER PROJECT PHOTOGRAPH COLLECTION, UNIVERSITY OF WASHINGTON SPECIAL COLLECTION

for renovation or improvement in living conditions.[70] The Loudspeaker interrupts, chastising Schulz for speculating and profiteering with little regard for his tenants, to which Schulz retorts by explaining that all landlords speculate if they expect to get anything out of their investment, affirming that 'land, land,

---

70   Arent, *One-Third of a Nation: A Living Newspaper about Housing*, Act One, Scene Two.

LAND!' is where profits are made.⁷¹ Mr. Rosen protests, and Schulz explains that if you can only afford $24 rent per month, then you will have to live in one of his tenements, and in order to discover why this is, one has to 'go back in history and discover why NYC real estate became the most profitable speculation on the face of the earth'.⁷² This opening scene shows the blame for the fire shifting from the tenant to the landlord to the fire department to the city officials, before settling firmly on 'history'.

This beginning is comparable with the opening of *Injunction Granted* that detailed slave labour, bonded labour and migration to the US as forms of primitive accumulation. By travelling back into the past and registering an origin point for the subject at hand, both Living Newspapers established a moment from which subsequent scenes and the crisis of the present unravel. As with the mapping of dispossession in *If You Lived Here ...*, documentary as genre is mobilised in order to index the past as a usable guide to the present. The scenes that go 'back in history' in *One-Third of a Nation* detail how the parish of Trinity Church acquired huge swathes of land in New York City during the eighteenth century. The accumulation of wealth by the landowning classes as they increased rents to new migrants is shown, and like *Injunction Granted*, this grounds the play in an American origin story that nevertheless wholly neglects to acknowledge the foundational dispossession of an indigenous population. During the ensuing scenes of land accumulation, a town crier continuously interrupts with facts about population growth, industrial development and political changes, here substituting for the Loudspeaker in providing a historical context for the growing exploitation of tenants at the hands of landowners. The Loudspeaker's inquiring speech re-appears towards the end of the scene, asking a landowner how much wealth he has accumulated. When the landowner smugly affirms that his brave faith and investment in the growth of the city enabled his financial success, the Loudspeaker contradicts him, stating that all he did was 'sit' whilst the industry of '696,000 people developed the metropolis', referring to those very proletarians whose wages provided his wealth in the form of rent.⁷³ It is here that the audience is first presented with the contradiction between land value and productive labour as a question of morals, to which the landowner responds by comparing himself to dynastic patriarchs of New York such as Robert Goelet and John Jacob Astor. Goelet and Astor subsequently appear on stage and explain how they made their fortunes, making claims of heroism due to their pioneering faith in investment.

---

71   Ibid.
72   Ibid.
73   Arent, 1938. Act 1, Scene 3.

FIGURE 28 'The city grows', *One-Third of a Nation*, New York City, 1938
COURTESY OF THE FEDERAL THEATRE PROJECT COLLECTION, SPECIAL COLLECTIONS AND ARCHIVES, GEORGE MASON UNIVERSITY LIBRARIES

As with the references to Heinz and Hearst in *Injunction Granted*, these figures stood as real individuals capable of representing a realist 'type' to the audience, personifying the entire landowning class – from slum landlord to property magnate – as immoral and exploitative. These first scenes were played in front of projections of photographs and drawings of nineteenth-century New York City, producing an immersive origin story for the present housing crisis. (Fig. 28)

The Little Man appears for the first time in the next scene, where he assumes the role of a confused audience member, walking down the aisles before ascending to the stage through the pit, and stating that he wants some information about housing. The interruption proceeds with the Loudspeaker questioning what he's doing in 'those clothes', explaining to the Little Man that 'they look 1938', and that the scene which just finished was 1845.[74] In response, the Little Man states that 'Every time something happens that I don't understand I'm going to stop the show and ask questions'.[75] We learn that his curiosity stems from his own housing problems, and after having observed the drama onstage, his dissatisfaction with how the parcelling up of land in New York City between private interests was not prevented. The colliding temporalities

---

74   *One-Third of a Nation: A Living Newspaper about Housing*, 1938 Act 1, Scene 4.
75   Ibid.

between the Little Man's (and the audience's) present woes and the history of eighteenth and nineteenth century property accumulation is established as a chain of causation, with the Little Man modelling comprehension of this dynamic for the audience. In response to the Little Man's frustrations at the history he has just witnessed, the Loudspeaker explains that 'Those were the good old days when nobody did anything about anything'. From here, the Little Man is increasingly employed to guide the audience, as the play settles into its didactic role of analysing and proposing solutions to the housing crisis.[76] Despite formal innovations in the set, and the deployment of numerous interruptions aimed at breaking the fourth wall very much in the style of the Blue Blouses or Brecht's *Lehrstücke*, *One-Third of a Nation* is more simplistic and didactic in its borrowing of those techniques than *Injunction Granted*. While the subversive ridiculing of the courts, police and big business in *Injunction Granted* worked to produce an overall picture of how capital and state intersect in their oppression and exploitation of the proletariat, *One-Third of a Nation* is instead marked by a solid belief in reform, with the Little Man positioned as a cipher for the morality of labour, which the state must protect against immoral financial speculators and landowners. To put this differently, wage labour is pitted here as a redeemable feature of capitalism, in contrast with the degeneracy of finance. This reformist tone is encapsulated in how the Little Man is primarily portrayed as a victim of circumstance, an honest everyman who does his job and works hard but has been forgotten by the barons of speculation. He is individuated in a way that less situates him as representative of a class, and more as an aspirational figure who tries to better his circumstances.

This change in tone from the more militant register of earlier WPA-FTP Living Newspapers is not incidental, but rather marks ideological shifts within the Communist Party USA (CPUSA) and the cultural front during the period of the 'Democratic Front' that followed the Popular Front or – in its Americanised version – the 'People's Front'. If the People's Front was an Americanised version of the Comintern policy of a Popular Front (initiated in 1935), then in 1937 the CPUSA headed further down this path with the Democratic Front. The May 1938 Party convention marked these changes, with the *Star-Spangled Banner* opening proceedings and the stars and stripes hung alongside the red flag. Politically, this period saw the Party support Roosevelt and the New Deal more directly and, as Hemingway notes, involved significant discursive shifts, such as the ill-defined category of the 'people' supplanting the

---

76   Ibid.

working class in affirmations of political agency.[77] The Little Man's whiteness is also notable here, with the unabashed patriotism of the Democratic Front tied to the promotion of a usable past that occluded settler colonialism, slavery and the ethnic diversity of the working class, in order to attempt a communist nationalism grounded in the figure of a white, working-class, Anglo-Saxon male.[78]

Following on from the discussion in Chapter Two about the mobilisation of pre-industrial metaphors in Segal's dance work, this appeal to a usable past within the cultural front also involved searching for more holistic examples of community, with urban centres figured as a corrupting influence, as in the description of slums within *One-Third of a Nation*. Act 1, scene 4 shows an Irish family who have recently immigrated to the US. The daughter in the family is a teenager, and the mother worries about her, stating that it 'Don't take cream long to get sour in this neighborhood'.[79] In the Detroit production, Edith Segal played the teenage daughter in this family and also choreographed several scenes, including one that incorporated *Dance of the Washerwomen*, discussed in Chapter Two. (Fig. 29 and 30) Elsewhere, in Act 2, we are presented with a correlation between poor housing, sexual abuse and juvenile delinquency through a fight between two boys, Frank and Sammy. Frank accuses Sammy of breaking his 'skooter' (sic) and threatens to beat him up. Sammy's failure to square up leads Frank to tease him, saying that 'ya can't expect nothin' out of a guy that has to sleep in the same bed as his big sister, kin ya?' Sammy explains there isn't any room in his home, and Frank responds more aggressively, asking what his sister is like, asking if he gets 'a nice little feel in sometimes when she don't know it'.[80] This teasing continues until Sammy reaches bursting point, and throws a punch. The Little Man asks 'Is that kid unusual or is it the result of where he lives and what he sees?' and then invites the Loudspeaker to give the facts, which leads to a litany of statistics about juvenile delinquency levels in various cities, and how it links to poor housing and slum living.[81] Scenes follow of couples arguing over whether or not to have a baby, details about infant mortality, and discussions of the spread of meningitis and diphtheria in the slums, episodes that coalesce to give an overall picture of the deterioration of family life and gender roles. The Little Man's thwarted attempts to get himself and his

---

77 Hemingway 2002, p. 103.
78 Notably, the Democratic Front found ideological bolster in the patriotic rhetoric accompanying the policy of 'Socialism in One Country' in the Soviet Union.
79 Arent, 1938, Act 1, Scene 4.
80 Arent, 1938, Act 2, Scene 2A.
81 Ibid.

FIGURE 29   Irish family scene, in *One-Third of a Nation*, Detroit production 1938
COURTESY OF THE JEROME ROBBINS DANCE DIVISION, NEW YORK LIBRARY
FOR THE PERFORMING ARTS

wife, Mrs. Buttonkooper, into one of the new housing developments also punctuates the drama, with specific reference made to the modernist Williamsburg Housing Project that were built through the Housing section of the PWA. The Little Man's disappointment evidence the limitations of the New Deal housing schemes in relation to this cycle of historical episodes, with the audience learning that the Williamsburg Project was oversubscribed by 19,000 applications for 1622 apartments.

FIGURE 30   Dance of the Washerwomen, choreography by Edith Segal, in *One-Third of a Nation*, Detroit production, 1938
COURTESY OF THE JEROME ROBBINS DANCE DIVISION, NEW YORK LIBRARY FOR THE PERFORMING ARTS

By the end of the second scene, the attention turns towards racism in housing provision as the Little Man travels uptown to Harlem. This aspect of *One-Third of a Nation* is most transparently tied to the political legacies of the Popular Front, and links closely with the concerns of the Photo League Feature Group's 'Harlem Document', to be discussed in the following chapter. *One-Third of a Nation* focused on the phenomenon of 'hot beds' in Harlem where people sleep in shifts, and showed that Black people were charged higher rents than white people.[82] (Fig. 31) This scene is also the first to display militancy and direct action, as two Black men discuss their woes and propose a rent strike. This is also the only point in the play where we see forms of community emerge through struggle, in contrast with the static misery arising from different social groups being forced to share space based on class, or more prominently, ethnicity as in the scenes which show newly arrived Jews, Italians and the Irish. As one of the men in this scene proclaims, 'When you don't like the way things are, and you want to change 'em, don't try to do it all by yourself. You can't ... You got to get 'em all together – and then you gotta do somethin' TOGETHER!'[83] Here, the drama of *One-Third of a Nation* sees agency emerge less from comprehending the incessant regaling of historical and present-day facts, but rather from lived experience. This distinction is crucial in beginning to reckon with the limits of a social documentary centred on 'facts', and indeed, as I will elaborate, the cognitive map.

The following scenes show the Harlem Rent Strike of 1936 when 300 tenants picketed landlords and other rent strikes in the Bronx and Brooklyn are referred to, all of which are highlighted as having been primarily organised by women.[84] Following the rent strikes, things begin to improve and a number of philanthropic solutions to the housing crisis are detailed, including the Dixie Houses in Memphis and Hull House in Chicago.[85] When attention turned to the present and the new proposals for government-sponsored housing, Straus appears on stage, opposing the claims that this provision would be unconstitutional by arguing that almost all reforms are initially thought of as unconstitutional. The following scene detailing the Wagner-Steagall Housing bill introduces a number of other politicians and as the audience sees the act being passed into law, they learn that it was an adulterated version of the legislation Straus and others had aimed for.[86] The Little Man, in one of the final scenes contemplates this, pacing back and forth, and states

> Do you realize that the Wagner Bill at the end of four years will have solved less than two per cent of the Housing problem in New York City? Do you

---

82   Arent 1938, Act 2, Scene 2C.
83   Arent, 1938, Act 2, Scene 2C.
84   These episodes relate to the struggles discussed in chapter two around the United Council of Working Class Housewives.
85   Arent, 1938, Act 2, Scene 3.
86   Ibid.

FIGURE 31   *One-Third of a Nation*, Philadelphia, Pennsylvania, 1938
COURTESY OF THE FEDERAL THEATRE PROJECT COLLECTION, SPECIAL COLLECTIONS AND ARCHIVES, GEORGE MASON UNIVERSITY LIBRARIES

realize that, at that rate, it will take us more than two hundred years before every slum in New York has been demolished? And by that time the ones they're building now will be slums and we'll be back just where we started.[87]

This is followed up by opinions from various housing 'experts' such as Helen Alfred, the Secretary and Executive Director of the National Public Housing Conference and Mayor La Guardia who bemoans that the Wagner Housing Act is merely a 'drop in the bucket'.[88] The blame for this is laid on 'inertia', an amorphous term that one imagines substituted for what the more radical writers of *One-Third of a Nation* may have preferred to call capitalism. The criticism of the 1937 Housing Act closes the play, and the final line was read by the Loudspeaker, stating that 'this could be Boston, New York, St Louis, Chicago,

---

87   Arent, 1938, Scene 5.
88   Ibid.

Philadelphia, but let's just call it, "one-third of a nation"', a closing utterance, which like the ideology of the Democratic Front, sought to stress nationhood as the ground for a shared experience over class or ethnicity.[89] Ultimately, as reported in the *Sunday Worker*, the play showed the need 'for slum elimination on a far greater scale than is proposed in the Wagner Housing Act'.[90] Yet, in contrast to the celebratory labour pageant hailing the formation of the CIO that closed *Injunction Granted*, *One-Third of a Nation* presented a more resigned, reformist view, with its teleological structure stressing New Deal era reforms as a starting point that might be built upon.

Despite this, Irwin Rhodes, general counsel for the WPA-FTP, claimed that *One-Third of a Nation* created more problems for him than any other Living Newspaper, including *Injunction Granted*, the swiftly cancelled *Ethiopia*, or even *Triple-A Plowed Under*, which caused uproar by featuring Earl Browder, leader of the CPUSA. This was because it played out scenes verbatim from congressional records related to the passage of the Wagner Housing Act, naming senators and regaling quotes to the audience. However, because all this material was reproduced as factual evidence, Arthur Arent and the other writers were far less vulnerable to accusations of communist propaganda, as had been levelled at *Injunction Granted*.[91] This illuminates the use of 'evidence' by the Living Newspaper unit as based in the contemporaneous legitimation of documentary as a form of social protest. As described by Haworth Jones, this was founded upon a 'meticulous attention to authenticity' with the recourse to history as usable past during the Depression operating under stringent terms that 'sought an objective version of history to provide guidelines for action'.[92] It was this cultural consensus over *One-Third of a Nation*'s claims to objectivity that sanctioned and protected its critique of the limits of New Deal reform, meaning that the play ultimately stood as a trickier target for censorship than the abrasive, polarising, surreal satire of *Injunction Granted*. Although *One-Third of a Nation* suggested the need for a more drastic political transformation than the continued tethering of state housing policy to private interests, it largely faltered in providing broader 'guidelines for action' beyond the expansion of the 1937 Housing Act.

Despite differences in form, *One-Third of a Nation* and *If You Lived Here* ... rest on similar principles and struggle with the same limits. Both projects construct a usable past as a pedagogical encounter for spectators and visitors to critically engage with the facts in order to develop guidelines for action.

---

89   Ibid.
90   'One-Third of a Nation', *Sunday Worker* Jan 23rd 1938, p. 12.
91   Brown and O'Connor, p. 169.
92   Haworth Jones, p. 715.

Yet, despite the 'meticulous attention to authenticity' demanded by such an approach, unmapped areas, blind spots and dead ends persist. In part, this is linked with the contradictory production and reception of these works. *One-Third of a Nation* was created through, but critical of the state and *If You Lived Here...* was riddled with the paradoxes of being sited in a SoHo art gallery whilst addressing the gentrification of New York City. Despite these contradictions, both projects form collective attempts to draw, teach and read from a cognitive map. But in the map's reliance on the forms of knowledge sanctioned and endorsed by the structures of oppression which prompted the need for such a map in the first place, both projects falter in their capacity to rest for a moment in seeking out more speculative and militant modes of working and thinking together.

The function of the discursive aspect in *If You Lived Here...* at least in part operated to remedy such omissions in providing an arena for the development of action, as did the contrasts between different image registers that marked the exhibition's cognitive demand upon the viewer. In comparison, the Little Man as personification of *One-Third of a Nation's* ambitions was far simpler in the demands he placed on the audience. Unlike the satirical, unruly and sometimes violent interruptions that marked the more eruptive Living Newspaper *Injunction Granted*, the only militant moment in *One-Third of a Nation* is the rent strike. Moving outwards from the scene of the hotbeds in Harlem, this scene offered an emotive picture of collective struggle. The rent strikers did not begin that action because of a lesson learned from the facts of history, but because their collective living conditions had become unbearable. This begins to mark out the limits to social documentary and the cognitive map as aesthetic modes that diminish the speculative and the emotional in favour of a usable past, which is less romantic in its recourse to history, and instead seeks out objective authenticity. In turning towards the exhibition *Roofs for 40 Million*, and the centrality therein of documentary photography as another response to the Wagner-Steagall Housing Act in the opening of chapter four, we can better think through the historical limitations to such a process of mapping. Or in other words, we can begin to see how the model of a usable past might end up merely repeating, rather than reigniting unresolved struggles of the past, and thus disallowing the creation of a militant imaginary based on, as Bloch writes, prevented futures. In picking up on this aspect of the Depression era quest for a usable past in relation to the impetus towards a socially useful art practice in the 1990s, the final chapter of this book begins to indicate more precisely the limits to social documentary as a seedbed for social practice in its emphasis, above all, on 'the facts' as a means towards social transformation, asking how we might supplement the cognitive map with more utopian and multi-temporal, rather than utilitarian and linear visions.

CHAPTER 4

Race, Nation and Usable Pasts

I want to begin by reiterating that the only militant moment of community formation in *One-Third of a Nation* is the rent strike. Moving outwards from the hotbeds in Harlem, those scenes dramatise the formation of an oppositional community through the struggle for better living conditions. Rather than the organic romanticism that underpinned dominant, Depression era transpositions of community onto nation, here we see how community is formed in resistance to the violence and domination that is the bedrock of the nation. Following this logic, it must be noted that alongside New Deal era housing reforms such as the Wagner-Steagall Act, the period also saw the continued legal enshrinement of racist conditions of access to mortgages and homeownership. As the 1938 Federal Housing Authority Underwriting Manual states, 'If a neighborhood is to retain stability, it is necessary that properties shall continue to be occupied by the same social and racial classes. A change in social or racial occupancy generally contributes to instability and a decline in values'.[1] Such covenants prohibited African Americans from homeownership to a large degree, and rental markets were no less exclusionary. As Horace Cayton wrote in 1940, 'Negro residents of the Chicago "Black Belt" pay as much per cubic foot per room as that paid by wealthy residents for equivalent space of the Lakeside Drive'.[2]

The rent strike scene in *One-Third of a Nation* disrupts the national-populist dimensions within the New Deal that primarily sought to overcome social divisions through the unifying labour of rebuilding the nation. In this sense, the scene also relates to how struggles around living conditions and social reproduction frequently assume some autonomy from those waged at work. As David Harvey notes, in the US, urban politics have largely emphasised individual and group identification with ethnicity, race and territoriality rather than class, while in Ira Katznelson's analysis, this 'American exceptionalism' frequently results in a 'radical separation in people's consciousness, speech, and activity of the politics of work from the politics of community'.[3] This does not mean that class politics are absent from US political life, but rather, that they are frequently isolated to the arena of work relations. Within struggles around

---

1   Federal Housing Administration 1938.
2   Cayton, p. 18.
3   Harvey, 1989, p. 87 and Katznelson, p. 6.

housing, ethnic, religious or regional community ties are often emphasised over class identification. Therefore, housing and living conditions constitute a critical category for understanding how communities are formed by material domination and exclusion, as well as through social bonds that extend beyond the nuclei of the family and the workplace.

This chapter begins with a discussion of works by Berenice Abbot and the Photo League Feature Group that were displayed in the exhibition *Roofs for 40 Million* (1938). The analysis of those works and the exhibition allows for a sharpening of focus on the nationalist dimensions of the quest for a usable past within documentary practice. Following on from this, the chapter turns to the Feature Group's *Harlem Document* (1938–9) and Richard Wright's *12 Million Black Voices* (1941) as works that have a more complex relationship to the pursuit of an idealised teleology and nationalist rhetoric within the latter period of the Cultural Front. Although both *Harlem Document* and *12 Million Black Voices* fall within the bounds of a documentary practice, their tone and method are markedly different to both *Roofs for 40 Million* and the works discussed in the previous chapter. Importantly, both works put the subjectivity of their makers into the picture in a way that confronts the viewer/reader more directly, and in doing so these works do not seek to paper over social divisions or assume any neutrality. The second half of the chapter turns to Rick Lowe's *Project Row Houses*, begun 1993 in Houston, Texas, a work that seeks to position art as a direct mediator for the formation of communities. *Project Row Houses* has significantly altered the fabric of the Third Ward in Houston. In doing so, it exists as a tentative contradiction to the world that surrounds it, a quality that also produced the necessity to step into the realm of the 'practical' through engaging directly with urban planning. During its lifetime, *Project Row Houses* has often wavered between the utilitarian and the utopian. By closing with *Project Row Houses*, I aim to centre a case study that prioritises speculative and relational modes of working and thinking together, while also addressing the instrumentalising of such practices. In staying with projects that examine the perpetual housing crisis in the United States, this chapter shifts focus from economic modes of exploitation through land speculation, towards stressing the ways in which community formation in the United States is so intimately bound up with processes of racialisation.

1   Documentary and Nationalism

Roofs for 40 Million was a group exhibition organised by An American Group Inc. and held at the galleries of La Maison Française in the Rockefeller Centre, and thus prominently displayed in Midtown Manhattan.[4] Established by artists Stuart Edie, Robert Phillip, Frederic Knight, Anatol Shulkin, Jacob Getlar Smith and Chuzo Tamotzu in 1931 to organize exhibitions for young, lesser-known artists, An American Group's exhibition scheduling was more exclusive and prioritised professional interests over concerns with political organising, in contrast with the two other main CPUSA associated organisations for visual artists, the American Artists' Congress and the Artists' Union.[5] However, like these groups and the broader CPUSA culture, An American Group aimed for an 'esthetic united front' and was dominated by Communist artists and fellow travellers such as Raphael Soyer, Anton Refregier, Stuart Davis and Philip Evergood.[6] These artists all exhibited in *Roofs for 40 Million*, which encompassed 200 works by over 100 artists that addressed housing, homelessness and poor living conditions through sculpture, architectural models, painting, prints and photography. In tandem with the exhibition, An American Group organised a symposium that hosted speakers from the NYCHA, the Tenants League, as well as engineers and architects. The work in the exhibition was largely in a documentary mode, and like *One-Third of a Nation*, criticised New Deal housing policy, in particular the limitations of the Wagner-Steagall Housing Act. The relationship between public talks, documentary and exhibition practice within *Roofs for 40 Million* corresponds to the structure of *If You Lived Here ...* and clarifies that the reshaping of exhibitions as projects and as a type of discursive practice in the 1990s was not without earlier precedents.

New Masses reported on *Roofs for 40 Million* over two issues in April 1938, with the first article including reproductions of ten of the prints and paintings, alongside a feature on the housing crisis by Sidney Hill, who had also authored a CPUSA pamphlet entitled *Housing Under Capitalism* in 1935. The following issue printed a review of the exhibition by Elizabeth Noble, pseudonym of the critic Elizabeth McCausland. McCausland said that she was reluctant to speak of specific works due to the volume of contributions, and instead heaped praise on the cooperative organisation of the exhibition, expressing admiration that the organisers charged visitors 15 cents for entry, rather than asking artists for exhibition fees.[7] Alongside the political example *Roofs for 40 Million*

---

4 There's an irony that *Roofs* was displayed in the Rockefeller Centre, a prime example of capitalist urban renewal that had replaced six square blocks of deteriorating brownstones. Such contradictions can be viewed as foreshadowing Rosler's anxiety about staging *If You Lived Here ...* at the Dia Foundation. See Gilmartin et al. 1987, p. 30.
5 Hemingway 2002, p. 133.
6 Ibid.
7 Elizabeth Noble 1938, p. 26.

set for artist-run efforts, McCausland noted that the exhibition looked 'remarkably well, especially in view of the tremendous amount of material gotten into the seventh floor galleries', emphasising that the photography room was 'particularly happy in design'.[8] During the 1930s in the United States, photographic culture on the left was primarily focused around the Workers' Film and Photo League (founded in 1930), which after 1933 simply became the Film and Photo League. In 1936, the group split between filmmakers and photographers, and the Photo League was formed.[9] Photographers with heterogeneous aesthetic approaches were involved with the earlier incarnation of the Workers' Film and Photo League, as well as in the post-1936 Photo League. Both formations included committed Communist Party members alongside fellow travellers, with these photographers taking up a range of visual approaches, from aestheticism to social documentary.[10] The Photo League is comparable with the Dance League, the Workers' Theatre movement and the John Reed Clubs discussed in earlier chapters, and, as mentioned previously, it is helpful to think of these formations as 'transmission belts', a Leninist term Theodore Draper uses to analyse the US communist movement.[11] There were frequent crossovers between these cultural groupings within the context of the Popular Front, as exemplified by Anne Tucker's description of Photo League fundraisers held at venues like the left-wing cabaret Café Society, which featured entertainment by the Katharine Dunham dancers and folk groups like the Weavers and Almanac Singers.[12] Many of the photographers included within *Roofs for 40 Million* were important figures within this milieu, and the exhibition exemplifies the increasing centrality of that medium to the Cultural Front as the 1930s progressed.

McCausland viewed *Roofs for 40 Million* as an advance on previous displays about housing such as MoMA's 'America Can't Have Housing?' exhibition of 1934, and the 1937 installation of a typical slum tenement in the apse of the Cathedral of St. John the Divine in New York. Unlike these efforts, *Roofs for 40 Million* was described as provoking action in the viewer. The MoMA exhibition had been based around sociological displays that outlined slum clearances and possibilities for low-cost housing, charting the evolution of the tenement from a 'prize-winning design in 1879' to the entropic decline of these buildings as they became known as the 'Old Law Tenements'.[13] In contrast, McCausland

---

8   Ibid.
9   Levy 2011, p. 63.
10 For an overview of the League's history and its demise, see Tucker 2011.
11 Draper 1960, p. 182. See Hemingway 2002 for an account of the John Reed Clubs.
12 Tucker 2001.
13 Lyman Paine Jr. 1934, pp. 75–7.

explained that *Roofs for 40 Million* provoked 'a strong and passionate protest against the evils portrayed', thankfully avoiding the sentiment of 'How horrible this is!' and instead prompting the viewer to feel that 'I must do something about this!' Again, the relationship to *If You Lived Here ...* is striking in the sense that Rosler was intent on not mounting a 'pity show'. In avoiding this, both projects sought to develop a multi-dimensional map of the issue at hand. Overall, McCausland's review of *Roofs for 40 Million* stressed that when art is 'used in this spirit', it 'can really function as a weapon', a view that had been a mainstay within CPUSA writings on art and culture since before the Third Period, and centred on affirming representations of proletarian experience as a means to galvanise political action.[14] In contrast with the earlier emphasis on social realist painting and printmaking, McCausland singled out photography as the vanguard of Democratic Front aesthetics through its claims to objectivity and realism, as well as its reproductive potential. This chimed with the majority of reviews of *Roofs for 40 Million* in emphasising the photographic work within that exhibition, and exemplifies how that medium was foregrounded as uniquely capable of being weaponised through its claims to objectivity.[15] Yet, the stress on 'facts' within McCausland's review should not be taken as reducible to photography – as we have seen in the discussion of *One-Third of a Nation* – but rather as encapsulating the ways in which documentary was positioned as the primary method for attaining the 'evidence' valorised within the quest to establish a usable past.

By the 1930s, photography already existed as a medium highly capable of indexing the past and invoking residual forms of pre-industrial life, either as a usable past or savage remnant. Jacob Riis's *How the Other Half Lives: Studies among the Tenements of New York* (1890) is paradigmatic of how photographers invoked the past to represent and reinforce spatial and temporal disjuncture between communities, with the tenement forming a 'type' to express difference. Riis was a Danish-born immigrant who became a journalist, assigned to work with the police. As an extension of his photographic work, he began running lantern slide shows, acting as a mediator between his predominantly Christian, bourgeois audience and the 'other half' that were documented in his images, immigrant inhabitants of tenements and slums. Riis assumed the role of adventurer, a trope related to the contemporaneous nineteenth-century literary convention of viewing the modern city as so fragmented that certain

---

14 Noble (McCausland) 1938.
15 In this respect, the inclusion and stress on photography within *Roofs for 40 Million* meant An American Group were pointing to their forthcoming obsolescence as painters of social realism.

quarters could be rendered as 'another country', or as dating to a different time.[16] Through Riis, we can see that the practice of mapping mobilised within *If You Lived Here ...* and by the Little Man in *One-Third of a Nation* can also take a reactionary, paternalistic turn. Within *Roofs for 40 Million*, the mapping of tenements and slums as sites of social dislocation took on conflicting registers, negotiating between the emergent moralism of the Democratic Front and the Photo League's oscillating allegiances to aestheticism and didacticism.

There were 12 photographers who displayed work in *Roofs for 40 Million*, all of whom were associated with the Photo League. Prominent participants included Sid Grossman, the Communist co-founder of the League who was nicknamed 'Commissar' for his uncompromising politics and critique of aestheticism.[17] On the other hand, Berenice Abbot, who had emerged from the Parisian modernist avant-garde and bohemian Greenwich Village scene into the Photo League as a fellow traveller, also showed a large selection of works. She had 12 images in the photography section of *Roofs* whereas all the other photographers had no more than four works on display. The photographs were primarily drawn from her *Changing New York* series, produced whilst she was employed by the WPA-FAP, although she also displayed photographs of mining families in West Virginia and New England farmhouses that were taken on her travels throughout the USA with McCausland, who was her partner. Abbot's New York photographs included shots of skyscrapers such as the *Daily News Building* (1935) and representations of slums and makeshift housing such as *Huts and Unemployed* (Fig. 32), (1935) alongside portrayals of the dispossessed (*Shelter on the Water Front, Coenties Slip, Pier 5, East River, Manhattan*). (Figs. 33)

Huts and Unemployed shows a man lighting another man's cigarette in front of two adjacent huts. An upright broom stands between them, leaning against the wall of the wooden hut, with the door of the hut left ajar to reveal a table that holds tins of food and a bucket resting on the ground. The interior of the door has been pasted over with what looks like wallpaper, a decorative gesture echoed in the framed pictures that bedeck the neighbouring hut. We presume that these men live here, with their sharing of a cigarette working along similar lines as the decoration that personalises their dwellings. Both aspects serve to humanise these men, displaying a sense of life continuing among the dereliction. Two oil drums with grills placed over them sit at the foreground of the photograph, with the bashed-in metal of the larger drum forming a strange, human-like face. This sense of rough materiality – along with the stacked-up

---

16   Stange 1989, p. 13.
17   Klein 2011, p. 17.

FIGURE 32 Berenice Abbot, *Huts and Unemployed*, from the series *Changing New York*, (Federal Art Project) 1935
COURTESY OF THE NEW YORK PUBLIC LIBRARY

wooden boards that form the roofs of the huts – indicates Abbot's allegiances with surrealism, whilst the two men at the centre form the subjects of social documentary. In this sense, Abbot's photograph can be compared with the contribution of Aaron Siskind and the Photo League Feature Group, *Portrait of a Tenement*, also included in *Roofs for 40 Million*, and similarly bridging the gap between modernism and social documentary.

The Feature Group was a sub-section of the Photo League set up by the modernist photographer Aaron Siskind to conduct studies of different neighbourhoods in New York. From 1936–40, they made four long-term collaborative projects on social issues around housing. These projects were entitled *Portrait of a Tenement* (1936), *Dead End: The Bowery* (1937), *Harlem Document* (1937–40) and *Park Avenue North and South* (1938). In 1938, aspects of *Portrait of a Tenement* were shown in *Roofs for 40 Million*, with the photographs included in the exhibition mostly showing bare, run-down interiors without their inhabitants, and instead zooming in on architectural details, signs of domesticity or a crucifix that rests above a single, iron-frame bed. In their study of the tenement interior, these works adhered to the overall aim of *Roofs for 40 Million* to produce a sociological study of poor housing, with this ambition relying on the

FIGURE 33 Berenice Abbot, *Shelter on the Water Front, Coenties Slip, Pier 5, East River, Manhattan* from the series *Changing New York*, (Federal Art Project) 1938
COURTESY OF THE NEW YORK PUBLIC LIBRARY

representational tendencies of a dominant, depression-era documentary that had led the tenement to stand as a 'type' by the late 1930s. Yet, unlike a Lukácsean idea of the type as a de-reifying force, Abbot's *Huts and Unemployed* and the Photo League's *Portrait of a Tenement* struggle to counter the naturalised, utilitarian history of such representations.

Earlier, literary attempts at representing tenement life within the CPUSA were less formally constricted, and in writing by Mike Gold we can see the potentially revolutionary force – contra Riis – of *affirming* the tenement as 'another country'. Here, the tenement forms a container for struggles that dramatise psychic experience along lines that surpass the instrumentalising of 'art as a weapon'. For Gold, the founding editor of *New Masses*, novelist, and foremost literary critic of the CPUSA, growing up in a tenement informed his development of a proletarian aesthetic that he hoped could become a 'religion of the masses'.[18] Particularly notable is his 1921 Whitman-influenced manifesto *Towards Proletarian Art*, which stated that 'All that I know of Life I learned in the tenement', declaring that that 'tall somber mass, holding its freight of obscure human destinies is the pattern in which my being has been cast'.[19] The significance Gold affords the tenement connects with Lukácsean typification, as evidenced in passages that state 'I am not an individual: I am all that the tenement group poured into me during those early years of my spiritual travail'.[20] Gold poses the tenement as a wellspring for the expression of suffering, insisting that 'Art is the tenement pouring out its soul through us … Life for us has been the tenement that bore and molded us through years of meaningful pain'.[21] Here, the idea of 'meaningful pain' should not be understood as martyrdom, but rather as the spur to further action. Indeed, lived experience distils and takes on the magnitude of social history in its capacity to prompt solutions, with this working in a similar vein to the rent strike in *One-Third of a Nation*.

We can also see the tenement as the stimulus for transformation in Gold's fictionalised autobiography *Jews Without Money* (1929). The character of Gold's mother, Katie Gold, organises a rent strike against the corrupt and negligent landlord, Mr. Zunzer. She begins by describing Zunzer as a 'yellow faced murderer' and hopes that 'his false teeth choke him to death next week!'[22] Some tenants respond to the misery of living in Zunzer's property by searching for new dwellings, but find none that are unoccupied and affordable. At that point, one woman laments that 'The tenements are the same everywhere, the landlords the same … I have seen places today an Irisher wouldn't live in, and the rents are higher than here'.[23] This drama culminates with Katie Gold refusing to pay rent and invoking the Angel of Death against Zunzer, with militancy and religion posed as the paths through which pain is made meaningful. As well as the tenement forming a type potentially capable of encompassing *all* proletarians, we also see that all landlords are 'the same everywhere', with this form of typification working in similar ways to the role of the police in Lacy's *The Oakland Projects*, or the judges in *Injunction Granted*, as discussed in Chapter

18   Hemingway 2002, p. 14.
19   Gold 1972, p. 64.
20   Ibid.
21   Gold 1972, p. 65.
22   Gold 1930, p. 254.
23   Gold 1930, pp. 254–5.

One. Furthermore, the 'tenement group' described by Gold in *Towards Proletarian Art* is nuanced in *Jews Without Money*, appearing not as a singular mass but rather a series of interlocking but isolable worlds differentiated by ethnicity and degrees of suffering: as the woman in *Jews Without Money* dismissively notes, 'I have seen places today an Irisher wouldn't live in'. Such separation also permeates *One-Third of a Nation*, where communities overwhelmingly emerge through the forms of domination and exploitation that shape place and ethnicity.

This returns us to the 'American exceptionalism' described by Katznelson at the outset of this chapter. I want to stress that in response to the nationalistic promise of a communal wholeness proffered by the New Deal and supported by the Democratic Front, the 'exceptionalism' that marks the separation between the politics of work and the politics of community offered a crucial terrain of struggle. The limitations of Abbot and the Feature Group's work in *Roofs for 40 Million* primarily rests upon the exhibition's attempt to paper over the contradictions of urban living, class struggle and ethnic difference through appeals to liberal notions of equality and nationhood. *Roofs for 40 Million* sought to invoke a 'usable past' and mobilise documentary as 'a weapon', albeit one which sought to incorporate individuals and groups into a monolithic, de-fanged notion of 'the people' that ultimately harmonised with the dominant New Deal national ideology.

McCausland and Abbot's plan to produce a photo-book of the nation together, images from which were included in *Roofs for 40 Million*, is exemplary of the nationalistic impulse behind the drive to find a 'usable past' as it took shape within the Democratic Front. The project began with the two women exchanging letters where Abbot declared her 'passion' for New York. McCausland responded by affirmatively listing her adoration of 'brownstone stoops', 'funny facades in Troy, N.Y.', as well as her 'fantastic passion' for 'Nantucket and Cape Cod, and all the little hill towns in the Sangre de Cristo mountains'. She closes this mawkish list by emphasising, above all, her 'fantastic passion for AMERICA'.[24] In this project, McCausland and Abbot sought to capture the nuances of the US, set within an over-arching affirmation of the nation. Such appeals to a usable past were frequently articulated as a means to posit the so-called levelling effects of the Depression through affirming national, rather than class or ethnic experience, thus standing as an attempt to override the American exceptionalism described by Katznelson.[25]

---

24 Weissman 2011, p. 90.
25 Haworth Jones 1971, p. 718.

As we shall see in *Harlem Document*, the limitations of this can be most forcefully registered in the disjuncture between appeals to a 'usable past' and the experience of African Americans. However, I should clarify that my argument is not one that proposes a wholesale failure of photography or social documentary, but rather seeks to expose the limitations of a political and aesthetic imaginary that affirms unobtainable wholeness over the very contradictions that clarify the experience of oppression and exploitation. While the episodic structure and dialogical quality of *If You Lived Here ...* and *One-Third of a Nation* at least in part foreclosed the affirmation of an exclusionary 'wholeness', the static rendering of the dispossessed and the tenement as types by Abbot and the Feature Group faltered in their capacity to de-reify those representations and socialise their implications. The limit point of documentary becomes even more apparent in *Harlem Document*, as the mode of production used to generate that work explicitly sought to 'build community', an impossible venture writ large on the surfaces of the images themselves.

2 Blackness and the Limits of a Usable Past

Ann Petry's novel, *The Street* (1946) is set in and among the tenement houses, nightclubs and bars of Harlem in the 1940s. The novel tracks the thwarted attempts of Lutie Johnson to move herself and her son, Bub, off the fabled 'street', a site marked by 'slums and dirt and poverty', in the words of the lawyer Lutie employs to try and get Bub out of trouble. Lutie's life is marked by the experience of being 'hemmed into an ever-narrowing space', blocked by a wall 'built up brick by brick by eager white hands'.[26] Throughout the novel, Petry conveys the intense claustrophobia of tenement living in Harlem as a central feature of African American experience during the 1940s, following the first great migration North. In making *Harlem Document*, the Feature Group sought to engage and capture such experiences and stories.

In contrast with *Portrait of a Tenement*, the length of production for *Harlem Document* meant the work extended into several areas of study and was far more comprehensive than other Feature Group projects on housing.[27] Planned as a book that was never published, the initial idea was to organise the publication into chapters on labour, health, housing, religion, recreation, society, youth

---

26 Petry 1946, pp. 323–4.
27 Berger 2011, p. 30.

and crime.²⁸ *Harlem Document* began with an invitation to Siskind from a man who presented himself as a sociologist called Michael Carter, but was actually a journalist called Milton Smith. Carter's invitation was framed in terms of a project that would involve the Feature Group making photographs to accompany a text he was writing, with the combination of these elements intended to help 'build community' in Harlem.²⁹ In response to Carter's invitation, Siskind assembled a group of photographers including Lucy Ashjian, Richard Lyon, Jack Manning, Miller Simon and Sol Prom. Aside from Carter, who was African American, all the other participants involved in the production of *Harlem Document* were white and mostly Jewish. *Harlem Document* presented an opportunity for the Feature Group to create new situational modes of working with their subjects in line with their aim of building community, and the project relied on an extended period of collaborative, on-site work that Siskind described as 'preparation in excess'.³⁰ Feature Group members would regularly travel uptown to visit various sites, take notes, research the history of Harlem and engage in casual conversation as well as formal interviews with subjects, whilst consistently taking photographs and reviewing this material along the way. Because the material was being prepared for a book, we should understand the photographs not as finished works, but rather as material evidence of a process that would eventually need editing to accompany Carter's text.

Clearly, the emphasis on research, process and dialogue with subjects foreshadows key tenets of later social practice. Moreover, in distinction to the view of documentary valorised by McCausland in *Roofs for 40 Million*, and aimed for within *One-Third of a Nation*, Siskind wrote that the Feature Group were not trying to capture an 'objective' view of Harlem, but rather to record a 'feeling', and index the experiences they gained in the production of this work.³¹ In this sense, they went beyond the dominant ambitions and conventions of documentary during the period. The collaborative nature of the project, as well as the emphasis on process, returns us to some of the principles that guided *If You Lived Here ...* as well as Lacy's *The Oakland Projects*. Furthermore, Siskind's disavowal of objectivity is important in relation to the dynamic between the Feature Group photographer and their subjects. Just as social practice artists profess political and ethical qualms today about speaking on behalf of, or

---

28   Later, in 1981, Aaron Siskind published his own version that encompassed photographs from 1932–1940, not all of which were taken during the Feature Group project. See Siskind.
29   Blair, p. 32.
30   Blair, p. 24.
31   Ibid.

representing participants, *Harlem Document* anticipates those anxieties, with Siskind stressing that the project was based around a series of highly particular encounters rather than aiming to produce a structural and objective view, which was the usual ambition of documentarians during the period. In thinking specifically about photography, it is also notable that Feature Group members did not use the miniature cameras popular with most documentarians at the time. Whilst those cameras enabled the photographer to be less obviously intrusive, capturing an image from a removed position, Siskind was described as travelling through Harlem with a view-type camera and tripod. In Joseph Entin's account, this bulky equipment was part of how Siskind sought to establish a dialogue in the production of *Harlem Document*, with the ambition of securing a situational encounter between subject and photographer forming the backbone of the project.[32]

Akin to *If You Lived Here ...* and the works by Lacy discussed in the first two chapters, *Harlem Document* also had multiple audiences that accessed the project through different routes. These included the mass media, local settings and institutions established by the Photo League such as their magazine *Photo Notes*, which provided extensive coverage of the project. The Feature Group met every Friday at Siskind's house, and *Harlem Document* was the primary discussion point from 1938–1940, as registered in the announcements published in *Photo Notes*. Although the photographs from *Harlem Document* were always attributed to individuals in displays and reproductions, the weekly meetings presented an opportunity to explore more collective modes of production through sharing recent work, planning assignments as well as working on circulation.[33] One can also speculate that these meetings formed an important aspect of the project in terms of reflecting upon its aims and possibilities, both politically and aesthetically.

The first public outing for *Harlem Document* took place at the 135th Street YMCA in February 1939, roughly six months into the project. The Feature Group showed 40 prints, and the National Urban League, a liberal civil rights organisation for African Americans whose objective was to help rural migrants adapt to city living, sponsored the exhibition. Siskind wrote in *Photo Notes* that the first showing of the project was viewed as an opportunity for the Feature Group to gain 'the advice and assistance of the people who live in Harlem' on how to proceed.[34] This approach towards display and the circulation of images differs significantly from the dominant practices of documentary during the

---

32 Entin 2007, p. 115.
33 *Photo Notes*, December 1938, p. 1.
34 *Photo Notes*, Feb 1939, p. 1.

period. If most documentarians recorded poor living conditions in particular neighbourhoods for audiences other than the subjects represented, the Feature Group attempted to produce the *Harlem Document* for the community it represented. This use of the exhibition as a mediator between the Feature Group and their subjects/audience was recounted in *Photo Notes*. Following the close of the exhibition, *Photo Notes* reported that 'Instead of assigning someone to review the "Harlem Document" exhibition ... we are letting the people of Harlem give their comments as they wrote them down in the guest book'.[35] Over two pages in *Photo Notes* a variety of comments were reproduced. Many viewers registered the contrast between the poor housing of Harlem and the rest of New York, with several commentators hoping the project would assist in transforming those conditions. One visitor stated that the *Harlem Document* 'should move all to action', and others affirmed that the pictures ought to 'open the eyes and pocketbooks of the lucrative exploiters of the poor'.[36] Akin to the way the Living Newspaper sought to establish a bloc between audiences and performers, *Harlem Document* strove for a similar affinity between Harlemites and the Feature Group (as representatives of the Cultural Front.) However, several visitors strongly opposed the exhibition, stating in their comments that representing Harlem in such a negative light would produce further barriers to progress and emancipation. In particular, the focus on housing was criticised despite being 'true and factual'. Instead of dwelling on poverty, commentators remarked that the Feature Group should have paid attention to the intellectual and cultural side of Harlem 'such as the thousands at night schools, the various churches and forums, the library and its avid readers'. Others disparaged the aesthetic of the photographs, claiming they lacked 'artistic value'.[37] The partly hostile reception at the YMCA was taken seriously by the Feature Group, and following this outing they returned to Harlem to shoot 'good looking' housing, local artists, performers and churches in order to present a more balanced view.[38]

With regards to the aim of shaping *Harlem Document* in a way that was sympathetic to the community it represented, a symposium was organised following the exhibition to gain further feedback. A mix of speakers were invited to contribute to a dialogue around the project; these including Reverend J. Brown, a local Unitarian minister, James Flood, a housing expert and director of the Harlem River Houses, Lemuel Foster from the WPA and James Hubert from the

---

35   'Feature Group's "Towards a Harlem Document"', pp. 1–2.
36   Ibid.
37   Ibid.
38   Berger 2011, p. 33.

Urban League. James Ford, the Vice-Presidential candidate for the CPUSA also spoke, although he is only listed as a 'union leader' in the *Photo Notes* account of the event, most likely in an attempt to downplay links to the Party. There was a strong emphasis on health within the symposium, with speakers from the WPA Tuberculosis Center, as well as a presentation from William Traynham, an executive at Harlem Hospital.[39] The symposium afforded the Feature Group another opportunity to hear reactions to the project, as well as to deepen their understanding of social issues in the community as they proceeded to expand their subject matter. The symposium formed one component of the emphasis on process within Harlem Document. Like the public programming of *If You Lived Here ...* and the symposium of housing that formed part of *Roofs for 40 Million*, the integration of such events within art projects and exhibitions forms a central strategy in attempting to transform an audience into participants.

The exhibition and symposium for *Harlem Document* was strongly characterised by its Popular Front era collaboration between the Urban League, the CPUSA, government branches and local religious groups. During the Third Period, African American Party activists had generally treated reform organisations and the church with deep hostility. Mark Naison describes this as resulting from the ultra-left, sectarian line of the Sixth Comintern Congress, noting that prominent black Communists such as Charles Alexander and Cyril Briggs would openly deride the NAACP, National Urban League and the church as the 'lap dogs at the table of the imperialists'.[40] As described in Chapter Two, the CPUSA did not make significant inroads into the African American community in Harlem until the period of the Popular Front, when the Party emerged as a focal point of political and cultural activity among Harlem intellectuals. However, towards the latter half of the 1940s – notably after the attempted Communist nationalism of the Democratic Front – several leading black intellectuals such as Claude McKay, Chester Himes and Richard Wright, who had joined the party or been fellow travellers during the Popular Front, would attack the CPUSA for cynically cultivating a relationship with African Americans for

---

39 'Symposium on Harlem Document', p. 1.
40 Naison describes this strategy as primarily emerging through directives formed within the Sixth Comintern Congress. Although the Soviet Union influenced such politics, I believe hostility towards bourgeois reform associations and the church by African American Communists must also have emerged through their own experiences and dissatisfaction with those channels and non-revolutionary politics. If nothing else, it seems reductive of Naison to attribute the adoption of an ultra-left line on race relations by African American Communists entirely to the influence of the Comintern. See Naison 1983, p. 36.

votes.⁴¹ Despite the waning of attention towards race in favour of an affirmation of the false unity of 'the people' within the Democratic Front, the overall relationship between the CPUSA and African Americans from the 1920s to 40s is rich and complex. From Harry Haywood's 1928 'Self-Determination for the Black Belt' thesis which advocated a secessionist movement for African Americans, to the period of the Popular Front, there was always dissent within the CPUSA against its official analysis and political position around the so-called 'Negro question'. In its collaboration with the National Urban League, churches and CPUSA leaders such as James Ford, *Harlem Document* is exemplary of a cultural milieu where the Party had gained a significant foothold. At least in part, this happened through nurturing a relationship with established pillars of the Harlem community, the Party's internationalism on issues such as the Italian invasion of Ethiopia, as well as through partnering with nationwide reform organisations.

In terms of other modes of distribution that reached beyond Harlem, some of Siskind's photographs for *Harlem Document* were reproduced in *Fortune* magazine in July 1939, alongside a text by Carter. Forming part of a larger feature about New York City that studied different neighbourhoods, Carter's essay was remarkably critical for the context of a business-oriented magazine with a largely white readership. Carter described how the over-population of Harlem produced profits for the overwhelmingly white landlords who owned the tenements, noting that the median rent across New York was $35 a month, whilst in Harlem it was $50 due to over-demand.⁴² Like the depiction of poor housing in Harlem in *One-Third of a Nation*, Carter also reported on the 'hot beds', detailing how 50 cents was the cost for an eight-hour sleeping shift. The article repeatedly highlights how white ownership of businesses maintained severe levels of inequality even among the affluent, explaining that 'Even the Savoy ballroom, gay birthplace of the Lindy Hop, though managed by a $20,000-a-year black, is owned by a $100,000-a-year-white'.⁴³ Following the display at the YMCA, it is clear Carter and the Feature Group also used the space in *Fortune* to present Harlem in a positive light, and the report included coverage of religious organisations, sports, entertainment and successful black doctors, lawyers and business owners.⁴⁴ Still, the most poignant line in the article is where Carter states that 'Harlem is simply a vast rooming house' registering the way poor housing conditions tended to eclipse all other aspects of life, a quality that per-

---

41   Naison 1983, p. 193.
42   Carter 1939, p. 78.
43   Carter 1939, p. 170.
44   Ibid.

meates the psychic and material environment of contemporary novels such as Petry's *The Street*, and Gold's statement that 'Life for us has been the tenement ...'[45]

The tone of the May 1940 *Look* feature on *Harlem Document* was even more confrontational to its readers. Here, Carter's writing provided captions to the images that occasionally, taken out of context, could be understood to be speaking, not in a critical, but in a white-supremacist voice. For example, above a large reproduction of a woman scrubbing the floor, the title reads 'Harlem's People at Work – on jobs that keep them in their place'. This tone underpins the link made in *Look* between the Feature Group's photographs of Harlem and Richard Wright's recently published *Native Son* (1940). The plot of *Native Son* follows Bigger Thomas, a young black man from the slums of the Chicago South Side, as he commits violent crimes against both the white ruling class and members of his own community. Entitled '244,000 Native Sons', the *Look* article portrayed Bigger Thomas as a 'victim of his environment' and explored how the living conditions in Harlem were comparable to those depicted by Wright. For example, next to a photograph of a group of young boys the caption reads 'Harlem delinquents in the making', and even the images of leisure were described in terms of relief from drudgery. Maurice Berger describes the *Look* coverage as a refusal by Carter and the Feature Group to downplay the realities of poverty and racism in the North, relating this to the usual presentation of these problems in *Look* as limited to the South.[46] The predominantly white, affluent, Northern readership was thus faced with a reality much closer to their own geographically, but a world apart socially.

In this light, the presentations of *Harlem Document* in *Look* and *Fortune* could be viewed as repeating the documentary trope of enabling viewers to witness a world drastically different from their own, often portrayed negatively as nonsynchronous or foreign, as in the work of Riis discussed earlier. However, *Harlem Document* in *Look* takes on a sharp, critical function towards the parcelling out of the city, with the relationship between the headlines, images and text engineered to confront the reader with their own prejudices and complicity. This works like Wright's *Native Son*, or Ann Petry's description of the poverty of Harlem as 'no accident', but rather as 'the North's lynch mob', or Peter Marcuse's statement that 'Homelessness exists not because the system is not working but because this is the way it works', painted on the walls of Dia during *If You Lived Here ...* Such statements capture the totality structuring the

---

45   Carter 1939, p. 78. Gold 1921, p. 64.
46   Berger 2011, p. 32.

conditions of dispossession in a manner that goes far beyond the invocation of a usable past as providing guidelines for action in *One-Third of a Nation*, or the documentary conventions guiding the photography presented in *Roofs for 40 Million*. *Harlem Document* refused the consignment of white supremacy to the South, as well as the idea that contemporary African American experience was on the up, by stressing the synchronic reproduction of white supremacy within the forms of employment and living conditions available to African Americans in the North.[47] This brought the seemingly nonsynchronous living conditions of African Americans into the bourgeois homes of the readers of *Look* and *Fortune*, and if this came with an air of impending threat and disjuncture, it should be read as related to the so-called 'Protest Fiction' of Wright and Petry, rather than as sensationalising violence and misery.[48]

This critical sense of disjuncture was internal to the practice of *Harlem Document*. The attempt of the Feature Group to establish a dialogue between photographer and subjects and help build community can be felt in several of the photographs and rarely appears ameliorative. The mood is frequently strained, recording tense social interactions between white photographers and black subjects. The photograph by Siskind of the Brotherhood of Sleeping Car Porters union members stands out in this regard. (Fig. 34) Showing a group of seated railroad workers, mostly facing forwards, presumably towards a stage outside the picture frame, the photograph appears to have been taken at a meeting or rally. However, some faces turn towards Siskind expressing suspicion, amusement or surprise at his presence, recording the photographer's presence within a community he was not part of. This produces an estrangement between viewer, audience and photographer and here, the Feature Group's aim to form a bloc with their subject falters. A similar effect appears in Siskind's photographs of a Store Front church. (Fig. 35)[49] The woman seated on the far right scowls contemptuously towards the camera as it focuses on another woman in the centre of the frame, holding an infant and in the throes of religious fervour. These photograph can be read as showing the rebuffed attempts of outsiders to assist in 'building community', and their presence amongst other images which record more typical scenes of impoverished domestic life, or the white patron-

---

47 Petry 1946, p. 323.
48 For an overview of the 'protest novel', see Ward Jr.
49 The curators of the George Eastman House, which provided the reproduction of this image for publication here informed me that all known extant prints that Siskind made at the time of the *Harlem Document* project crop out the woman in question and that the reproduction published here is from a print made in 1980 by Michaela Allan Murphy under the supervision of and signed by Aaron Siskind.

FIGURE 34 Aaron Siskind, 'Brotherhood of the Sleeping Car Porters', from *Harlem Document*, gelatin silver print, ca. 1935, George Eastman Museum, gift of Aaron Siskind
© VIRGINIA MUSEUM OF FINE ART

age of Harlem night spots, registers the mixed success of the Feature Group's attempt to go beyond documentary conventions, present a new picture of Harlem and build community.

For most writers, the photographing of black subjects by white photographers in *Harlem Document* has prompted questions about the ethics of the project.[50] Instead, I suggest we can register the aesthetic and political meaning of *Harlem Document* in how the photographs truly did capture non-recognition between white artists and black communities, with the Feature Group's attempt to overcome this making it all the more pronounced. This holds more weight than simply accusing the project of being an example of bad photographic 'ethics'. Furthermore, through this lens of analysis, the reference to *Native Son* in the *Look* feature has relevance beyond the crude use of the novel as a diagnostic tool for the social problems facing young male Harlemites. As described by Frantz Fanon, Bigger Thomas' fear of his own aggression was produced by social expectations about black men being violent, much like the *Look* depiction of Harlem as populated by 'delinquents in the making'.[51] On first glance, the citation of *Native Son* by Carter and the Feature Group would

---

50 See Berger 2011, Blair 2007, and Entin 2007.
51 Fanon 1986, p. 107.

FIGURE 35 Aaron Siskind 'Church Interior', 1938, from *Harlem Document*, gelatin silver print, printed 1980 by Michaela Allan Murphy under the supervision of Aaron Siskind. George Eastman Museum, Gift of LIGHT Gallery
© VIRGINIA MUSEUM OF FINE ART

appear to reproduce the patterns the novel critiques. But might we more usefully ask how the failed attempt of Mary Dalton and her Communist boyfriend Jan Erlone to befriend Bigger Thomas relates to the Feature Group's role in the making of *Harlem Document*?

Newly employed as the driver for the liberal, philanthropic Henry Dalton after a spate of petty crime, Bigger is supposed to drive Mary to university, but instead she directs him to take her to meet her boyfriend Jan Erlone. Once Jan joins Mary inside the car, they ask Bigger to take them to an African American restaurant on the South Side. Jan tries to engage Bigger on the topic of politics, pushing a variety of CPUSA pamphlets as they drive, before Mary begins to cry when Bigger repeatedly refuses their invitations to dinner. The whole encounter is excruciatingly tense and Mary and Jan's supercilious but well-intentioned gestures prompt shame, irritation and fear in Bigger, triggering an even greater feeling of hatred and alienation than the day-to-day racism, violence and poverty he consistently experiences. This catalyses a searing self-awareness and capacity for violence. The patronisingly proffered hand of friendship, violently rejected, relates to the disdainful looks prompted by

Siskind's camera, clarifying the chasm the Feature Group faced in attempting to 'build community' through *Harlem Document*.[52] In this sense, *Harlem Document* is not isolated from the problematic aspects of the CPUSA's drive to recruit African Americans that Wright would later sharply criticise in his article 'I Tried to Be a Communist'.[53] Yet, rather than viewing *Harlem Document* and *Native Son* as reducible to a representation of the Party's underestimation of the depths to which proletarian experience was racialised, by looking at Wright's photo book *12 Million Black Voices* we can hone in on the specific historical limitations of the drive towards an aesthetic wholeness that marked Democratic Front culture from 1938. *12 Million Black Voices* was published in 1941, when Wright was still involved with the CPUSA but becoming increasingly dissatisfied. His text, coupled with Edwin Rosskam's editorial command over FSA photographs, consistently evokes a unified voice for African American experience that necessarily rests upon an ambivalent relationship to the notion of a usable past as it was being promoted within the Cultural Front.

As the foreword states, *12 Million Black Voices* 'accepts as basic and centrally historical those materials of Negro life identified with the countless black millions who made up the bulk of the slave population during the seventeenth, eighteenth, and nineteenth centuries'.[54] The book proceeds through a series of types that make up the 12 million, many of which establish the book's dynamic as centrally concerned with the great migration North. The types include the maid, the industrial worker, the stevedore and the dancer. Urban life is described in terms that occasionally pastoralise what was left behind in the South. This is particularly pronounced along gender lines, as women are described as having 'fared better' after emancipation because they had 'worked in houses and learned to sew'.[55] Similarly, the text plays into other aspects of paternalism, pronouncing that 'We ... needed the ritual and guidance of institutions'.[56] The refrain of 'we' is repeated throughout the book, and Jeff Allred characterises this as typical of much Depression-era culture such as 'the pious yet ordinary heroes of Frank Capra's films, such as *Mr Smith Goes to Washington* (1939), or the chanting audience-turned-chorus in Clifford Odets's *Waiting for Lefty* (1935)'.[57] We can also observe this holistic trope in the Living Newspaper through the character of the Little Man in *One-Third*, or the unified labour

---

52   Wright 2000.
53   Wright 1944.
54   Wright and Rosskam 1941, p. 6.
55   Wright and Rosskam 1941, p. 35.
56   Wright and Rosskam 1941, pp. 94–5.
57   Allred 2006, p. 549.

pageant at the climax of *Injunction Granted*. As Allred notes, this invocation in 1930s culture generally conforms to the racial, classed and even geographically specific profile of rural whites with 'tattered clothes and empty bellies whose mouths are nonetheless filled with a rough eloquence'.[58] These are precisely the kind of figures conjured by Abbot in *Huts and Unemployed*, with their humanity emanating from one man lighting another's cigarette. Wright's 'we' contradicts this image precisely because it extends an 'alien' yet domestic voice, and therefore in Allred's account, offers a significant challenge to the dominant national-populist structure of feeling which shaped culture in the latter years of the 1930s across a variety of political stripes.[59]

Allred's argument is strongly based in an analysis of the 'we' in *12 Million Black Voices* as a form of historical knowledge that makes present the barely discernible origins of how that 'we' came about. For the purposes of this discussion, perhaps the most significant aspect of *12 Million Black Voices* is the following description, paired with a photograph of sleeping children (Fig. 36)

> The kitchenette scatters death so widely among us that our death rate exceeds our birth rate, and if it were not for the trains and autos bringing us daily into the city from the plantations, we black folk who dwell in northern cities would die out entirely over the course of a few years.[60]

This quote makes explicit the connection between reproduction of life and reproduction of racial capitalism through the pairing with the photograph and setting in the kitchenette on the one hand, and the trains and automobiles that funnel 'black folk' from the plantations to the city on the other. The tone is deathly, registering the necessity of internal migration from South to North as a means to reproduce exhausted labour power, with the progress of new transportation technologies cast under the relations associated with slavery. This returns us to the discussion in previous chapters concerning the continued presence of slavery in the material and ideological formation of 'community' in the US, as well as the place of social reproduction within this. Moreover, the metaphors of organic and inorganic hurtle off the page throughout *12 Million Black Voices*, as seen in the descriptions of the 'gigantic factories and mills', counter-posed with the statement that 'we have never been allowed to become an organic part of this civilization'.[61] Repeating aspects of Gold's *Jews*

---

58   Ibid.
59   Allred 2006, p. 550.
60   Wright and Rosskam 1941, p. 106.
61   Wright and Rosskam 1941, p. 127.

The kitchenette is the seed bed for scarlet fever, dysentery, typhoid, tuberculosis, gonorrhea, syphilis, pneumonia, and malnutrition.

The kitchenette scatters death so widely among us that our death rate exceeds our birth rate, and if it were not for the trains and autos bringing us daily into the city from the plantations, we black folks who dwell in northern cities would die out entirely over the course of a few years.

FIGURE 36   Russell Lee, *Bedroom*, Chicago, FSA, Taken from Richard Wright and Edwin Rosskam, *12 Million Black Voices: A Folk History of the Negro in the United States*, New York: Viking Press, 1941
PHOTOGRAPH: EMILE EBRAHIM KELLY

Without Money, Petry's *The Street* and the *Look* feature on *Harlem Document*, we encounter the Northern city as a parcelled-out series of historical, ethnic and geographic cells in *12 Million Black Voices*. As Wright describes, 'after working all day in one civilization, we go home to our Black Belts and live, within the orbit of the surviving remnants of the culture of the South, our naïve, casual, verbal, fluid folk life'.[62]

---

62   Wright and Rosskam, 1941, p. 127.

In *Native Son*, Bigger Thomas is described as never having 'felt a sense of wholeness' in his entire life.[63] Despite its very different mode of address and folksy appeal to the 'we', *12 Million Black Voices* ultimately delivers the same sentiment. In James Baldwin's essay on *Native Son*, this aspect of Wright's novel was criticised as a failure to articulate an over-arching black sensibility, or tradition. Baldwin's criticism, however, also points to the success of *Native Son*, and for that matter *12 Million Black Voices*. As he wrote, 'a tradition expresses, after all, nothing more than the long and painful experience of a people; it comes out of the battle waged to maintain their integrity or, to put it more simply, out of their struggle to survive'.[64] This also sits close to Gold's stress on tenement living as providing 'meaningful pain', and in Irving Howe's response to Baldwin's criticisms of *Native Son* he argued that in criticising Wright's refusal to present a 'Negro world with fullness, balance or nuance', Baldwin had succinctly pinpointed the militancy of the novel.[65]

The correspondence between history and militancy in Wright's work counters the teleological and occasionally saccharine notion of a 'usable past' that tends to permeate *One-Third of a Nation*, as well as much of the work exhibited within *Roofs for 40 Million*. In *Harlem Document*, the intractable relationship between the Feature Group and their subjects that emerges through the project's ambitions to 'build community' forces us to reckon with the question of precisely how community can be 'built' in the world described by Wright. The internal tensions within the Popular Front, as it declined into the reformist nationalism of the Democratic Front, sought out an instrumentalised, utilitarian art that could not reckon with the political pressures of the moment. This prompted the aesthetic and political problems around ethics and misrepresentation that we see in *One-Third of a Nation, Roofs for 40 Million* and *Harlem Document*, issues that remain very much alive within much social practice today. I have tried to focus on the capacity of these works to illuminate how struggle emerges and is necessitated by the forms of life reproduced by capital. In thinking through their shortcomings, it becomes clear that a sense of absolute rage and tension is fundamental to rejecting the unobtainable notions of communal wholeness that characterised the Democratic Front's recourse to a usable past, and returns today, often appearing in both instances under the

---

63   Wright, 2000, p. 271.
64   Baldwin was critical of *Native Son*, and the protest novel more generally, viewing Wright as trapped by the American image of black life, a criticism similar to those leveled at Claude McKaye's *Home to Harlem* by W.E.B. Du Bois. See Baldwin 1970, p. 129.
65   Howe 1957, p. 143.

guise of an ethical engagement that seeks to sweep aside difference. The final section of this chapter turns to Rick Lowe's *Project Row Houses*, an ongoing work that has continually reckoned with such conflicts within its history. Located in the urban South, it presents a different set of historical and geographical coordinates to the Northern works discussed in this chapter and the previous, and offers a perspective on the ambition of 'building community' that responds to the task quite literally, through the project's emphasis on urban planning.

3   Project Row Houses

Project Row Houses was co-founded in 1993 by artists Jesse Lott, James Bettison, Bert Long, Floyd Newsum, Bert Samples, George Smith and Rick Lowe. Within this group, Lowe has been most central to the maintenance of the project as he took on the role of director early on. The project exists as a series of renovated 'shotgun houses' in the mostly African American Third Ward of Houston that includes community spaces, residencies for artists and a young mothers' programme. (Fig. 37) *Project Row Houses* is also partnered with a Community Development Corporation (CDC) that builds low-income housing in the neighbourhood. Viewed as an exemplary project by many critics, curators and artists associated with the growth of social practice since the early 1990s in the USA, *Project Row Houses* also directly inspired the creation of *Watts House Project* in Los Angeles, which I discuss briefly in the conclusion to this book. Over the last decade, Lowe has become an increasingly well-established artist both within the USA and beyond; in 2013 he was elected to President Obama's National Council on the Arts and in 2014, he received the MacArthur Foundation 'Genius' grant.

Lowe was born into a sharecropping family in rural Alabama and studied art at Columbus State University in Georgia. Attracted by the livelier art scene in Houston, he moved to the city in 1985. Prior to *Project Row Houses*, Lowe was making what he describes as activist art which took the shape of installations composed by figurative painting and cut-out sculpture on struggles related to race and class, as well as environmental concerns. He showed these in galleries as well as community centres and was always concerned with working both inside and outside the art world. However, after a visit to his studio from a group of high school students in 1990, his practice changed direction. One of the students was excited by the political urgency of his work but griped that it only *showed* what was going on in the neighbourhood rather than offering solutions; the boy believed artists were in a good position to imagine answers. Following this encounter, Lowe describes how his ambitions grew into making art 'that

FIGURE 37 Aerial view of Project Row Houses in 2015
PHOTOGRAPH BY PETER MOLICK COURTESY OF PROJECT ROW HOUSES

is poetic and symbolic but at the same time has a practical application'.[66] In this sense, I introduce *Project Row Houses* not only for its focus on housing, but also for its relation to the varied notions of how art can become politically useful that runs through all the works discussed in this book. In comparison to those works already discussed, *Project Row Houses* steps even more dramatically into the realm of usefulness, leaping over the belief that representation, or dialogue could suffice and instead actualising a material transformation to the urban fabric of the Third Ward.

At the time of the above encounter with the student visiting his studio, Lowe lived on the West side of Houston but was doing volunteer work at the SHAPE community centre in the Third Ward, where he had prior connections from an art project addressing police brutality. As part of his role there, he was invited on a bus tour of the neighbourhood for city and county officials where sites of neglect and danger in the Third Ward were identified for demolition. During the tour, empty and abandoned houses were highlighted as particular hubs

66   Rick Lowe, personal interview, 19 September 2013.

FIGURE 38 Row houses before renovations
PHOTOGRAPH BY SHERYL TUCKER VASQUEZ COURTESY OF PROJECT ROW HOUSES

for prostitution and drug dealing, with the site where *Project Row Houses* now stands described as the most dangerous area in the neighbourhood. Following the tour, Lowe began to think through the aesthetic possibilities of the shotgun shacks and how they could be repurposed for art-based community projects (Fig. 38). Alongside the encounter with the young man who proposed that artists work on solutions to social problems, the experience of the tour prompted Lowe to rethink how his practice could use social interaction as a medium. Initially, he registers that his only real reference point for artworks that functioned in this manner was Joseph Beuys and the notion of 'social sculpture' he had encountered at art school. However, by beginning with the shotgun shack, Lowe connected his early ideas for *Project Row Houses* to a whole range of references that went beyond thinking in terms of medium, but rather worked to connect with past communities and ways of life in the Third Ward in order to produce a usable past.

George Lipsitz's account of *Project Row Houses* emphasises such connections. He begins by describing the history of black power in the district, focusing on how the twenty-one year old activist Carl Hampton had spent time in Oakland, California during the late 1960s and had been inspired by the Black Panther Party's efforts in feeding, clothing and providing self-organised medical care to the community. Deciding to return to the Third Ward, Hampton established the People's Party II in 1969, modelled after the Black Panthers, which swiftly gained support in the neighbourhood, despite intense hostility from the police.[67] On 26 July 1970, Hampton spoke at a rally composed of around 100 attendees that took place amidst an ongoing battle between the police and community members that had begun 10 days earlier. This particular conflict began after Hampton confronted two police officers who were attempting to prevent a young People's Party II member from selling the Black Panther's newspaper outside the Party's Headquarters in the Third Ward. When Hampton spoke to the officers, they noticed an unconcealed .45 calibre automatic pistol strapped across his shoulder. Although it was legal to carry a weapon in public, Hampton was charged. After the arresting officer reached for his gun, the situation escalated, and several People's Party II members emerged from the Headquarters with their own weapons. When the police radioed for back-up, Hampton and the other members barricaded themselves inside, which led to a 10-day siege during which 2,000 residents from the Third Ward formed a barricade outside the headquarters, while 30 police cars continuously patrolled Dowling Street with a warrant for Hampton's arrest. The siege ended at the rally on 26 June when sharpshooters opened fire at Hampton. He died the next morning, several others in the crowd were injured and sixty arrests were made.[68] The People's Party II had sought to carve out some autonomy for the Third Ward by establishing basic services such as education and healthcare, and the destruction of this by the police marked the continuation of entrenched, racist barriers to social reproduction in the neighbourhood.

During the early 1930s the Third Ward had one of the highest population densities in the USA and was inhabited by a mix of whites and blacks, including many Jews.[69] In the post-war years, the demographics of the Third Ward were re-shaped via the discriminatory land-use policies and redlining practices of the Home Owners Loan Corporation and Federal Housing Administration. As described at the opening of this chapter, such legislation was crucial to the production of welfare as a racialising force during the New Deal. This led to the Third Ward becoming almost entirely African American, alongside the Fourth and Fifth Wards, all of which suffered from disproportionate municipal neglect in the following two decades. By the early 1950s, the constricted housing market for African Americans in Houston was further diminished by the con-

---

67   Lipsitz 2011, p. 149.
68   Lipsitz 2011, p. 150.
69   Lipsitz 2011, p. 153.

struction of the Gulf Freeway that demolished the eastern part of the Fourth Ward.[70] This was no accident, but might be viewed in light of the suggestion in the 1936 Federal Housing Authority Underwriters Manual that 'A high-speed traffic artery or a wide street parkway may prevent the expansion of inharmonious uses' with this meaning not only 'the infiltration of business and industrial uses' but also 'lowerclass occupancy, and inharmonious racial groups'.[71] During these years where the racial formation of the Third, Fourth and Fifth Wards was sculpted by law and capital, shotgun shacks, or row houses, proliferated as the architectural staple in those neighbourhoods, as they make efficient use of small spaces and can house large families. They are also usually constructed with minimal materials and work well in Houston's humid climate, as with both doors open a breeze can blow through the house. Despite the shotgun shack's appearance in the Third Ward as resulting from discrimination and limited resources, Lipsitz argues that they produce 'egalitarian solidarity and inclusion' amongst inhabitants.[72] However, as with those aspects such as the rent strike in *One-Third of a Nation*, as well as the drive of *Harlem Document* and *12 Million Black Voices* to show community formation as inseparable from a limited and exclusionary housing market, the row houses can also be taken to signify limited choice and freedom. In its attention to housing as a mediator for the formation of communities, *Project Row Houses* inherits this conflicted history, as well as the struggle to create autonomous means of social reproduction such as those initiated by People's Party II.

Following the bus tour of the Third Ward, Lowe and the group of artists listed above decided to investigate the status of the twenty-two row houses designated as the most dangerous street in the neighbourhood. Quickly realising that they were all uninhabited and abandoned, Lowe hunted down the owner who was in Taiwan and was eventually able to acquire a lease agreement with an option to purchase. These initial stages also involved applying to the NEA for funding and Lowe attributes the group's success with this – despite their lack of experience – to the fact that the NEA was particularly keen to fund 'social' projects during the early 1990s.[73] As discussed in the introduction and previous chapter, this directive from the NEA involved a stress on utility as a means to mediate the aftermath of the culture wars, and cohered into the 1997 *American Canvas* report by Gary Larson. The success of *Project Row Houses* in gaining

---

70 Lipsitz 2011, p. 151.
71 Federal Housing Administration 1936.
72 Ibid.
73 Rick Lowe, personal interview, 19 September 2013 and Larson 1997.

FIGURE 39 Drive by Exhibit at Project Row Houses – Installation of work by Israel McCloud 1993
COURTESY OF PROJECT ROW HOUSES

support from the NEA anticipates that report and direction in policy, and shows that from the outset, Lowe and his collaborators were implicated in a national vision for the arts that is marked by utilitarian impoverishment, both in terms of its sense of what art can be, as well as how this became imbricated with the welfare reforms enforced by President Clinton discussed in Chapter Two. However, as we shall see, Lowe's relationship to the utilitarian aspects of *Project Row Houses* remains ambivalent.

Once this 'seed money' had been obtained from the NEA, Lowe describes how the project began by cleaning up the houses every weekend, a task made easier by the carpentry and building skills of Lowe's studio mates. After a few weeks, increasing numbers of people from the neighbourhood – particularly parents and children – began to join in. Once the houses were in a decent enough state, an exhibition was staged to clarify that the project was not solely about regeneration, but that the aim was for artists to carry out projects in and around the houses. Whilst working on the building, the windows had to be boarded up, and the artist Jesse Lott suggested that these spaces be used as framing devices in what he called a 'drive-by' exhibition. (Fig. 39) Anxieties from Third Ward residents – let alone the city's broader art audience – meant *Project Row Houses* set up this first exhibition on the boarded up windows so people could drive by and look without getting out their cars.⁷⁴ The double meaning of drive-by in this context pokes fun at such anxieties without dismissing their basis in reality and, moreover, connects to the dominant yet contradictory car culture of the United States discussed in Chapter One as marked by metaphors of escape and freedom, as well as the real bisection of communities by sprawling freeways such as those that demolished part of the Fourth Ward.

In Lowe's description of these early stages of *Project Row Houses*, it is clear that the social aspects of rehabilitating the houses, and the projected production of artworks around them, were fairly separate. However, as the project moved forward, the spatial aspects of the Third Ward and the form of the shotgun shack solidified into a conceptual base for extending the aesthetic ambitions of the project into a broader social process. These developments happened in response to dialogue with Third Ward residents and led the project towards providing housing and social programmes as well as space for artists. As Lowe explains, the initial reaction of Third Ward residents to *Project Row Houses* was largely one of support, albeit with some scepticism towards the 'art' content of the work, which to many seemed unimportant in contrast with social issues such as housing, crime and education. This led Lowe and his collaborators to question how they could establish a housing programme that retained an aesthetic dimension and was 'symbolic' of a wider crisis rather than an attempt to solve the problem.⁷⁵ Eventually, seven of the initial twenty-two houses were developed into homes for young mothers, as this was a demographic particularly lacking in housing and welfare support. The establishment of a supportive infrastructure for these families provided an alternative to the way young mothers, especially young African American mothers, were demonised within the media and government policy, as exemplified by the history of welfare reform discussed in Chapter Two. (Fig. 40)

According to Lowe, the artists' project programme has been increasingly shaped by the lessons learned in the young mothers' programme about collaborative work. Since 2013, the application procedure for the artists' programme now mirrors that of the young mothers' programme, existing as an 'expanded artist residency program' that functions like a 'laboratory', in Lowe's terms.⁷⁶ This fluidity also extends to how those working around *Project Row Houses* often cross over from one aspect to another, with some of the young

---

74   Rick Lowe, personal interview, 19 September 2013.
75   Ibid.
76   Ibid.

FIGURE 40 Young Mothers Residence at Project Row Houses
PHOTOGRAPH BY PETER MOLICK COURTESY OF PROJECT ROW HOUSES

mothers who were residents becoming artists, beginning work in the education programme or assisting on the exhibitions and public programming. This emphasis on not denying different experiences to those who participate in *Project Row Houses* is attributed by Lowe to his mentor and collaborator, Jesse Lott, whose desire to diminish the boundaries between different aspects of life is related to his disavowal of barriers between 'high art' and 'vernacular' or 'folk' art within his own practice. Lott's insistence on speculation and creativity as a form of experience often unavailable to many residents in the Third Ward is probably his most significant contribution to *Project Row Houses*.[77] If day to day struggle has tended to dominate life in the Third Ward, enabling experiences beyond that remains a radical gesture in the context, with the row house positioned as a container in which new ways of living can be imagined.

Lowe often talks about the 'symbolic' qualities of *Project Row Houses* and this primarily relates to the shotgun shack representing utopian possibilities of transforming housing and living arrangements in relation to African Amer-

---

77   Ibid.

ican history. In this respect, the painter John Biggers provided a key influence. Biggers was a muralist and important figure in the black community art movement of the 1960s, particularly in Houston where he taught at Texas Southern University. His work thematised black southern life and from 1957 also incorporated West African themes, following a UNESCO grant that enabled him to spend six months travelling and studying in West Africa where he visited Ghana, Benin, Togo and Nigeria. This led to the formation of a usable past through new visual mythologies and histories. As Biggers described, 'My concern was how to create an archetype for people who didn't have one of their own, but hated what they did have'.[78] The shotgun shack became an important component of Biggers's aesthetic, with the naming of that architectural form not only related to the usual story that if a shotgun was fired through the front door it would pass straight through the house and out the back. Instead, he believed the titling of the shotgun shacks was a corruption of the word *shogun*, a Yoruba word meaning 'God's House'. Biggers cultivated a similar aesthetic of creolisation in his paintings from the late 1950s onwards, as most clearly expressed in works such as the mural *Birth from the Sea* (1966), where imagery of West African dress and music is combined with an underwater, otherworldly environment that recalls science-fiction depictions of outer space, standing as a proto Afro-Futurism.[79] The mural diptych *Ascension* and *Origins* for the Delta Arts Center in Winston Salem, North Carolina (1990) further exemplifies Biggers' syncretism through spatial arrangements that reference West African folklore and the cosmic, alongside depictions of everyday aspects of the Southern American landscape such as row houses and train tracks.

Robert Farris Thompson describes how Biggers was particularly inspired by the ornamentation of the row houses, noting that residents frequently place jugs, jars, baskets, and pots on their porches and adorn trees and the outside walls with bottles, mirrors, pinwheels, figurative icons and tires.[80] Following on from this, Lipsitz affirms that the serial quality of the row houses produces solidarity, but also allows for 'dynamics of difference, for individual impro-

---

78   Theisen 2010, p. 71.
79   Biggers' aesthetic can be seen to prefigure aspects of what has been dubbed Afro-Futurism by Mark Dery, an aesthetic that blends science fiction, Afro-centricity and historical fiction to address the emergence of the African diaspora and speculate on the future. Prominent novelists associated with the genre include Samuel Delaney and Octavia Butler. The musicians Sun Ra and Parliament Funkadelic, as well as the techno duo Drexciya, are also seen as seminal to the development of this aesthetic. See Dery 1994.
80   Thompson 1995, p. 110.

visation, ornamentation, and expression'.[81] Lipsitz and Thompson therefore both attempt to establish a 'usable past' in their description of how the shotgun shack is mobilised by Biggers, and later in *Project Row Houses*, with this connecting to Ernesto Laclau's assertion that the 'symbols and ideological values' from a place of origin by rural migrants provides a 'natural' and 'populist' reaction to the experience of capitalist legality and exploitation.[82] Though superficially this might appear as 'the *survival* of old elements', Laclau writes that in reality, they conceal a '*transformation*' whereby remnants become the 'raw materials' for expressing 'new antagonisms'.[83] Such a view clearly connects with Bloch's idea of non-simultaneity as a radical, rather than reactionary force, with the positioning of the row house as of West African origin less about establishing a linear, 'objective' usable past, or nostalgia, and more, as Biggers describes, about creating an 'archetype for people who didn't have one of their own, but hated what they did have'. The production of this mythic archetype did not seek to paper over its destruction and dislocation via the transatlantic slave trade, and in understanding the apparently folksy, harmonised 'we' in *12 Million Black Voices* as presenting a challenge to the dominant rhetoric of a usable past in the 1930s, this also supports the possibility of theorising Biggers' and *Project Row Houses*' investment in the row house as more complex than a straightforwardly idealised vision of a severed past.

Clearly, the shotgun shacks remain rich with potential for a meeting of historical resonance with utopian projection in *Project Row Houses*, and the idea of these constructions forming containers for art that worked socially in the Third Ward was partly drawn from Biggers' aesthetic. The emphasis on autonomy also ties to historical efforts to build community as a form of political resistance as attempted by the People's Party II. However, with this building a 'neighborhood as practice' being so based on architectural and cultural tropes that offer up a highly conflicted image of a 'usable past', Lowe explains that tensions have inevitably arisen over the attachment *Project Row Houses* has to these legacies. As he explains 'There are some African Americans that don't want to own that legacy, the history of struggle and so on. There are ones that when they get to the middle class they don't want to look back'.[84] This relates to the split opinion on whether focusing on slum conditions in *Harlem Document*, violence in *Native Son*, or the African past in Biggers' paintings, erected further barriers to eman-

---

81 Lipsitz 2011, p. 154.
82 Laclau 1977, p. 157.
83 Ibid.
84 Rick Lowe, personal interview, 19 September 2013.

cipation. Lowe's comment highlights that ideas of social progress attempting to break from the past can lapse into individualised quests for success and class mobility.

Within *Project Row Houses*, this conflict over emancipatory politics and class mobility has been closely linked to the urban processes that have taken place around the site since its inception. Inevitably, the success of *Project Row Houses* and its subsequent support by local government, the NEA and Non-Governmental Organizations such as the Nathan Cummings Foundation and the Bruner Foundation, have attracted a lot of interest in the neighbourhood. Alongside the efforts of *Project Row Houses* in renovating buildings and supporting the community, the Third Ward began to appear increasingly attractive to property developers due to its proximity to Texas Southern University, Riverside Hospital and downtown Houston. Split off from Midtown and the Museum District by a tributary of freeways, a lack of zoning laws in Houston encouraged speculation in the Third Ward from the late 1990s. For some, including those who Lowe describes as not wanting to 'own' the legacy of struggle, these transformations may have been welcome. But for Lowe and *Project Row Houses*, this interest in property development in the Third Ward pushed them to expand the infrastructure and resources they were offering to the neighbourhood. Subsequently, the Project Row Houses Community Development Corporation was established in 2003 in order to acquire and renovate buildings for low-income, residential renting. Through the 2000s, the Community Development Corporation continued to grow in response to the targeting of the Third Ward for wholesale redevelopment. In addition to renovating existing buildings, it began to build low-income rental units, attempting to stand as a bulwark against the displacement of long-term residents and promote community self-management.[85]

However, in 2013 Lowe began to distance the art and education aspect of *Project Row Houses* from the Community Development Corporation, as he felt increasingly disconnected from the aesthetic aspect of the project. As the Community Development Corporation grew to encompass 70 rental units, Lowe became concerned that the 'symbolic' quality of the project had diminished. Moreover, he was frustrated by the knowledge that the Community Development Corporation could never solve the housing crisis in the Third Ward, nor was that what he set out to achieve.[86] At the 2013 Creative Time summit, an important annual event within the field of social practice, Lowe was keen to

---

85 Lipsitz 2011, p. 159.
86 Austen.

challenge the formalisation of 'place-making' and 'social practice' into genres of art that stress usefulness and impact above the aesthetic. Speaking in conversation with Creative Time's chief curator, Nato Thompson, Lowe asked 'Is social practice gentrifying community arts out?', clearly identifying himself with the tradition of the latter category.[87] If we think of gentrification in the way it was addressed by Rosler in *If You Lived Here ...* and analysed by Deutsche and Gendel Ryan as a process of neo-colonialism, how does this serve the kind of periodisation Lowe is arguing for? Firstly, Lowe emphasised that young artists are increasingly graduating with 'credentials' from 'social practice', 'art in the community' or 'art and the public sphere' MFA programmes that enable them to access resources inaccessible to long-established cultural organisations. How does the professionalisation of social practice – an issue I return to in the conclusion of this book – resonate with Rosler's comments that utopian thinking seemed 'illicit' in the context of 1970s USA, and even more so by the early 1990s and *If You Lived Here ...?*

The aesthetic of *Project Row Houses* is rooted in the pursuit of speculative practices that do not attempt to reconcile present conditions as the inevitable result of historical development, or to establish a linear narrative for the past, but rather collide different moments and histories. This strategy works differently than the modes of historical mapping in *One-Third of a Nation* and *Roofs for 40 Million*, and instead sits closer to the situational work of *Harlem Document*, or the fundamentally collaborative aspects of Lacy's *Oakland Projects*, Segal's dances, and Rosler's *If You Lived Here ...* History is stitched together through different experiences, viewpoints and symbols. Crucially, the appeal to the 'symbolic' through the row house might act as a usable past, but straightforward nostalgia is largely inadmissible within critical, African American cultural production. In this light, we can return to the significance of Bloch's notion of non-simultaneity. In appealing to Biggers' mythologising of the shotgun shack as a container to build community, *Project Row Houses* could be seen as attempting to conjure up 'sentimentally or romantically, that wholeness and liveliness from which communism draws genuine material against alienation'.[88] Yet, wholeness remains unobtainable and tradition, as Baldwin writes, is a 'struggle to survive'.[89] I suggest, therefore, that the meaning of invoking a 'usable past' in *Project Row Houses* is the role this plays as a speculative history that mediates, or pushes back against the functionalist submission of the aesthetic to utilitarian concerns.

---

87   Rick Lowe in conversation with Nato Thompson at the 2013 Creative Time Summit.
88   Bloch 1977 p. 35.
89   Baldwin 1970, p. 129.

If *Roofs for 40 Million* responded to the housing crisis of the late 1930s with direct criticism of government policy, it offered little in the way of imagining a future. *Harlem Document* detailed the crisis in housing and homelessness and made a further step by attempting to construct a community, both through its production and circulation. Both these projects stress utility in some form or another, whether through positing art as a weapon in contesting the housing crisis, or by attempting to build community. *Project Row Houses* leaps even further into this realm of usefulness through its provision of actual housing yet manages to sustain a way of living that is different from that projected – materially and ideologically – for residents of the Third Ward. However, once the project's utility was expanded through the Community Development Corporation, *Project Row Houses* reached a point where the aesthetic dimension of the work risked disappearance, and the political dimension faced dissolution into the functional austerity of a world it struggles against. To return to the central question that has threaded through this chapter, how do these works – as responses to the racialised politics of housing and living conditions in the US – chart historical change, as well as the shifting possibilities of art to mediate the formation of communities? If we begin with *Project Row Houses*, this work is marked by a duration and scale that can be observed at a reduced level in the other works discussed in this chapter. With *Harlem Document*, the Feature Group attempted to work with the subjects of their photographs in a durational manner, repeatedly visiting the neighbourhood to engage the people living there, while within *Roofs for 40 Million*, documentary is mobilised for its supposedly objective capacities to map a crisis. Yet the production and reception of these works was contradictory. The desire for photography to act as a weapon within *Roofs for 40 Million* was compromised by the increasingly reformist politics of the Democratic Front, as well as the ways that the conventions of social documentary had been absorbed within mainstream Depression-era culture. *Harlem Document* made work with and for the 'community', but also for the mostly white, affluent readership of popular magazines. Finally, *Project Row Houses* sought to carve out some autonomy around artistic practice and living conditions in the Third Ward, only for the success of this to begin disrupting those ambitions.

In each instance, such ambitions and contradictions are internal to their aesthetic and political orientation, but also related to the particular state formations and histories within which they emerged. The pedagogical orientation of *Roofs for 40 Million* was marked by didacticism and a moralising attitude towards slum inhabitants, with its proposed solutions to the housing crisis – like *One-Third of a Nation* – limited to pleas for an expansion of the 1937 Housing Act. With *Harlem Document*, the attempt of the Feature Group to work with a community outside their own produced a chasm that is registered in both the photographs and the reception of the project. *Project Row Houses* would initially appear to close that chasm through its sustained presence in the Third Ward and its ability to cohere with contemporaneous NEA (and other) funding policies for the arts; however, its aesthetic and political import suffers in ways prefigured by the functionalism of the earlier works. As we saw with McCausland's valorisation of documentary photography, that debate on aesthetics and politics in the late 1930s links with the emphasis on ethics that underpins the present 'impact' agenda of social practice, as noted by Lowe. By considering the slippage of militancy into moralism, we can register how social documentary cohered with the liberal, reformist position the left were backed into by the dawn of the 1940s in the US. In comparison with the trajectory Lowe criticises – the 'gentrification' of community art by social practice – we arrive at the historically specific contradiction of art that actively attempts to address and propose solutions to social issues in the present. Unlike the avant-garde trope of dissolving art into life, the attempt to subsume life under the category of art in the works discussed means art risks becoming simply another arena of administered, measurable life under capital. In the final chapter, this book closes by examining the contemporary stakes of this dilemma, seeking to outline limits as well as capacities for arts expansion into the social field, after the deepening institutionalisation of social practice since the 2000s.

Coda: Utility and Social Practice

With this book I have attempted, firstly, to provide a corrective to the short-sighted and linear history that has characterised accounts of the growth of social practice in the US since the 1990s. Secondly, I have tried to address the dynamic between state formation and socially engaged culture in the United States. By positioning social reproduction as foundational to the ways community formation interacts with the state, I examine the various ways artworks mediate this process, stressing the relationship between material, historical limitations and the social possibilities that cultural forms are able to engage.

The practices I have discussed typically produce multiple mediations between artists, participants, the state, the art institution, the Party and so on that I believe are often in excess of the forms of mediation produced by artworks that pose a more conventional subject-object encounter. Each of the 'bodies' that mediate the Living Newspaper, Segal's dance works, Lacy's *The Oakland Projects*, the Feature Group's *Harlem Document*, Rosler's *If You Lived Here ...* and Lowe's *Project Row Houses* interact with one another in different ways, meaning the sole category that sustains their mutual engagement is the aesthetic, or at the very least, the fact that a cultural project producing these multiple interactions. The socialised artwork is the conduit for a range of experiences that take place temporally – often, as we have seen, nonsynchronously – across groups and individuals, metabolised at different rates, with those processes internal to the meaning of a work.

These systems of mediation point to the dialectical tension that lies at the centre of the practices I have examined. As Alfred Schmidt, writing about labour and nature, explains –

> One cannot, without falling into error, conceive things in a metaphysically rigid way as finished and unchangeable. Equally however, one cannot dissolve things completely into the moments of the social process which mediates them, for this would amount to the same metaphysical error with reversed premises.[1]

Schmidt's dialectic is suggestive for analysing the ever-present possibility within social practice of a wholesale collapse into the social processes that mediate a work's ongoing production. As social practice moves beyond a pro-

---

1 Schmidt 1971, p. 67.

cessing point for experience in 'the real world' – into pre-determined forms, or the utilitarian logic of the world it is attempting to mediate – I believe the aesthetic experience promised by such works risk ossifying into a formula.

To shore up what I mean by this, I want to refer again to the discussion in the previous chapter about art and utility, and argue that the troubled and incomplete descent of Democratic Front aesthetics into utilitarianism is comparable with the dilemma faced by Lowe as *Project Row Houses* expanded into a Community Development Corporation. In this coda, which attempts to speak to the recent past of social practice, I point toward the necessity of historicising the recent turn towards 'usefulness' with regards to the works discussed in this book. Before offering a closer examination of what 'usefulness' entails in recent work by arguably the two most prominent social practice artists working today, Tania Bruguera and Theaster Gates, let us briefly return to Mother Art's *Laundry Works* in order to clarify the particular stakes of affirming art's 'usefulness' in relation to social reproduction.

As discussed in Chapter Two, a large portion of Mother Art's *Laundryworks* project simply involved doing laundry, yet, as I have stressed, the project is not comparable with the aesthetic nominalism of Mierle Laderman Ukeles. This is because Mother Art *affirmed* the tasks carried out under the aegis of *Laundryworks* along moral lines, and sought to transform the alienation and boredom of the commercial laundry by designating the activities carried out within them as art. This positioning of art as a means to improve mundane, gendered labour taking place in spaces oriented toward commercial gain carried through into Mother Art's organisation of the protest/performances *Mother Art Cleans Up City Hall* and *Mother Art Cleans Up the Banks* (1978), both staged in response to reactionary criticisms of *Laundryworks* in the popular press, as well as the reduction of arts funding in California. By scrubbing and dusting the exterior of civic and commercial buildings, these performances sought to highlight the 'real source of waste and corruption of public interest'.[2] As such, Mother Art performed a *moral* affirmation of art and domestic labour as 'useful', opposed to the 'useless' activity of the state and banks.

The political stakes of this moral dichotomy correspond to the polarisation within social reproduction feminism over the valorisation of activities associated with social reproduction. On the one hand, writers such as Silvia Federici have affirmed the tasks associated with gendered social reproduction and care as the ground for reimagining life, seeking to elevate those activities that have

---

2 Liss 2009, p. 2.

historically been denigrated as unproductive.³ On the other hand, this strategy has been rejected as reinforcing normative experiences of womanhood, and, in recent years, problematised as accommodating the burden of social reproduction as forms of state support are withdrawn – a similar conundrum to the one facing social practice.⁴

This schism also loops back to the question of whether social practice should abandon its attachment to the historical categories of art and aesthetics as hopelessly bound up with normative, constrained forms of experience. Conversely, such forms of abandonment – attempts by artists to 'leave art' – have been criticised as naïve for their failure to recognise that this may point to a process of subsumption rather than an overcoming of categories. As Stewart Martin suggests, the attempt to produce an identity between life and art will not necessarily produce social transformation, as life needs to be understood within the context of capitalist life – as a subsumption of life by capital.⁵ The current aesthetic dilemma of social practice partly emerges from this renewed pressure on the particular meaning of affirming or negating social practice *as art*, with this dynamic underpinning the particular relationship of social practice artworks to social reproduction. As this book has shown, the stakes, limits and potentialities for art that centres on the social continually shifts according to the particular alignment between state, capital and citizen, with those changing alignments also determining who can legitimately lay claim to the last category. In this light, the worst possible outcome in the present would be the formalisation of standards, or an attempt to implement a model of 'best practice' that could be serialised and uniformly 'applied' as policy in response to austerity and the forms of social emergency that have proliferated since the 2007–8 financial crisis. Yet, it is precisely this type of formalisation that characterises the more recent emphasis on usefulness within the field.

As a start, I want to outline the shortcomings that arose following the franchising of *Project Row Houses* into *Watts House Project* in Watts, Los Angeles. An area best known for the 1965 riots, Watts remains a primarily working class and largely Latinx and African American neighbourhood. Watts also has a rich history of community art projects, including the well-known Watts Towers, built by Simon Rodia between 1921 and 1955, which form the frame for the Watts Towers Art Center. Opened in 1970, the Art Center became a central institution for the Black Arts Movement in Los Angeles.⁶ In 1996, prior to initiating

---

3   Federici 2012.
4   For a discussion of the polarisation between these positions, see Endnotes 2013.
5   Martin 2009, pp. 481–94.
6   Jones 2017.

the Community Development Corporation, Lowe began thinking about how he could expand *Project Row Houses* into a model that could work in other cities, including St Louis and Los Angeles. Lowe was commissioned by the Los Angeles Museum of Contemporary Art to produce a project that would replicate aspects of *Project Row Houses* in Los Angeles, and he decided to work in Watts.[7] Edgar Arceneaux, then an art student, collaborated with Lowe on community organising in the neighbourhood and after the MOCA commission ended, Lowe handed responsibilities over to Arceneaux in 1999, and distanced himself from the project after returning to Houston, saying that he 'didn't understand the politics of L.A.'[8]

As a profoundly critical article in the *Los Angeles Times* explains, *Watts House Project* has consistently been received with suspicion in the neighbourhood, and often viewed as a tremendous waste of money.[9] *Watts House Project* seems to have suffered both politically and aesthetically because the project did not work with what was specific about Watts, but rather fixated on replicating the 'useful' architectural component of *Project Row Houses* by attempting to redesign the row houses surrounding Rodia's towers. When I visited *Watts House Project* in September 2013 the forthcoming plans for the project were pinned on the 'Virtual Redevelopment Project'. This is a piece of software that would apparently enable 'homeowners to work creatively with artists, architects, and designers to redesign the colors and shapes of fences, outside walls, landscaping, front doors, and other exterior areas of the virtual home'.[10] At that time, it seemed that the 'virtual' arena could prevent further issues arising between *Watts House Project* and community members, many of whom were seriously dissatisfied with the project, primarily due to its financial mismanagement. Although *Watts House Project* is a charity, Internal Revenue Service tax law means the renovations cannot be done free of charge by the Project, as they might benefit private interests. Becoming aware of this only after the renovations began, the *Watts House Project* board attempted to comply with the law by drafting contracts stating that residents would be required to 'reimburse' project costs, should they sell their homes. This aspect was not clear to residents, or apparently Arceneaux and the board, before the initial renovation work had begun. Among others, resident Moneik Johnson refused to sign the

---

7   McKenna 1997.
8   George 2008, and Brynjolson p. 218.
9   Finkel 2015.
10 See *Watts House Project* website at http://wattshouseproject.org/virtual-redevelopment/. This website is now archived, and appears to have been inactive (as does the project) since 2013, Noni Brynjolson reports that the project officially closed in 2014.

contract, explaining that 'From Day 1, I thought this would be a gift ... You can't go telling people it's going to be a gift and then two or three years later change your mind and say: If you ever have a sale then you have to repay the amount. That's not what I call a gift'.[11]

The damaged relationship between residents and *Watts House Project* seems to have been accelerated by the lack of dialogue between Arceneaux and the Watts Towers Art Centre. By the time of my visit, this had degenerated to the point where there was minimal dialogue between the two projects, despite the fact that they are within meters of one another. In the end, the project stands as a flawed attempt at seriality, a failed franchise. The aims of generating a formula for a nationwide model of social practice bypassed existing histories and promised 'outcomes' that cannot match up to the changing realities of how art is able to mediate the social.

In recent years, and again within the arena of social practice's collision with housing, comparisons have been made between Lowe and the work of the Chicago-based African American artist Theaster Gates, most notably in a December 2013 *New York Times* article.[12] The comparison rests on Gates' avowal of *Project Row Houses* as an inspiration, as well as their shared choice of medium in renovating public spaces and housing. However, like the trajectory of *Watts House Project*, the differences between the work of Gates and Lowe tells us much more about current state of social practice, and links directly to Lowe's criticism that recent social practice is 'gentrifying community arts out'.[13] In 2013, Gates was described by *Art Review* as a 'popularizer' and the 'Mick Jagger of social practice'.[14] His rise to prominence has been swift, following his appearance in the Chicago Museum of Contemporary Art's 'Emerging Artists' show in 2009 and subsequent representation by the White Cube gallery, more commonly associated with the work of the Young British Artists. His social practice work began with refurbishing buildings on Chicago's South Side and hosting cultural events, which subsequently grew into the Rebuild Foundation, a non-profit redevelopment agency with satellite projects in Omaha and St Louis. This work is linked to his lucrative studio practice through what Gates describes as a 'circular ecological system', with the renovated buildings partly financed by his commercial success, and the material from those buildings frequently appearing in his sculptures.[15] Despite their shared interest in African

---

11   Finkel 2015.
12   Gregory Sholette writes about these comparisons in Sholette 2017, p. 135.
13   Ibid.
14   'The Power 100'.
15   Wei.

American cultural history and the relationship between art and housing, Lowe has described Gates as a wildcat businessman, and in contrast declared that he is not an entrepreneur.[16] These criticisms chime with Lowe's distancing of himself from *Watts House Project* and rest on separating the qualities he identifies with successful studio artists from those required of social practice artists.[17] Arguably, this is also a political distinction based upon different notions about how social transformation might be achieved.

Gates' 'circular ecological system' exposes the vexed nature of 'usefulness' within the current discourse on social practice, and points towards the increasing shift of many projects into quasi-Non-Governmental Organisations (NGO). Though Gates has largely elided the usual ethics vs. aesthetics debate due to his mainstream art world success, his practice invites criticism along the lines of argumentation that view the 'usefulness' of his Rebuild Foundation as based on compliance with the system that perpetuates the social issues it attempts to improve. Put cynically, Gates' 'circular ecological system' mobilises the Rebuild Foundation as a feel-good money laundering facility for the commercial art world and corporate developers, thereby enabling his status as a 'popularizer' for social practice. Notably, Gates uses the term 'place-making' to describe his practice, which aptly expresses the transient qualities of his work. As he explains,

> The act of place-making feels like a kind of sacrifice, because I'm the catalyst for action in places in St. Louis, Omaha and Chicago that I'm developing with my Rebuild Foundation, which means I'm always going somewhere else.[18]

Following on from this, Gates' description of his practice as 'real-estate art' signals the artist as property speculator; a very different comparison to the usual parallels made between artists such as Lacy and Lowe with social workers, community organisers, educators or researchers.[19] Of course, as Marina Vishmidt notes, 'anything which transpires in the field of art, even if it is identical in form to what transpires anywhere else, is very different in *function*: its function

---

16 Austen.
17 Finkel.
18 Wei 2011.
19 For example, compare with Lacy's statements cited in Chapter Two that *Expectations* rested upon 'the sheer effort to provide personal support and social services before education and making art became possible'. See Lacy 2013, p. 88.

may alter or be erased altogether'.[20] The point then is less that there is a different status between the artworks produced by Lowe and Lacy in comparison to Gates, but rather, as this book has attempted to show, thinking through the way these practices relate to non-artistic activity is something which needs addressing in relation to the mechanisms governing those spheres, be it the state or the property market. As Vishmidt and Kerstin Stakemeier elaborate, 'useful art' (read: social practice more generally) will 'remain thoroughly dependent on its institutional-material premises and can only jettison its artistic framing as an artistic gesture'.[21] So, when Bruguera decides to make useful art and disavows its artfulness, or Lacy decides to entitle her book *Leaving Art* or Lowe describes the origin story of *Project Row Houses* as one which involved leaving a more traditional (albeit already politicised) studio practice behind, these decisions become part of the artwork itself.

Coming back to Lowe's argument that current social practice involves an arms-length separation from political struggle and existing cultural initiatives in favour of generating financial support from viable donors, we could point to the chasm between Gate's projects in Chicago and the Chicago South Side Community Art Center (SSCAC).[22] The SSCAC has been open non-stop since 1940, since its formation via the WPA-FAP Community Art Center programme. The project is steeped in the black radicalism of 1940s Chicago, and was vital to the formation of Communist, Cultural Front artists including Elizabeth Catlett and Charles White. The Center continues to act as an exhibition space, cultural hub, and location for art classes and it sits roughly five miles away from Gates' Dorchester Projects. When I visited in 2012, the Center seemed to be running on a shoestring budget, although since then, in 2019, it has been promised a two-million-dollar fund from the State of Illinois.[23] What does it mean when a project like Gates' establishes a pipeline to profitable financial resources and a cosy relationship with the city's reactionary then-Mayor Rahm Emanuel just down the road? To not deal with the discrepancy of assets and political clout between similar projects in such proximity involves subscribing to the right-wing myth of trickle-down economics, and blindness to the uneven dispersion of power and privilege that operates in the purportedly 'progressive' world of social practice. Through this comparison, we can clarify Lowe's use of gentrification as a metaphor to describe the current state of the field; it shows us that the

---

20 Stakemeier and Vishmidt 2016, p. 44.
21 Stakemeier and Vishmidt 2016, p. 68.
22 See video of Lowe's conversation with Nato Thompson at the 2013 Creative Time Summit here: https://www.youtube.com/watch?v=IoloNoVKDXE (Accessed 26 January 2015).
23 Jones 2019.

metaphor signals not only a spatial problem, but also a desire for social mobility at the expense of ignoring or erasing the past, thus reinforcing precisely those forms of cultural amnesia Lippard observed in her experiences during the Culture Wars, as discussed in the introduction to this book.

The present moment of social practice stands as a de-politicised shift towards the banal, 'post-political' smoothness that typifies the art world at large, with the perceived usefulness of projects resting on their ability to maintain existing social relations, or to offer incremental reforms in a non-antagonistic manner. This orientation towards a moralising liberalism typifies the outlook of major players in the field such as Gates as well as Nato Thompson, former chief curator of Creative Time, the foremost commissioning organisation within social practice. In two recent articles, Thompson proposes similarities between the strategies of General Petraeus and the US military during the last Iraq war, the Black Panthers, Suzanne Lacy and Saul Alinsky.[24] He fails to distinguish between the political meaning and material effects of these examples, but instead concocts an argument suggesting that the military have learned certain tactics of 'soft power' from the cultural field, and that it is now time for culture, particularly social practice, to learn from the military. The equivalences that Thompson proposes epitomise the turn towards usefulness in social practice as one where history is posited less as the repository of usable pasts (whether nostalgic or militant) than as an undifferentiated field of options which might be blended into new, technocratic policies. Moreover, Thompson, like Gates, eschews arguments for structural analysis and change in favour of a belief in individualised 'empowerment' as the means by which our social reality might be transformed. As Vishmidt writes, this involves subscribing to the idea that 'there is actually enough justice in the system to recognize the claims of the dispossessed'.[25]

In outlining how the current political codification and foregrounding of 'usefulness' in social practice impacts on its aesthetic possibilities, it is worth referring to the Cuban artist Tania Bruguera. Since 2010, Bruguera has transitioned from a performance-based practice within the circuits of the art world to a central figure within the current wave of social practice. Bruguera's project *Immigrant Movement International* outwardly declares its usefulness and is described as an 'artist-initiated socio-political movement'.[26] Funded by Creative Time and the Queens Museum of Art, *Immigrant Movement International*

---

24   Thompson 2013a and Thompson 2013b.
25   Vishmidt 2013.
26   See description of the project on the Creative Time website: http://creativetime.org/projects/immigrant-movement-international/.

was based out of a community space in Corona, Queens in New York City which has since transitioned into an independently run organisation called Centro Corona.[27] Bruguera titles IMI *'Arte Útil'*, or useful art, and has also founded the *Asociación de Arte Útil*, which lays out eight criteria that projects must meet if they are to be deemed useful and gathers works fitting the bill on its website and in exhibitions such as the Museum of Arte Útil, held in 2013–2014 at the Van Abbe Museum in Eindhoven. The Museum of Arte Útil exhibition showcased Bruguera's work alongside Theaster Gates' Dorchester Projects and other works by a variety of activists, artists and NGOs. The criteria for Arte Útil include points such as 'Be implemented in the real and actually work', 'Have practical, beneficial outcomes for its users', 'Replace authors with initiators and spectators with users' and 'Pursue sustainability whilst adapting to changing conditions'.[28]

Tellingly, the tone of the criteria is less like an artist's manifesto, and more like a mission statement for a non-profit organisation. The writer and activist Dylan Rodriguez authored a significant critique of what he describes as the 'non profit industrial complex', drawing on Antonio Gramsci's concept of hegemony to describe how such organisations assimilate dissent into a 'social movement industry' approved by the state.[29] Operating as a non-profit may assist in introducing a relative stability in infrastructure and funding, as was the case for *Project Row Houses*. However, for Rodriguez, the formal constitution of social movements into non-profits involves a funnelling of activism into discrete, single-issue campaigns that create an epistemological barrier to the possibility of imagining and working towards social transformation.

Along similar lines, the majority of artworks contained under the banner of Arte Útil are positioned as 'useful' precisely because they help to maintain a necessary level of social reproduction in otherwise adverse conditions. For example, Bruguera's *Immigrant Movement International* helps migrants access services that ease their entry into the American legal system. As another example, the Vienna-based collective WochenKlausur, who featured prominently in the Museum of Arte Útil, produce projects such as their Women-led Workers' Cooperative in Drumchapel, Glasgow, an area with high levels of poverty and unemployment. The social issues in Drumchapel led WochenKlausur to form a cooperative for a group of unemployed women, who subsequently decided to address the health problems that affected many in the

27 See: https://www.facebook.com/CentroCorona/.
28 See the criteria for the Museum of Arte Útil here: http://museumarteutil.net/about/. Accessed 20 March 2015.
29 Rodriguez 2007, p. 29.

area as a result of poor diet. WochenKlausur and the women's cooperative opened a shop selling 'meal bags' that contained fresh fruit and vegetables and simple recipes to encourage healthy cooking; the project also provided skills development for the women in business planning, marketing and accounting.[30] In this project there are two stages of dealing with faltering social reproduction. The women who WochenKlausur engaged were not earning and faced barriers to employment, with the project they produced encouraging higher levels of social reproduction within a relatively impoverished neighbourhood. Overall, WochenKlausur worked with a population viewed as a 'burden' by the British state – the unemployed – at a time when measures such as the introduction of workfare in 2011 sought to re-purpose and make 'useful' that social group.[31] While the example of WochenKlausur strays from this book's focus on the US, it is exemplary of how the turn to usefulness has been marked by processes of 'parachuting in'. As in the attempted franchising of *Project Row Houses*, a circuit akin to the mainstream art world has begun to develop for social practice artists to behave as international 'consultants' in places where they may have little prior engagement with the social issues they are being asked to address.

The orientation of WochenKlausur's project, as with Bruguera's *Immigrant Movement International*, suggests that the issues at hand can be 'usefully' overcome. In other words, such work affirms that art can introduce change through its continued expansion into life, advancing until projects arrive at an identity with the paradigmatic social form they engage. This presents a significant contrast with *The Oakland Projects, If You Lived Here ...* and *Project Row Houses*. Although Lacy's, Rosler's and Lowe's projects also involved aspects of social reproduction, notably childcare, education and housing, those processes were *staged* in relation to issues that stood outside day-to-day experience, and through this they explored a meaningful chasm between the art work and dominant social reality. Similarly, Segal's dance works and *Injunction Granted* did not operate as, for example, a union for performers, nor, for example, did *Harlem Document* act solely as evidence or a case study for social workers or housing reformers. Rather, they triangulated social struggles with aesthetic processes in order to fruitfully examine how both art and life – and the relation between these categories – might be transformed.

---

30   WochenKlausur, 'Women's-led Workers' Cooperative', details available on the WochenKlausur website here: http://www.wochenklausur.at/projekt.php?lang=en&id=41.

31   I present an extended discussion of this with regards to the United Kingdom and recent theoretical developments within the field of accelerationism in Abse Gogarty 2017.

Within Arte Útil, Bruguera writes that 'failure is not a possibility. If the project fails, it is not Arte Útil'.[32] Through this, Bruguera implies that the stakes are higher, and the possibility for experimentation lower, in the art she promotes. This is encapsulated in how Gates' practice ensures the reproduction of capital through kick-starting property and land speculation in otherwise condemned neighbourhoods, a process from which Lowe explicitly sought to distance *Project Row Houses*, and with which Rosler had already grappled in *If You Lived Here* … Through these examples, we can see more clearly how the reproductive and 'useful' dimensions of social practice function today by attempting to excise problems of mediation. This occurs firstly through avowing 'empowerment' as an individualised and non-antagonistic mode of social transformation, and secondly by presenting a total collapse into the social arena that projects relate to, with this often marked by the adoption of the operational framework of a non-profit organisation. The attempted serialisation of *Project Row Houses*, the poverty of utilitarianism in Bruguera's manifesto and Gates' circular ecology as property speculation, all point in this direction. Following Martin's assertion that new processes of aesthetic subsumption represent a rational and instrumentalised flipside to the ambitions of the historical avant-gardes, we can say that the current tendency is to discourage questions about how we might assess contemporary practices as art, and to instead compel us to assess them as forms of life.

The current stakes of working 'socially' in a context where artists are required to enable forms of social reproduction, and arguably to assist in the reproduction of capital, is undoubtedly linked to recent austerity measures, the withdrawal of state services and the current crisis of social reproduction. We can posit the recent emphasis on usefulness as an attempt to re-animate an apparent heyday of social welfare, here transposed onto the activity of artists and art institutions. This is why the New Deal remains such a powerful lens through which to analyse the works discussed here, and to think through the future of how art mediates between the state and communities in the US. For many liberals, and those aligned with the centre-left, the idea of the New Deal maintains a psychic pull in articulating the possibility of social change in the US. But as I hope to have illuminated here, this model – this usable past – will only serve to absorb and perpetuate class antagonisms, white supremacy and other tools of social division if it remains a nostalgic mythology emphasising past national glory. In other words, this deployment of a New Deal imaginary could risk repeating the reactionary processes at play in the invocation of a

---

32 Bruguera 2012.

usable past during that period, rather than standing as a means to create a militant imaginary based on, as Bloch writes, prevented futures.[33]

This book has sought to examine how artists have engaged social dynamics and processes of community formation as material and medium. By going beyond the current periodisation and analysis of such work as centred on the affirmation or negation of an avant-garde lineage, I have focused on the conditions that made these works possible, thinking through how older forms resonate and make new meaning in the present. My aim has been to work less at the level of analogies, and to refuse to identify the critical purchase of works in their ability to simply reflect the social circumstances they engage. Instead, as explained in this coda, I am interested in how these practices act as mediating forces. Faced with the present situation, I would argue, we might still strive for an art of the social, that instead of subsuming aesthetic experience into life, can imagine ways of abolishing the system that makes such subsumption necessary in the first place. The historical collisions and divergences mapped here offer one way to confront the ongoing relations of violence and exploitation that artists have sought to mediate, allowing us to criticise both nostalgia and the excision of the past in the histories we have received.

---

33   Fordism acts in a similar manner in much contemporary discourse, particularly for liberals and reformist socialists, as explored by Martin 2017.

Bibliography

Books, journal articles and periodicals

Abse Gogarty, Larne 2017, '"Usefulness" in Contemporary Art and Politics', *Third Text*, 31, 1: 117–32.

Abse Gogarty, Larne and Hannah Proctor 2019, 'Communist Feeling', *New Socialist*, 13 March, available at https://newsocialist.org.uk/communist-feelings-lessing-gornick/.

Adorno, Theodor and Horkheimer, Max 1998 [1947], *Dialectic of Enlightenment*, translated by John Cumming, New York: Continuum.

Alexander, Michelle 2010, *The New Jim Crow: Mass Incarceration in the Age of Colorblindness*, New York: New Press.

Althusser, Louis 1971, *Lenin and Philosophy and other essays*, translated by Ben Brewster, London: New Left Books.

Allerhand, Ruth 1935 'The Lay Dance' *New Theatre*, April, p. 26.

Allred, Jeff 2006, 'From Eye to We: Richard Wright's *12 Million Black Voices*, Documentary and Pedagogy', *American Literature*, 78, 3: 549–83.

Anonymous 1938 'One-Third of a Nation' 1938, *Sunday Worker* Jan 23rd. 12.

Anonymous 1947 'National Affairs: Barrel No. 2' *Time*, Vol. XLIX, No. 25. June 23, p. 5.

Arruza, Cinzia 2013, *Dangerous Liaisons: The Marriages and Divorces of Marxism and Feminism*, translated by Marie Lagatta and Dave Kelly, London: The Merlin Press Ltd.

Wallis, Brian (ed.) 1991, Artists' Life/Work: Housing and Community for Artists in *If You Lived Here ...: The City in Art, Theory and Social Activism*, Seattle: Bay Press.

Associated Press 1988, 'Reagan says some homeless sleep on grates from own choice', *Los Angeles Times*, 23 December. Available online at http://articles.latimes.com/1988-12-23/news/mn-549_1_homeless-people

Austen, Ben 2013, 'Chicago's Opportunity Artist', *New York Times*, 20 December, available online at http://www.nytimes.com/2013/12/22/magazine/chicagos-opportunity-artist.html.

Baker, Ella and Marvel Cooke 1935, 'The Bronx Slave Market', *The Crisis*, 42, November.

Baker-White, Robert 1999, *The Text in Play: Representations of Rehearsal in Modern Drama*, Lewisburg and London: Bucknell University Press.

Baldwin, James 1970 [1950], 'Many Thousands Gone', in *Richard Wright's Native Son: A Critical Handbook*, edited by Richard Abcarian, Belmont, CA: Wadsworth Publishing Company.

Baxandall, Rosalyn 1993, 'The Question Seldom Asked: Women and the CPUSA', in *New Studies in the Politics and Culture of U.S. Communism*, edited by M. Brown, R. Martin, et al., New York: Monthly Review Press.

Bellamy Foster, John and Fred Magdoff 2009, *The Great Financial Crisis: Causes and Consequences*, New York: Monthly Review Press.

Bentley, Joanne 1988, *Hallie Flanagan: A Life in the American Theatre*, New York: Alfred A. Knopf Press.

Beradi, Franco 'Bifo' 2009, *Precarious Rhapsody: Semiocapitalism and the pathologies of the post-alpha generation*, New York: Minor Compositions.

Berger, Maurice 2011, 'Man in the Mirror: *Harlem Document*, Race, and the Photo League', in *The Radical Camera: New York's Photo League 1936–1951*, edited by Mason Klein and Catherine Evans, New Haven and London: Yale University Press.

Bernes, Jasper, Joshua Clover, and Juliana Spahr 2014, 'Elegy, or the poetics of surplus', in *Jacket 2*, available at http://jacket2.org/commentary/elegy-or-poetics-surplus.

Biles, Roger 1990, 'Nathan Straus and the Failure of U.S. Public Housing', in *The Historian*, 53, 1 (September): 33–46.

Bernstein, Irving 2010, *The Turbulent Years: A History of the American Worker, 1933–1940*, Chicago: Haymarket Books.

Bishop, Claire 2004, 'Antagonism and Relational Aesthetics', *October*, Fall, 51–80.

Bishop, Claire 2006, 'The Social Turn: Collaboration and its Discontents', *Artforum*, 44, 6 (February): 178–83.

Bishop, Claire 2012, *Artificial Hells: Participatory Art and the Politics of Spectatorship*, London: Verso.

Blackburn, Robin 2008, 'The Sub Prime Crisis', *New Left Review*, 50, March–April, 63–106.

Blair, Sara 2007, *Harlem Crossroads: Black Writers and the Photograph in the Twentieth Century*, Princeton and Oxford: Princeton University Press.

Bloch, Ernst 1991 [1935], *Heritage of our Times*, translated by Neville and Stephen Plaice, Cambridge: Polity Press.

Boal, Augusto 2009 [1974], *Theatre of the Oppressed*, London: Pluto Press.

Bourriaud, Nicolas 1998, *Relational Aesthetics*, Dijon: Les presses du reel.

Brecht, Bertolt 1964 [1940], 'Short Description of a New Technique of Acting which Produces an Alienation Effect', in *Brecht on Theatre: The Development of an Aesthetic*, edited and translated by John Willett, London: Methuen.

Brecht, Bertolt 1977 [1967], 'Against Georg Lukács', translated by Stuart Hood, in Ernst Bloch et al., *Aesthetics and Politics*, London: New Left Books.

Brecht, Bertolt 1977, *The Messingkauf Dialogues*, translated by John Willett, London: Methuen.

Browder, Laura 1998, *Rousing the Nation: Radical Culture in Depression America*, Amherst: University of Massachusetts Press.

Brown, Lorraine and O'Connor, John 1980, *The Federal Theatre Project: Free, Adult, Uncensored*, London: Eyre Methuen.

Brynjolson, Noni 2020 'Learning From Watts House Project: On Failure and Reparative Practice in Socially Engaged Art' *Public Art Dialogue*, 10:2, 218–242.

Buchloh, Benjamin 1999, 'In Conversation with Martha Rosler', *Martha Rosler: Positions in the Life World*, edited by Catherine de Zegher Cambridge, MA and London, England: The MIT Press.

Buchmann, Sabeth and Constanze Ruhm 2013, 'Subject put to the Test', *Texte zur Kunst*, 23, 90. Available at http://www.textezurkunst.de/90/buchmann-ruhm-subject-put-test/.

Burnshaw, Stanley 1935, 'The Dance', in *New Masses*, 26 February, p. 27.

Carson, Mina 1998, 'Settlement House Movement', in *The Reader's Companion to U.S. Women's History*, edited by Wilma Mankiller et al., Boston and New York: Houghton Mifflin Company.

Carter, Michael 1939, 'Harlem', *Fortune*, 20:78, 168–70.

Cayton, Horace R. 1940, 'Negro Housing in Action', *Social Action*, 6, 4 (5 April).

Chappell, Marisa 2010, *The War on Welfare: Family, Poverty and Politics in Modern America*, Philadelphia: University of Pennsylvania Press.

Cosgrove, Stuart 1985, 'The Living Newspaper: Strikes Strategies and Solidarity', in *Nothing Else to Fear: New Perspectives on America in the Thirties*, edited by Stephen Baskerville and Ralph Willett, Manchester: Manchester University Press.

Davis, Angela Y. 1983, *Women, Race and Class*, New York: Vintage Books.

Davis, Angela Y. 2003, *Are Prisons Obsolete?* New York: Seven Stories Press.

Day, Gail 2011, *Dialectical Passions: Negation in Postwar Art Theory*, New York: Columbia University Press.

Denning, Michael 1997, *The Cultural Front: The Laboring of American Culture in the Twentieth Century*, London: Verso.

Denning, Michael 2010, 'Wageless Life', *New Left Review*, 66 (November–December): 79–97.

Deutsche, Rosalyn and Cara Gendel Ryan 1984, 'The Fine Art of Gentrification', *October*, 31 (Winter): 91–111.

Deutsche, Rosalyn 1996, *Evictions: Art and Spatial Politics*, Cambridge, MA. and London, England: The MIT Press.

Dimitrakaki, Angela and Kirsten Lloyd (guest eds.) 2017, 'Social Reproduction and Art', *Third Text*, 31, 144 (Jan).

Dolber, Brian 2008, 'Unmaking "Hegemonic Jewishness": Anti-Communism, Gender Politics, and Communication in the ILGWU, 1924–1934', *Race, Gender & Class*, 15, 1/2, 188–203.

Draper, Hal 2004, *The Adventures of the Communist Manifesto*, Alameda: Center for Socialist History.

Draper, Theodore 1960, *American Communism and Soviet Russia*, London: Macmillan & Co.

Dubofsky, Melvyn 1994, *The State and Labor in Modern America*, Chapel Hill: University of North Carolina Press.

Dubofsky, Melvyn 2000, *We Shall Be All: A History of the Industrial Workers of the World*, edited by J.A. McCartin, Champaign, Ill: University of Illinois Press.

Edwards, Steve 2010, *Martha Rosler: The Bowery in two inadequate descriptive systems*, London: Afterall.

Ellington, Duke 1993 [1931], 'The Duke Steps Out', *Rhythm*, republished in *The Duke Ellington Reader*, edited by Mark Tucker, New York and Oxford: Oxford University Press.

Ellington, Duke 1993 [1939], 'On Swing and its Critics', in *The Duke Ellington Reader*, edited by Mark Tucker, New York and Oxford: Oxford University Press.

Endnotes, 2013, 'The Logic of Gender' in *Endnotes*, 3. Available at http://endnotes.org.uk/articles/19.

Entin, Joseph B. 2007, *Sensational Modernism: Experimental Fiction and Photography in Thirties America*, Chapel Hill: The University of North Carolina Press.

Erenberg, Lewis 1999, *Swingin' the Dream: Big Band Jazz and the Rebirth of American Culture*, Chicago and London: University of Chicago Press.

Espiritu, Nicholas 2005, '(E)Racing Youth: The Racialized Construction of California's Proposition 21 and the Development of Alternative Contestations', *Cleveland State Law Review*, 52: 189–209.

Fanon, Frantz 1986 [1952], *Black Skin, White Masks*, translated by C.L. Markmann, London: Pluto Press.

'Feature Group's "Towards a Harlem Document"' 1977 [1939], *Photo Notes*, April, pp. 1–2. Republished by the Visual Studies Workshop, Rochester, New York.

Federici, Silvia 2012 [2010], 'Feminism and the Politics of the Common in an Era of Primitive Accumulation', in *Revolution at Point Zero: Housework, Reproduction, and Feminist Struggle*, Oakland: PM Press.

Finkel, Jori 2015, 'Watts House Project under fire', *Los Angeles Times*, 8 April. Available online at http://articles.latimes.com/2012/apr/08/entertainment/la-ca-watts-house-project-20120408/3.

Foster, Hal 1996, 'Obscene, Abject, Traumatic', *October*, 78 (Autumn): 106–24.

Flanagan, Hallie 1973, 'Introduction' to *Federal Theatre Plays*, edited by Pierre de Rohan, New York: Da Capo Press.

Florida, Richard 2002, *The Rise of the Creative Class and how It's Transforming Work, Leisure, Community and Everyday Life*, New York: Basic Books.

Franko, Mark 2002, *The Work of Dance: Labor, Movement and Identity in the 1930s*, Middletown, Connecticut: Wesleyan University Press.

Fraser, Andrea 1997, 'What's Intangible, Transitory, Mediating, Participatory, and Rendered in the Public Sphere?' *October*, 80 (Spring): 111–16.

Freire, Paulo 1970, *Pedagogy of the Oppressed*, London: Penguin.

Freeman, Joshua B. 2000, *Working-Class New York: Life and Labor since World War Two*, The New Press: New York.

Fried, Michael 1998 [1967], 'Art and Objecthood', in *Art and Objecthood: Essays and Reviews*, Chicago: University of Chicago Press.

Fuoss, Kirk W. 1997, *Striking Performances/Performing Strikes*, Jackson: University Press of Mississippi.

George, Lynell 2008, 'Watts House Project: art meets architecture near the towers', *Los Angeles Times*, 2 November. Available online at http://www.latimes.com/entertainment/la-ca-watts2-2008nov02-story.html#page=2.

Giles, Dennis 1983, 'The Outdoor Economy: A Study of the Contemporary Drive-In', *Journal of the University Film and Video Association*, 35, 2 (Spring): 66–76.

Gilmartin, Gregory. Stern, Robert A.M. and Mellins, Thomas 1987 *New York 1930: Architecture and Urbanism between the Two World Wars*, New York: Rizzoli.

Gilmore, Ruth Wilson 2006, *Golden Gulag: Prisons, Surplus, Crisis, and Opposition in Globalizing California*, Berkeley: University of California Press.

Gilroy, Paul 2001, 'Driving while Black', in *Car Cultures*, edited by Daniel Miller, Oxford: Berg.

Giroux, Henry 2001, 'Mis/Education and Zero Tolerance: Disposable Youth and the Politics of Domestic Militarization', *Boundary 2*, 28, 3 (Autumn): 61–94.

Gold, Michael 1930, *Jews without Money*, London: Noel Douglas.

Gold, Michael 1972 [1921], 'Towards Proletarian Art', in Mike Gold, *A Literary Anthology*, edited by Michael Folsom, New York: International Publishers.

Goldberg, Roselee 2001, *Performance: Live Art 1909 to the Present*, London: Thames and Hudson.

Goldman, Wendy Z. 1993, *Women, The State and Revolution: Soviet Family Policy and Social Life 1917–1936*, Cambridge: Cambridge University Press.

Goldman, Wendy Z. 1996, 'Industrial Politics, Peasant Rebellion and the Death of the Proletarian Women's Movement in the USSR', *Slavic Review*, 55, 1 (Spring): 46–77.

Graff, Ellen 1997, *Stepping Left: Dance and Politics in New York City, 1928–1942*, Durham and London: Duke University Press.

Green, Martin 1988, *New York 1913: The Armory Show and the Paterson Strike Pageant*, New York: Collier Books.

Gugliemo, Jennifer 2002, 'Italian Women's Proletarian Feminism in the New York City Garment Trades, 1890s–1940s', in *Women, Gender, and Transnational Lives: Italian Women Around the World*, edited by Donna R. Gabaccia and Franca Iacovetta, Toronto: University of Toronto Press.

Halpern, Rick and Jonathan Morris 1997, 'The Persistence of Exceptionalisn: Class Formation and the Comparative Method', in *American Exceptionalism? US Working-Class Formation in an International Context*, edited by Rick Halpern and Jonathan Morris, London: Macmillan Press Ltd.

Stefano Harney and Fred Moten 2013, *The Undercommons: Fugitive Planning and Black Study*, Wivenhoe and New York: Minor Compositions.

Harris, Jonathan 1995, *Federal Art and National Culture: The Politics of Identity in New Deal America*, Cambridge: Cambridge University Press.
Harris, Paul 2011, 'Oakland Police: Controversial History sets Tone for City's Discord', *The Guardian*, Wednesday 26 October, available at: http://www.guardian.co.uk/world/blog/2011/oct/26/oakland-police-department-black-community.
Hartman, Andrew 2015, *A War for the Soul of America: A History of the Culture Wars*, Chicago and London: The University of Chicago Press.
Harvey, David 1982, *The Limits to Capital*, Basil Blackwell: Oxford.
Harvey, David 1989, *The Urban Experience*, Baltimore: The John Hopkins University Press.
Harvey, David 2002, 'The Art of Rent: Globalisation, Monopoly and the Commodification of Culture', *Socialist Register*, 38: 93–110.
Haworth Jones, Alfred 1971, 'The Search for a Usable American Past in the New Deal Era', *American Quarterly*, 23, 5 (December): 710–24.
Hayden, Dolores 1981, *The Grand Domestic Revolution: A History of Feminist Design for American Homes, Neighbourhoods, and Cities*, Cambridge, MA and London, England: The MIT Press.
Hays, R. Allan 1985, *The Federal Government and Urban Housing: Ideology and Change in Public Policy*, Albany: State University of New York Press.
Hemingway, Andrew 2002, *Artists on the Left: American Artists and the Communist Movement 1926–1956*, Yale University Press.
Henderson, Mary C. 1991, 'Against Broadway: The Rise of the Art Theatre in America (1900–1920)', in *1915, the Cultural Moment*, edited by Adele Heller and Lois Rudnick, New Brunswick, New Jersey: Rutgers University Press.
Houser, Craig, Leslie C. Jones et al. (eds.) 1993, *Abject Art: Repulsion and Desire in American Art*, New York: Whitney Museum of Art.
Howe, Irving 1970 [1963], 'Black Boys and Native Sons', in *Richard Wright's Native Son: A Critical Handbook*, edited by Richard Abcarian, Belmont, CA: Wadsworth Publishing Company.
Howe, Irving and Lewis Coser 1957, *The American Communist Party: A Critical History (1919–1957)*, Boston: Beacon Press.
Hughes, Robert 1995, 'Why America Shouldn't Kill Cultural Funding', *Time*, August 7.
Hutchins, Grace 1934, *Women who Work*, London: Martin Lawrence Ltd.
Hyde, Lewis 1999, 'The Children of John Adams: A Historical View of the Fight over Arts Funding', in *Art Matters: How the Culture Wars Changed America*, edited by Julie Ault, Brian Wallis et al., New York: New York University Press.
Inman, Mary 1940, *In Woman's Defense*, published by the Committee to Organize the Advancement of Women, Los Angeles, California.
Inman, Mary 1942 *Woman Power*, published by the Committee to Organize the Advancement of Women, Los Angeles, California.

Irish, Sharon 2010, *Suzanne Lacy: Spaces Between*, Minneapolis and London: University of Minnesota Press.
Isserman, Maurice 1982, *Which Side Were You On? The American Communist Party during the Second World War*, Middletown, Conn.: Wesleyan University Press.
Jackson, Shannon 2011, *Social Works: Performing Art, Supporting Politics*, New York and London: Routledge.
Jameson, Fredric 1970, 'The Case for George Lukács', *Salmagundi*, 13, 3–35.
Jameson, Fredric 1991, *Postmodernism, or, The Cultural Logic of Late Capitalism*, Durham: Duke University Press.
Jones, Chris 2019, 'Pritzker bill dangles millions for Illinois arts spending – here are some of the winners', *Chicago Tribune*, 5 June. Available at https://www.chicagotribune.com/entertainment/theater/ct-ae-spending-arts-jones-0609-story.html.
Jones, Kellie 2017, *South of Pico: African American Artists in Los Angeles during the 1960s and 1970s*, Durham and London: Duke University Press.
Jowitt, Deborah 1984, 'Dance: Frontline', *Village Voice*, 10 July.
Katznelson, Ira 1981, *City Trenches: Urban Politics and the Patterning of Class in the United States*, Chicago and London: The University of Chicago Press.
Kelley, Robin D.G. 1990 *Hammer and Hoe: Alabama Communists during the Great Depression*, Chapel: University of North Carolina Press
Kester, Grant H. 2004, *Conversation Pieces: Community and Communication in Modern Art*, Berkeley, Los Angeles, London: University of California Press.
Kester, Grant H. 2006, 'Another Turn' *Artforum*, 44, 9 (22 May).
Kester, Grant H. 2011, *The One and the Many: Contemporary Collaborative Art in a Global Context*, Durham, NC and London: Duke University Press.
Klehr, Harvey 1984, *The Heyday of American Communism: The Depression Decade*, New York: Basic Books Inc.
Klein, Mason 2011, 'Of Politics and Poetry: The Dilemma of the Photo League', in *The Radical Camera: New York's Photo League 1936–1951*, edited by Mason Klein and Catherine Evans, New Haven and London: Yale University Press.
Kracauer, Siegfried 1995 [1926], 'The Mass Ornament', in *The Mass Ornament: Weimar Essays*, translated and edited by Thomas Y. Levin, Cambridge, MA. and London, England: Harvard University Press.
Kristeva, Julia 1982, *Powers of Horror: An Essay on Abjection*, New York: Columbia University Press.
Kwon, Miwon 2002, *One Place After Another: Site Specific Art and Locational Identity*, Cambridge, MA and London, England: MIT Press.
Laban, Rudolf 1966, *Choreutics*, London: Macdonald and Evans.
La Berge, Leigh Claire 2019, *Wages against artwork: decommodified labor and the claims of socially engaged art*, Durham and London: Duke University Press.
Laclau, Ernesto 1977, *Politics and Ideology in Marxist Theory*, London: New Left Books.

Lacy, Suzanne 1994, 'Affinities', in *The Power of Feminist Art: The American Movement of the 1970s, History and Impact*, edited by Norma Broude and Mary D. Garrard, New York: Harry N. Abrams Inc.

Lacy, Suzanne 1995, *Mapping the Terrain: New Genre Public Art*, Seattle: Bay Press.

Lacy, Suzanne and Ann Wettrich 2010 [2002], 'What it Takes', in Suzanne Lacy *Leaving Art: Writing on Performance, Politics and Publics 1974–2007*, Durham, NC: Duke University Press.

Lacy, Suzanne and Lucy R. Lippard 2010 [1985], 'Political Performance Art: A Discussion', in Suzanne Lacy, *Leaving Art: Writing of Performance, Politics and Publics 1974–2007*, Durham: Duke University Press.

Landy, Avram 1943, *Marxism and the Woman Question*, New York: Workers' Library Publishers, July.

Lazzarato, Maurizio 1996, 'Immaterial Labor', in *Radical Thought in Italy: A Potential Politics*, edited by Paolo Virno and Michael Hardt, Minneapolis: University of Minnesota Press.

Lenin, V.I. 1914, 'The Taylor System – Man's enslavement by the Machine' in *Put Pravdy*, 35, 13 March. Available online: http://www.marxists.org/archive/lenin/works/1914/mar/13.htm.

Lenin, V.I. 1919, 'A Great Beginning' in *Collected Works*, 29. Available online at http://www.marxists.org/archive/lenin/works/subject/women/abstract/19_06_28.htm.

Levy, Michael 2011, 'Paper World', in *The Radical Camera: New York's Photo League 1936–1951*, edited by Mason Klein and Catherine Evans, New Haven and London: Yale University Press.

Lippard, Lucy 1999, 'Too Political? Forget it', in *Art Matters: How the Culture Wars Changed America*, edited by Julie Ault, Brian Wallis et al., New York: New York University Press.

Lipsitz, George 1994, *Rainbow at Midnight: Labor and Culture in the 1940s*, Urbana, Illinois: University of Illinois Press

Lipsitz, George 2011, *How Racism Takes Place*, Philadelphia: Temple University.

Liss, Andrea 2009, *Feminist Art and the Maternal*, Minneapolis: University of Minnesota Press.

Lloyd, Norman 2003, 'Living Newspaper Unit, New York', in *Voices from the Federal Theatre*, edited by Bonnie Nelson Schwartz, Madison: University of Wisconsin Press.

Lukács, Georg 1962, *The Meaning of Contemporary Realism*, translated by John and Necke Mander, London: Merlin Press.

Lukács, Georg 1971 [1920], *History and Class Consciousness*, translated by Rodney Livingstone, London: Merlin.

Lukács, Georg 1972 [1948], *Studies in European Realism: A Sociological survey of the Writings of Balzac, Stendhal, et al.*, translated by Edith Bone, London: The Merlin Press.

Lukács, Georg 1977 [1938], 'Realism in the Balance', in *Aesthetics and Politics*, London: New Left Books.
Lukács, Georg 1994 [1920], *The Theory of the Novel: A historico-philosophical essay on the forms of great epic literature*, translated by Anna Bostock, Cambridge, MA and London, England: MIT Press.
Lukács, Georg 2011 [1968], 'Life and Work', in *Lives on the Left*, edited by Francis Mulhern, London: Verso.
Lunn, Eugene 1982, *Marxism and Modernism*, Berkeley, London and Los Angeles: University of California Press.
Lyon, James K. 1983, *Bertolt Brecht in America*, Princeton: Princeton University Press.
The Mad Housers 1991, 'Essential Shelter: The Mad Houser Hut', in *If You Lived Here: The City in Art, Theory and Social Activism*, edited by Brian Wallis, Seattle: Bay Press.
Males, Mike A. 1996, *The Scapegoat Generation: America's War on Adolescents*, Monroe, ME: Common Courage Press.
Mallon, Thomas 2006, 'An Empty Robe', *The New York Times*, 22 January. Available at http://www.nytimes.com/2006/01/22/books/review/22mallon.html?pagewanted =all.
Mally, Lynn 2008, *The Americanization of the Soviet Living Newspaper*, The Carl Beck Papers in Russian and East European Studies, Number 1903, February.
Manning, Susan 2004, *Modern Dance, Negro Dance: Race in Motion*, Minneapolis and London: University of Minnesota Press.
Marcuse, Peter and Keating, W. Dennis 2006, 'The Permanent Housing Crisis: The Failures of Conservatism and the Limitations of Liberalism', in *Right to Housing: Foundation for a New Social Agenda*, edited by Rachel Bratt, Chester Hartman and Michael Stone, Philadelphia: Temple University Press.
Martin, Laura Renata 2017, 'Historicizing White Nostalgia: Race and American Fordism', *Blindfield: A Journal of Cultural Inquiry*, 3 August. Available at: https://blindfieldjour nal.com/2017/08/03/historicizing-white-nostalgia-race-and-american-fordism/.
Martin, Stewart 2007, 'Critique of Relational Aesthetics', *Third Text*, 21, 4 (July): 369–86.
Martin, Stewart 2009, 'Artistic Communism – A Sketch', *Third Text*, 23, 4 (July): 481–94.
Martinot, Steve 2003, 'The Militarisation of the Police', *Social Identities: Journal for the Study of Race, Nation and Culture*, 9, 2: 205–24.
Martinot, Steven and Jared Sexton 2003, 'The Avant-Garde of White Supremacy', *Social Identities: Journal for the Study of Race, Nation and Culture*, 9, 2: 169–81.
Marx, Karl and Friedrich Engels 1998 [1848], *The Communist Manifesto*, London: Verso.
Marx, Karl and Friedrich Engels 1988 [1844], *Economic and Philosophical Manuscripts of 1844*, translated by M. Milligan, New York: Prometheus Books.
Marx, Karl 1990 [1867], *Capital: A Critique of Political Economy Volume 1*, translated by Ben Fowkes, London: Penguin Books.
McKenna, Kristine 1997, 'Causes and Effects', *Los Angeles Times*, 16 March. Available

online at: http://articles.latimes.com/1997-03-16/entertainment/ca-38656_1_melros e-place/3.

McLaughlin, Milbrey et. al. 2009, *Between Movement and Establishment: Organizations Advocating for Youth*, Stanford: Stanford University Press.

McNamara, Brooks et al. 1971, 'Paterson Strike Pageant', *The Drama Review: TDR*, 15, 3: 60–71.

Meyerson, Harold 2009, 'How the Golden State got Tarnished', *The Washington Post*, 28 May. Available online at: http://www.washingtonpost.com/wpdyn/content/artic le/2009/05/27/AR2009052702904.html.

Mittenzwei, Werner 1973, 'The Brecht-Lukács debate', in *Preserve and Create: Essays in Marxist Literary Criticism*, edited by G.C. LeRoy and U. Beitz, New York: Humanities Press.

Molesworth, Helen 2000, 'House Work and Art Work', *October*, 92: 71–97.

Möntmann, Nina 2009, '(Under) Privileged Spaces: On Martha Rosler's *If You Lived Here …*', *e-flux*, 9 October. Available online at http://www.e-flux.com/journal/09/61370/ under-privileged-spaces-on-martha-rosler-s-if-you-lived-here-8230/.

Moravec, Michelle 2003, 'Mother Art: Feminism, Art, Activism', *Journal of Mothering, Popular Culture and the Arts*, 5, 1 (Spring/Summer): 69–77.

Morley Cohen, Mary 1994, 'Forgotten Audiences in the Passion Pits: Drive-in Theatres and Changing Spectator Practices in Post-War America', *Film History*, 6, 4 (Winter): 470–86.

Moten, Fred 2003, *In the Break: The Aesthetics of the Black Radical Tradition*, Minneapolis and London: University of Minnesota Press.

Mullen, John 1936, 'A Worker Looks at Broadway', *New Theatre*, 3, 5 (May): 25.

Nadler, Paul 1995, 'Liberty Censored: Black Living Newspapers of the Federal Theatre Project', *African American Review*, 29, 4: 615–22.

Naison, Mark 1983, *Communists in Harlem During the Depression*, Urbana, Illinois: University of Illinois Press.

Noble (McCausland), Elizabeth 1938, 'Housing Exhibit and Harriton's Art', *New Masses*, April 19: 26–7.

Oakley, Helen 1993 [1943], '(Dance)', *Downbeat*, republished in *The Duke Ellington Reader*, edited by Mark Tucker, New York and Oxford: Oxford University Press.

Ocko, Edna 1935, 'The Dance League Recital', *New Theatre*, February: 25.

Ocko, Edna 1935, 'The Dance', *New Masses* 5 March, p. 26.

O'Connor, Brendon 2001, 'The Protagonists and Ideas behind the Personal Responsibility and Work Opportunity Reconciliation Act of 1996: The Enactment of a Conservative Welfare System', *Social Justice*, 28, 4 (Winter): 396–411.

Older, Daniel José 2014, 'Gentrification's Insidious Violence: The truth about American cities', *Salon*, 18 April. Available online at: http://www.salon.com/2014/04/08/ gentrifications_insidious_violence_the_truth_about_american_cities/.

Orleck, Annelise 1993, ' "We Are That Mythical Thing Called the Public": Militant Housewives during the Great Depression', *Feminist Studies*, 19, 1 (Spring): 147–72.

Orleck, Annelise, 1995 *Common Sense and a Little Fire: Women and Working-Class Politics in the United States, 1900–1965*, Chapel Hill and London: The University of North Carolina Press.

Paine Jr., G. Lyman 1934, 'Outline of the exhibition of Slum Clearance and Low-cost Housing of the City of New York', in *America Can't Have Housing*, edited by Carol Aronovici, New York: MOMA.

Pateman, Carole 2005, 'Another Way Forward: Welfare, Social Reproduction and a Basic Income', in *Welfare Reform and Political Theory*, edited by L. Mead and C. Beem New York: Russell Sage Foundation.

Pearlstein, Steven 2012, 'Shattering the Glass Steagall Myth', *The Washington Post*, 28 July. Available online at http://www.washingtonpost.com/lets-shatter-the-myth-on-glass-steagall/2012/07/27/gJQASaOAGX_story.html.

Petry, Ann 1946, *The Street*, Boston: Houghton Mifflin.

Photo Notes 1977 [1938], December, p. 1. Republished by the Visual Studies Workshop, Rochester, New York.

Photo Notes 1977 [1939], Feb, p. 1. Republished by the Visual Studies Workshop, Rochester, New York.

Pollin, Robert 2000, 'The Anatomy of Clintonomics', *New Left Review*, 3 (May–June): 17–46.

Potts, Alex 2013, *Experiments in Modern Realism: World Making in Postwar American and European Art*, New Haven: Yale University Press.

'The Power 100' 2013, *ArtReview*, 63, 65 (November): 126.

R.L. 2013, 'Wanderings of the Slave: Black Life and Social Death', *Mute*, 5 June. Available online at http://www.metamute.org/editorial/articles/wanderings-slave-black-life-and-social-death.

Reckitt, Helena 2013, 'Forgotten Relations: Feminist Art and Relational Aesthetics', in *Politics in a Glass Case: Feminism, Exhibition Cultures and Curatorial Transgressions*, edited by Angela Dimitrakaki and Lara Perry, Liverpool: Liverpool University Press.

Rhomberg, Chris 2004, *No There There: Race, Class and Political Community in Oakland*, Berkeley, London and Los Angeles: University of California Press.

Roberts, Adrienne 2013, 'Financing Social Reproduction: The Gendered Relations of Debt and Mortgage Finance in Twenty-first-century America', *New Political Economy*, 18, 1: 21–42.

Rodriguez, Dylan 2007, 'The Political Logic of the Non-Profit Industrial Complex', in *The Revolution will not be Funded: Beyond the non-profit industrial complex*, edited by INCITE! Women of Color Against Violence, Cambridge, MA: South End Press.

Roediger, David 1999, *The Wages of Whiteness: Race and the Making of the American Working Class*, London: Verso.

Rosler, Martha 1977, 'The Private and the Public: Feminist Art in California', *Artforum*, September, 66–74.

Rosler, Martha 1978, *Service: A Trilogy on Colonization*, New York: Printed Matter.

Rosler, Martha 1990, 'In, around and afterthoughts (on documentary photography)', in *The Contest of Meaning: Critical Histories of Photography*, edited by Richard Bolton, Cambridge, MA and London, England: MIT Press.

Rosler, Martha 1991, 'The Artists Home Ownership Program', in *If You Lived Here: The City in Art, Theory and Social Activism*, edited by Brian Wallis, Seattle: Bay Press.

Rosler, Martha 1991, 'Fragments of a Metropolitan Viewpoint', in *If You Lived Here: The City in Art, Theory and Social Activism*, edited by Brian Wallis, Seattle: Bay Press.

Rosler, Martha 2004, *Decoys and Disruptions: Selected Writings 1975–2001*, Cambridge, MA and London, England: The MIT Press.

Rosler, Martha 2014, *Culture Class*, New York and Berlin: Sternberg Press, in association with e-flux.

Roth, Moira 2001, 'Making and Performing Code 33: A Public Art Project with Suzanne Lacy, Julio Morales and Unique Holland', *PAJ: A Journal of Performance and Art*, 23, 3 (Sept.): 47–62.

Rounthwaite, Adair 2017, *Asking the Audience: Participatory Art in 1980s New York*, Minneapolis: University of Minnesota Press.

Schmidt, Alfred 1971, *The Concept of Nature in Marx*, London: New Left Books.

Schwartz, Frederic J. 2005, *Blind Spots: Critical Theory and the History of Art in Twentieth Century Germany*, New Haven: Yale University Press.

Schwartz, Herman M. 2009, *Subprime Nation: American Power, Global Capital and the Housing Bubble*, Ithaca and London: Cornell University Press.

Segal, Edith 1935, 'Children's Work', *New Dance*, March, p. 13. Courtesy of the Edith Segal papers (Box 2), Dance Collection, The New York Public Library, Astor, Lenox and Tilden Foundations.

Segal, Edith 1935, 'Mayday Script', *New Dance*, March, p. 19. Courtesy of the Edith Segal papers (Box 2), Dance Collection, The New York Public Library, Astor, Lenox and Tilden Foundations.

Segal, Edith 1935, 'Directing the New Dance', *New Theatre*, May, p. 23.

Sekula, Allan 1989, '"Gay-Bashing" as an Art Form: The Mapplethorpe affair reveals a linkage of quirky conservative impulses in art, economics and politics', *LA Times*, 21 October. Available online at http://articles.latimes.com/1989-10-21/local/me-246_1_art-world.

Shanin, Teodor 1983, 'Late Marx: gods and craftsmen', in *Late Marx and the Russian Road: Marx and 'the peripheries of capitalism'*, edited by Teodor Shanin, London: Routledge and Kegan Paul.

Shannon, David A. 1955, *The Socialist Party of America*, New York: Macmillan.

Sholette, Gregory 2011, *Dark Matter: Art and Politics in the Age of Enterprise Culture*, London: Pluto Press.

Sholette, Gregory 2017, *Delirium and Resistance: Activist Art and the Crisis of Capitalism*, London: Pluto Press.
Siskind, Aaron 1991, *Harlem: Photographs 1932–1940*, New Haven: National Museum of Art, Smithsonian Institution.
Smith, Neil 1992, 'Contours of a Spatialized Politics: Homeless Vehicles and the Production of Geographical Scale', *Social Text*, 33: 54–81.
Smith, Neil 1996 *The New Urban Frontier: Gentrification and the Revanchist City*, London: Routledge.
Stakemeier, Kerstin and Marina Vishmidt 2016, *Reproducing Autonomy: Work, Money, Crisis and Contemporary Art*, London: Mute Publishing.
Stange, Maren 1989, *Symbols of Ideal Life: Social Documentary Photography in America 1890–1950*, Cambridge: Cambridge University Press.
Straus, Nathan 1966 [1938], 'End the Slums', in *New Deal Thought*, edited by Howard Zinn, Indianapolis and Cambridge: Hackett Publishing.
Stimson, Blake and Gregory Sholette (eds.) 2007, *Collectivism after Modernism: The Art of Social Imagination after 1945*, Minnesota: University of Minnesota Press.
'Symposium on Harlem Document' 1977 [1939], *Photo Notes*, June, p. 1. Republished by the Visual Studies Workshop, Rochester, New York.
Taylor, Alexander 1936, 'The Theatre: Injunction Granted', *New Masses*, 4 August, p. 29.
Theisen, Olive Jensen 2010, *Walls that Speak: The Murals of John Thomas Biggers*, Denton, Texas: University of North Texas Press.
Thomas, Peter 2009, 'Catharsis', *Historical Materialism*, 17, 3: 259–64.
Thompson, Nato 2013a, 'The Insurgents, Part I: Community-Based Practice as Military Methodology', *e-flux*, 47. Available online at http://www.e-flux.com/journal/the-insurgen
ts-part-i-community-based-practice-as-military-methodology/.
Thompson, Nato November 2013b, 'The Insurgents, Part II: Fighting the Left by Being the Left', *e-flux*, 49. Available online at http://www.e-flux.com/journal/the-insurgen
ts-part-ii-fighting-the-left-by-being-the-left/.
Thompson, Robert Farris 1995, 'John Biggers's *Shotguns* of 1987: An American Classic', in *The Art of John Biggers: View from the Upper Room*, edited by Alvia J. Wardlaw, New York: Harry N. Abrams.
Ticker, Jill et al. 2014, 'Ferguson ruling sparks Oakland Freeway shutdown, looting', *SF Gate*, 1 December. Available online at http://www.sfgate.com/bayarea/article/Bay
-Area-protesters-voice-anger-at-Ferguson-5915541.php.
Toscano, Alberto 2008, 'The Open Secret of Real Abstraction', *Rethinking Marxism: A Journal of Economics, Culture & Society*, 20, 2: 273–87.
Treanor, Jill 2010, 'Obama takes on America's banks with new Glass-Steagall act', *The Guardian*, 21 January. Available at http://www.theguardian.com/business/2010/jan/
21/obama-bank-reform-glass-steagall.

Tucker, Anne Wilkes 2001, 'The Photo League: A Center for Documentary Photography', in *This Was the Photo League: Compassion and the Camera from the Depression to the Cold War*, Chicago: Stephen Daiter Gallery.

Tucker, Anne Wilkes 2011, 'A Rashomon Reading', in *The Radical Camera: New York's Photo League 1936–1951*, edited by Mason Klein and Catherine Evans New Haven and London: Yale University Press.

Valgemäe, Mardi 1972, *Accelerated Grimace: Expressionism in the American Drama of the 1920s*, Carbondale: Southern Illinois University Press.

Vishmidt, Marina 2013, 'Mimesis of the Hardened and Alienated: Social Practice as Business Model', *e-flux*, 43 (March). Available online at http://www.e-flux.com/journal/43/60197/mimesis-of-the-hardened-and-alienated-social-practice-as-business-model/.

Vogel, Lise 1983, *Marxism and the Oppression of Women: Toward a Unitary Theory*, New Brunswick, NJ: Rutgers University Press.

Von Osten, Marion 2010, 'Another Criteria ... or, What is the Attitude of a Work in the Relations of Production of Its Time?', *Afterall: A Journal of Art, Context and Enquiry*, 25 (Autumn): 56–69.

Ward Jr., Jerry W. 2004, 'Everybody's protest novel: The era of Richard Wright', in *The Cambridge Companion to the African American novel*, edited by Maryemma Graham, Cambridge: Cambridge University Press.

Weinstein, Megan 1998, 'The Teenage Pregnancy "Problem": Welfare Reform and the Personal Responsibility and Work Opportunity Reconciliation Act of 1996', *Berkeley Women's Law Journal*, 13: 117–52.

Weinstein, James 1967, *The Decline of American Socialism: 1912–1925*, New Jersey: Rutgers University Press.

Weissman, Terri 2011, *The Realisms of Berenice Abbot: Documentary Photography and Political Action*, Berkeley, Los Angeles and London: University of California Press.

Whyman, Rose 2008, *The Stanislavsky System of Acting: Legacy and Influence in Modern Performance*, Cambridge: Cambridge University Press.

Wilderson II, Frank B. 2003, 'Gramsci's Black Marx: Whither the Slave in Civil Society?' *Social Identities*, 9, 2: 225–40.

Wilderson II, Frank B. 2007, 'The Prison Slave as Hegemony's (Silent) Scandal', in *Warfare in the American Homeland: Policing and Prison in a Penal Democracy*, edited by Joy James, Durham and London: Duke University Press.

Wilding, Faith 1994, 'The Feminist Art Programs at Fresno and CalArts, 1970–75', in *The Power of Feminist Art: The American Movement of the 1970s, History and Impact*, edited by Norma Broude and Mary D. Garrard, New York: Harry N. Abrams Inc.

Williams, Raymond 1973, 'Base and Superstructure in Marxist Cultural Theory', *New Left Review*, 82 (Nov–Dec): 3–16.

Wacquant, Löic 2002, 'From Slavery to Mass Incarcaration: Rethinking the "race question" in the US', *New Left Review*, 13 (Jan–Feb): 41–60.

Wei, Lily 2011, 'In the Studio: Theaster Gates', *Art in America*, 99, 11 (December). Available online at http://www.artinamericamagazine.com/news-features/magazine/theaster-gates/.
Weigand, Kate 2001, *Red Feminism: American Communism and the Making of Women's Liberation*, Baltimore and London: John Hopkins University Press.
Wright, Richard and Edwin Rosskam 1941, *12 Million Black Voices: A Folk History of the Negro in the United States*, New York: The Viking Press.
Wright, Richard 1944, 'I Tried to Be a Communist', *The Atlantic*, 174, 2 (August).
Wright, Richard 2000 [1940], *Native Son*, London: Vintage Books.
Yúdice, George 1999, 'The Privatization of Culture', *Social Text*, 59: 17–34.
Zhang, Xudong and Fredric Jameson 1998, 'Marxism and the Historicity of Theory: An Interview with Fredric Jameson', *New Literary History*, 29, 3: 353–83.
Zumoff, Jacob 2014, *The Communist International and US Communism 1919–1929*, Leiden and Boston: Brill.
Zunser, Florence interview with Duke Ellington 1993 [1930], *New York Evening Graphic*, republished in *The Duke Ellington Reader*, edited by Mark Tucker, New York and Oxford: Oxford University Press.

Legal and Policy Documents

Federal Housing Administration 1938, Underwriting Manual, Washington, DC: Government Printing Office.
Harris, David A. 1999, 'Driving while Black: Racial Profiling on our Nation's Highways', An American Civil Liberties Union Special Report. Available online at: https://www.aclu.org/racial-justice/driving-while-black-racial-profiling-our-nations-highways.
Larson, Gary O. 1997, *American Canvas*, National Endowment for the Arts report. Available online at http://arts.gov/sites/default/files/AmericanCanvas.pdf.
National Endowment for the Arts 1996, Annual Report. Available online at https://www.arts.gov/sites/default/files/NEA-Annual-Report-1996.pdf.
Personal Responsibility and Work Opportunity Reconciliation Act of 1996, *Public Law 104/193*, 22 August, United States Statutes at Large. Available online at: http://www.gpo.gov/fdsys/pkg/PLAW-104publ193/pdf/PLAW-104publ193.pdf.

Personal Interviews

Suzanne Lacy, personal interview, 27 April 2012.
Suzanne Lacy, personal interview, 26 May 2013.
Rick Lowe, personal interview, 19 September 2013.
Martha Rosler, personal interview, 3 October 2013.

Oral Histories/Conference Transcripts

Lacy, Suzanne speaking at the 'Working in Public' seminar series at Robert Gordon University in 2007. See transcript online at: http://www2.rgu.ac.uk/subj/ats/ontheedge 2/workinginpublicseminars/seminar1_theOaklandDialogue.pdf.

Joseph Losey interview with Arnold Goldman, 30 April 1972, in Folder 1.5, Arnold Goldman Living Newspaper collection, Collection #C0173, Special Collections and Archives, George Mason University.

Rick Lowe in conversation with Nato Thompson at the 2013 Creative Time Summit. Available online at: https://www.youtube.com/watch?v=IoIoNoVKDXE.

Segal, Edith 1981, 'Music and dance and the Left in the 1930s', interview with B. Lemisch, February, Oral Histories of the American Left 1920–1980, Tamiment Library/Robert F. Wagner Labor Archives, New York University Libraries.

Segal, Edith oral history interview with Leslie Farlow, 1991, audiotape, Dance Collection, New York Public Library for the Performing Arts.

Scripts and Scores

Arthur Arent 1938, *One-Third of a Nation: A Living Newspaper about Housing*, Federal Theatre Project Works Progress Administration. Available online at: http://digilib.gmu.edu/dspace/handle/1920/4496.

Editorial Staff of the Living Newspaper Federal Theatre Project for New York City, 1936, *Triple-A Plowed Under*, Federal Theatre Project Works Progress Administration. Available online at: http://digilib.gmu.edu/dspace/handle/1920/3588.

Editorial Staff of the Living Newspaper, script of *Injunction Granted*, Federal Theatre Project Works Progress Administration 1936. Available online at: http://digilib.gmu.edu/dspace/handle/1920/4489 (Accessed 10 September 2013).

Score for Black and White in the Edith Segal papers (Box 2), Dance Collection, The New York Public Library, Astor, Lenox and Tilden Foundations. Undated.

Unpublished Material

Cosgrove, Stuart 1982 *The Living Newspaper: History, Production and Form*, PhD Thesis, University of Hull.

Lacy, Suzanne 2013, *Imperfect Art: Working in Public, A case study of the Oakland Projects 1991–2001*, PhD thesis, Robert Gordon University.

Archives

Arnold Goldman Living Newspaper collection, Collection #C0173, Special Collections and Archives, George Mason University.
Edith Segal papers, Dance Collection, The New York Public Library, Astor, Lenox and Tilden Foundations.

Online Resources

Bruguera, Tania, *Reflexions on Arte Útil*, November 2012. Available online at: http://www.taniabruguera.com/cms/592-0-Reflexions+on+Arte+til+Useful+Art.htm.
Dery, Mark 1994, 'Black to the Future: Afro-Futurism 1.0', first posted on the *rumori* mailing list. Available online at: http://www.detritus.net/contact/rumori/200211/0319.html.
Immigrant Movement International on the Creative Time website: http://creativetime.org/projects/immigrant-movement-international/.
Lacy, Suzanne, *The Roof is on Fire*. Available online at: http://theoaklandprojects.wordpress.com/the-roof-is-on-fire-1993-94/.
Ukeles, Mierle Laderman 1969, 'Maintenance Art Manifesto'. Available online courtesy of the Queens Museum at: http://www.queensmuseum.org/wp-content/uploads/2016/04/Ukeles_MANIFESTO.pdf.
Watts House Projects website: http://wattshouseproject.org/. This website is now archived and appears inactive.
WochenKlausur, 'Women's-led Workers' Cooperative', details available on the WochenKlausur website: http://www.wochenklausur.at/projekt.php?lang=en&id=41.
Womanhouse online archive: http://womanhouse.refugia.net/.

Video documentation

Video documentation of *The Roof is on Fire*, courtesy of Suzanne Lacy, 1994. Available online at: https://theoaklandprojects.wordpress.com/the-roof-is-on-fire-1994/.
Video documentation of *No Blood No Foul*, courtesy of Suzanne Lacy, 1996. Available online at https://theoaklandprojects.wordpress.com/no-blood-no-foul-1996/.
Video documentation of *Code 33*, courtesy of Suzanne Lacy, 1999. Available online at: http://theoaklandprojects.wordpress.com/code-33-1998-99-vid/.

Index

Abbot, Berenice   160, 164–66, 168–69, 180
Abu-Jamal, Mumia   41, 42, 45
Aesthetics   9, 11, 21, 24, 133, 142–43, 196, 199
   aesthetic form   26, 28, 81, 141
   aestheticism   164
   aesthetic nominalism   198
Aid to Families with Dependent Children   3, 21, 39, 74, 102–5
American Canvas report   15, 187
Arceneaux, Edgar   200–201
Arent, Arthur   6, 48, 148–49, 152, 155–57
Arte Útil   112, 205–207
Artists' Union   17, 161

Baldwin, James   182, 194
Biggers, John   178, 191–92, 194
Bishop, Claire   9–13, 19, 22, 124
Black Panther Party for Self-Defense   38, 41, 185–6
Bloch, Ernst   17–18, 21, 82–83, 89–91, 142, 158, 192, 194
Blue Blouse theatre troupe   4–5, 27, 151
Boal, Augusto   25, 28
Bourriaud, Nicolas   8–9, 113
Brecht, Bertolt   7, 20, 28–30, 36, 45–46, 49, 51, 62, 66, 69, 72, 142, 151
Browder, Earl   7–8, 98, 146, 157
Bruguera, Tania   23, 112, 198
   Bruguera's Immigrant Movement International   204–6
Burrough, Allison   85–91

Capp Street Gallery   73, 102, 107, 113–15, 119
Carter, Michael   170, 174–75, 177
Chicago, Judy   109–10, 116
Clinton, Bill   39, 102, 106, 117
Code 33 (The Oakland Projects)   20–21, 25, 28, 31–32, 37–48, 62, 66, 68–69, 72–73, 79, 101
   focus on police-youth relations   38–41
   performance of   37, 47
   video documentation of   44
Communist Party USA   4–5, 7–8, 21, 26, 29, 63–65, 75–76, 79, 87, 94–96, 99, 151, 157, 161, 166–67, 173–74, 178

Congress of Industrial Organizations   48, 63–64, 66–68, 99, 157
   theatrical productions   63
Cooke, Marvel   84
Creative Time   74, 193–194, 204
Cultural Front   3–4, 8, 16, 23, 144, 151–52, 160, 162, 172, 179
Culture Wars   1, 13, 15, 22, 127, 187, 204

Democratic Front   60, 151–52, 157, 163–64, 168, 173–74, 179, 182, 195, 198
Dia Art Foundation   127–28, 127, 130–32, 134, 137–38, 140, 161, 175
Documentary   22, 36, 123, 125–27, 129–31, 133, 135–37, 139, 141, 143, 145, 147, 149, 157, 160–61, 168–72
   documentary conventions   144, 170, 176–77
   documentary photography   125–126, 137–138, 158, 196
Domestic labour   21, 74, 91, 93, 96–97, 110–12, 120, 198
   domestic sphere   106, 119, 135, 141, 143, 146
   unwaged   100
   domestic work   92, 94–96, 98, 110–11, 116
Duke Ellington   4, 87, 89–91
Duncan, Isadora   75, 92
Dunham, Katharine   162

Engels, Friedrich   81, 96
Ethiopia (Living Newspaper)   4, 6, 85, 174
   cancellation of   157
Expectations (The Oakland Projects)   21, 48, 101–2, 106–7, 111–15, 117–18, 120–21
   Expectations exhibition   114
   Expectations summer school   103, 113, 117, 119

Fanon, Frantz   177
Federal Housing Administration   159, 186–87
Feminist Art Program   109
Flanagan, Hallie   5–7, 64–65, 147
Ford, James   173–74

INDEX 227

Foster, William Z.   87
Freire, Paulo   10

Gastev, Alexei K.   81
Gates, Theaster   23, 198, 201–2, 204–5, 223
Gentrification   22, 36, 39, 128–30, 138, 141, 158, 194, 196, 211, 218
Glass-Steagall Act   2–3
Gold, Mike   166–168, 175, 180, 182
Graham, Martha   12, 26–27
Group Material   127

Hampton, Carl   185–86
Hearst, William Randolph   60–61, 150
Holland, Unique   43–44, 102, 106–8, 114–15
Homelessness   21–22, 126–27, 130, 136, 138, 141, 161, 175, 195
   Homelessness and documentary   123, 125, 127, 129, 131, 133, 135, 137, 139, 141, 143, 145, 147, 149, 151
House Un-American Activities Committee   7

Industrial Workers of the World   31, 63
Injunction Granted (Living Newspaper)   20–21, 25–26, 28, 31–32, 48–53, 55–56, 58, 60–73, 79, 84, 144, 146, 149–51, 157, 167
Inman, Mary   21, 95–99, 110, 111, 120
International Ladies Garment Workers Organisation   62–63, 75–76, 77, 79, 92, 95

Jackson, Shannon   12–13
Jameson, Fredric   29–30, 46, 141–43
   cognitive mapping   22, 141–44, 155, 158
John Reed Clubs   162

Kaprow, Allan   27, 109
Kelly, Mary   110, 113
Kester, Grant   10–13, 42
Koch, Ed   128, 130–131
Kracauer, Siegfried   80–81
Kristeva, Julia   116
Kwon, Miwon   13

Laban, Rudolf   87
Lacy, Suzanne   2, 13, 20–29, 33–36, 38–46, 69, 73–74, 100–102, 105–9, 113–118, 138, 170–71, 202, 204
   Lacy's subjects   73
   Lacy's pedagogy   108
Laderman Ukeles, Mierle   110–13, 119
Landy, Avram   96–97, 99
Lenin   77, 98–99, 209, 216
   Leninist strategy   79
   Lenin Memorial Pageant   75
Lippard, Lucy   16–17, 23, 109
Living Newspaper   4–8, 20, 25, 48–50, 52, 54–61, 64–65, 69, 144, 146, 148–50, 157, 172, 179
Los Angeles Workers' School   96
Losey, Joseph   6–7, 48–49, 51, 62, 64–65
Lott, Jesse   183, 188, 190
Lowe, Rick   2, 13, 183–85, 187–90, 192–94, 196, 198, 200–202
Lukács, Georg   20, 28, 29–30, 46–47, 64, 72
   Lukács' aesthetics   142
   Lukács' dialectic   66
   Lukács' realism   29–30
   Lukácsean typification   72, 167
   Lukács and Brecht debate   29–30, 142

Mad Housers   138–40
Maintenance Art Manifesto   110–111
Marx, Karl   9, 80–81, 83, 96, 97, 100, 105–6, 109, 124–25
   Marxist-feminism   98–110
Mass incarceration   34–35, 69–71
McCausland, Elizabeth   161–64, 168, 170, 196
Mother Art   111–13, 198
Museum of Arte Útil   205

Nance, Marilyn   132
National Endowment for the Arts   1, 13–16, 39, 127, 187–88, 193
Nature Friends Dance Group   77, 92
Needle Trades Workers' Industrial Union Dance Group   63, 77–78, 83, 87, 89
New Dance Group   26, 77, 87
New Dance League   77
New Deal   1–4, 8, 66, 68–69, 102, 104, 123, 136, 138, 143, 145, 151, 153, 157, 159
New Duncan Dancers   77, 92–93
New Masses   26, 51, 67, 161, 167, 211, 218, 221

New Theatre 26, 29, 78
Newton, Huey 38, 89
Noble, Elizabeth (pseudonym of Elizabeth McCausland) 161–163

Ocko, Edna 26, 74
One-Third of a Nation (Living Newspaper) 144–58

Paterson Strike Pageant 31, 48, 63
People's Party II 186–87, 192
Personal Responsibility and Work Opportunity Reconciliation Act 21, 39, 102–7
Petry, Ann 169, 175–76, 181
Photo League Feature Group 23, 154, 160, 165–66, 169–77, 178–179, 182, 195, 197
Photo League Feature Group's *Harlem Document* 23, 154, 160, 165, 169–79, 181–82, 187, 192, 194–95
    Harlem Document and Native Son 179
    Harlem Document exhibition 172
Photo Notes 171–73
Popular Front 3, 6–7, 26, 29, 63, 71, 77, 87, 91, 94–95, 144, 151, 154, 162, 173–74
Project Row Houses 1–2, 23, 160, 183–85, 187–90, 192–96, 198–201, 205–6

Rand School 75, 94
Reagan, Ronald 209, 112
Red Dancers 26, 74, 77, 92–93
Relational Aesthetics 8–9, 113
Rice, Elmer 5–6
Rockland Palace Interracial Ball 85–88, 91
Roofs for Forty Million 160–65, 168, 170, 182, 194–95
The Roof is on Fire (The Oakland Projects) 20–21, 25, 28, 31–38
Rosler, Martha 2, 36, 110, 117, 130–31, 134, 137, 139–43, 163, 194, 197
Rosskam, Edwin 179–81

Segal, Edith
    Segal's formation 74–76
    Black and White 82–87
    Kinder Küche Kirche 91–95
    Dance of the Washerwomen 21, 92–93, 95, 152, 154
Siskind, Aaron 165, 170–71
    Siskind's photographs for *Harlem Document* 174–176

Social documentary 22–23, 123, 126, 136, 138–39, 141, 143–44, 155, 158, 162, 165, 169, 195–96
Socialist Party 61, 63, 75, 95
Social reproduction 21, 73–75, 77, 79, 81, 93–95, 99–101, 109–13, 117, 119–21, 124, 135, 186–87, 197–99, 205–6
Social Security Act 3, 21, 69, 74, 102, 104

Taft Hartley Act 67, 99
Temporary Assistance to Needy Families 103
Third Period 77, 87, 163, 173
Triple-A Plowed Under (Living Newspaper) 6–7, 48, 157

United Council of Working Class Housewives 94–95, 155
Unity House 75–77

Vogel, Lise 99–100

Wagner Act 63, 66–67
Wagner-Steagall Housing Act 144–45, 156–59, 161
Watts House Project 183, 199–202
Watts Towers 199
Watts Towers Art Center 199, 201
WochenKlausur 205–206
Wodiczko, Krzysztof 138
Womanhouse 109, 116–17
Workers' Alliance of America 20, 31, 65–66, 69, 95
Workers' Dance League 77
Workers' Film and Photo League/Film and Photo League 162–64, 171
Works Progress Administration 3, 6, 13, 16, 18, 25, 65, 104, 172
Works Progress Administration Federal Art Project 18, 165–66
Works Progress Administration Federal Theatre Project 1, 5, 7–8, 17–18, 20, 25–26, 29, 31, 62, 64–65, 95, 144, 147, 151, 157
Wright, Richard
    Wright's Native Son 175, 177, 179–182, 192
    Twelve Million Black Voices 23, 158, 160–65, 168, 170, 173, 176, 179–82, 194–95